W9-CCG-532

Praise for *Beyond Paycheck to Paycheck*

"The most straightforward financial planning book you'll find. Understandable by the financially clueless yet extremely beneficial to those who have already begun. Unique conversational format. Unbelievable glossary!"

—ARTHUR F. VON DER LINDEN, JR., CFP,®
FOUNDER AND PRINCIPAL, WINGATE FINANCIAL GROUP, INC.

"From managing your debt to investing for your future, *Beyond Paycheck to Paycheck* provides you with the tools and motivation necessary to intelligently pursue your financial dreams."

—CARL LEHMANN, ENTREPRENEUR, FORMER PRESIDENT,
TRAVELERS CHEQUE GROUP WORLDWIDE, AMERICAN EXPRESS COMPANY

"Refreshing, enlightening, and understandable. *Beyond Paycheck to Paycheck* stresses the message of personal finance without stressing the reader. I have read no other book as thorough, yet approachable, as this one. It is a critical read."

—STEPHEN P. AHERN, CPA/PFS, CFP,® MST,
PRESIDENT, WEALTH MANAGEMENT ADVISORS LLC

"I wish I could've read *Beyond Paycheck to Paycheck* when I was first starting out. But I can't wait to share Michael Rubin's wisdom with my daughters as soon as they join the workforce themselves. If you have any doubts whether this concise, cogent, and compelling book is for you (or your children), just read the preface. Now."

—B. JOSEPH PINE II, CO-AUTHOR, *THE EXPERIENCE ECONOMY:*
WORK IS THEATRE & EVERY BUSINESS A STAGE

"Thanks to *Beyond Paycheck to Paycheck,* procrastination and ignorance can no longer be your excuse. This candid and somehow humorous education is a must-read for anybody who wants to take their finances a step up—be it the first step or the next step." —STEVE C., 20+ YEAR CAREER IN INSURANCE SALES

Additional Praise for *Beyond Paycheck to Paycheck*

"How can you reach your mid-thirties and still be unaware of the most basic rules of money? Thanks to this book's conversational tone and sophisticated yet plainspoken content, I am both motivated and empowered to finally live *Beyond Paycheck to Paycheck!* —Tamara Cook, 35, Visual Merchandising

"With unexpected humor and healthy doses of sarcasm, the book teaches the financial lessons many of us wish we already knew—but don't." —Jenny Flax, 34, Entrepreneur

"It seems like everyone lives paycheck to paycheck, including many of my co-workers, the callers to my radio show, and the people I hang out with. But not me. After reading *Beyond Paycheck to Paycheck,* I have my financial act together. I don't read a lot of books, but when it comes to your future, you have to take action. Read this book. By the end, you'll change your habits and will be planning for your future. This is important, powerful stuff, even at my age." —Chase Daniels, 22, Afternoon Radio Host/Assistant Program Director

"To experience *Beyond Paycheck to Paycheck* is to suddenly find yourself sitting with a trusted family member infinitely knowledgeable about personal finance. *You* ask the questions and *you* get the honest answers. You'll find the resulting empowerment truly motivating." —Mark J. Alaimo, 24, Financial Planner

"Like having a true conversation with a patient expert. Michael is like the guy you wish you knew so you could learn the real deal. With *Beyond Paycheck to Paycheck* you finally get that conversation." —Shea Keisling, 33, Database Marketing Manager

"As I start a new career and buy a new home, *Beyond Paycheck to Paycheck* provides me with the understanding necessary to successfully develop and navigate my financial roadmap—a mortgage, student loans, 401(k) plans—and also enjoy today. I'm grateful for the confidence it's given me to move forward financially in my life. An invaluable resource!" —Vicki Simpson, 33, Physician Assistant

Have a comment you'd like to share? Let us know! Send your comments to feedback@beyondpaychecktopaycheck.com or visit: *www.totalcandor.com.*

BEYOND PAYCHECK TO PAYCHECK

A Conversation About Income, Wealth, and the Steps in Between

Michael B. Rubin
CPA, CFP,® MBA

First in a series from Total Candor

The information provided in this book is provided for informational purposes only and does not constitute legal, investment or accounting advice. You should consult a competent accountant, investment advisor or legal counsel, as applicable, in order to obtain specific advice tailored to your situation.

There is no endorsement, implied or otherwise, of the companies, web sites, or products mentioned in this book. Company information, such as web site addresses, may have changed since the publication of this book. Check *www.totalcandor.com* for periodic updates.

Published by Wachtel & Martin LLC   8/07
Portsmouth, New Hampshire
www.wachtelandmartin.com

Printed in the United States of America

For information on bulk purchases of *Beyond Paycheck to Paycheck,* including significant discount opportunities, please contact *bulksales@wachtelandmartin.com.*

For author availability for a specific date to lead a workplace event or university workshops, or for a calendar of public seminars, please contact *info@totalcandor.com* or visit *www.totalcandor.com.*

Publisher's Cataloging-in-Publication
(Provided by Quality Books, Inc.)

Rubin, Michael B.
    Beyond paycheck to paycheck : a conversation about
income, wealth, and the steps in between / by Michael B.
Rubin.
    p. cm.
    Includes index.
    LCCN 2006933773
    ISBN-13: 978-0-9787927-8-7
    ISBN-10: 0-9787927-8-5

    1. Finance, Personal.   I. Title. II. Title:
Income, wealth, and the steps in between.

HG179.R75 2007   332.024
                         QBI06-600365

SUMMARY TABLE OF CONTENTS

DETAILED TABLE OF CONTENTS

TABLE OF FIGURES

For my grandparents
Lillie and Jerome,
who teach more than they know.

For my parents
Arlene and Paul,
who teach everything they know.

For my wife
Laura,
who teaches there is always more to know.

PREFACE

YOU: *I have much less time these days for things I enjoy. If you want me to make time to read this book, you better convince me fast. Real fast. Like now.*

ME: Wow, it's like we're bonding already. Thanks for holding back. Here's the deal: The sooner you know what you're doing financially, the sooner you can begin to accumulate wealth.

YOU: *What?*

ME: You're probably not concerned about retirement planning yet and as far as investing—

YOU: *You're right about that. Retirement is at least thirty years from now, so who cares? And as far as investing goes, why does that matter if I have no money to invest in the first place? I'll deal with it when I have some. So I guess that's it—I'm putting the book down.*

ME: Wait a minute.

YOU: *My ride is going to be here any second.*

ME: I know you're in a hurry, but you need to understand that financial planning is about much more than retirement planning or investing. Most people don't realize that, so they think they don't have to worry about financial planning at all.

YOU:	*So financial planning isn't just for rich people?*
ME:	No! It's just that less affluent folks seldom understand how financial planning can benefit them.
YOU:	*Why can't I deal with this later? My older brother didn't bother with financial planning at my age and he drives a BMW.*
ME:	I don't know your older brother. However—
GARY:	**I know him. Just sold him an annuity last week. Great guy—didn't ask a lot of questions.**
ME:	Gary, butt out. This isn't your book.
YOU:	*Who's that?*
ME:	Just someone who *claims* to be looking out for you but often gets in the way of my helping you.
YOU:	*I see that already.*
ME:	As to your brother, one never really knows another person's true financial situation. However, *you* can and should proactively plan for *your* future. It is a rare person who does so at a young age, but the rewards for doing so are tremendous. I want you to be one of those people.
YOU:	*What if I already have credit card debt and student loans?*
ME:	I know. That's a common problem that can be overcome. We're going to talk about that. And I won't yell. But I will recommend what to do about it.
	Deal with your money situation now, whatever your current financial attitude. With this book, you have an opportunity to learn financial planning without someone like Gary trying to sell you an annuity, a mutual fund with a load, an insurance policy—
YOU:	*And—*
ME:	I, however, talk to you with *candor*—honesty, integrity, and lack of bias.
YOU:	*Candor?*
ME:	Total Candor.

INTRODUCTION

Few people at any age take the time to think about financial planning. Of those who do, many get only as far as "Huh? I don't know anything about this." As a result, procrastination is one of the biggest obstacles to successful financial planning.

Yet if overcoming procrastination is the key, why are many "Type A" people also in worse financial shape than they should be? Although they have the *desire* to take charge of their finances, they lack the *tools* to act effectively on their desire.

It's a tragedy that our society does not teach the most basic elements of personal financial planning. Most people don't learn it in junior high, high school, or even college. Sure, you might have one particularly motivated math or accounting teacher spend half a class on balancing a checkbook, but anything beyond that? Highly unlikely.

You might feel embarrassed by having chosen an educational path or a career that didn't prepare you for the basics of personal finance. You might think those who major in accounting or go into business already know this stuff. Nonsense! You don't learn squat about managing personal finances from such experiences. Despite my business degrees and work as an executive for a large company, my personal financial education came elsewhere.

OVERCOMING IGNORANCE

Lack of financial education results in a large number of stupid financial decisions being made by a large number of people. At least that's what I used to think. Now, I believe many of these financial decisions aren't so stupid after all.

Most people are curious yet somewhat intimidated by financial planning. As a result, my friends and family members were pretty excited years ago when they learned I had selected personal financial planning as my occupation. This meant they had someone they could ask questions of. There was now a financial planner "in the family."

Early on, all these people asking me questions flattered me. They trusted me with deeply personal information just so they could get my opinion! Friends and family asked me about mutual funds, income taxes, and their 401(k)s. I assisted clients with sophisticated estate planning strategies. At age 23 I became a Certified Public Accountant (CPA) and a CERTIFIED FINANCIAL PLANNER™ (CFP) professional. I worked for two of the largest and most prestigious public accounting firms as part of a team advising people often worth tens of millions of dollars.

Despite the large difference in wealth between my clients and my friends and family, I applied the same key principles of financial planning to assist them. Some days I found this extremely rewarding. But toward the end of my career at those public accounting firms I felt less satisfied. I realized my professional work was ultimately about making extremely rich people richer. The people who really needed my help could never afford to hire me. So off I went to grad school.

This book and the Total Candor business were born several years later. Rather than restrict myself to helping only those who could afford to pay me as an *advisor*, I built a company that helps others through financial planning *education*—the very benefit our society has historically failed to provide.

IT'S OKAY TO KNOW MORE
THAN YOU'RE EXPECTED TO

I select those words with great care. By definition, an advisor gives *advice,* or "guidance for a future action." This is very different from *education,* a word meaning "the imparting and acquiring of knowledge through teaching and learning."

Advisors are neither compensated by nor trained in the teaching of financial planning to their clients. Instead of education, advisors typically provide their clients with recommendations. As a result, many clients remain dependent on their advisors in their quest for financial success. Dependency is a fine relationship for some people, especially if they get a competent advisor with a high level of integrity. But that option isn't available to people who don't have wealth large enough to be attractive to a qualified advisor. This includes most people living paycheck to paycheck.

Think about it: if you were an advisor whose income was based on either sales commissions or as a percentage of money managed, would you seek clients with a lot of money to invest or those with just a little? This financial incentive alone explains why most advisors seek prospective clients who already have money.

On the other hand, you can choose to gain an understanding of basic personal finance. No longer financially ignorant, you will neither procrastinate nor make poor financial decisions. You will have the capacity and the motivation to live *Beyond Paycheck to Paycheck.*

Don't be embarrassed if you currently lack basic financial knowledge. Be proud. Why? Reading this book puts you way ahead of most of your peers. This is true regardless of your age. It is true whether you have a Ph.D. or didn't finish high school.

Knowledge is power no matter who you are or when you acquire it.

CHAPTER 1

The Basics:
Tell Your Money to Go to Work

"The beginnings of all things are small."
—CICERO

MONEY

Money is amazing. Look at any dollar bill. It's lightweight, rips easily, and flies away in a slight breeze. Yet you can go to any convenience store, hand a cashier this green piece of paper and walk out with a bag of chips. The cashier might even smile as you leave. To me, that's astounding.

Simply put, money has value because you can buy things with it. Depending on how much of it you have in your wallet, your money can buy you a steak dinner at a fancy restaurant or a side order of fries at a diner.

Money can sit in your wallet, desk drawer, pocket, or be buried in your couch. Money in these places is your **cash on hand** because that's where it is. You can access it and spend it, instantly. (Admittedly, it may be harder to access the cash buried in your couch, but you get the idea.) Because cash on hand is not invested, you can spend it now.

Like all education, the process needs a teacher and a student. You might not understand everything the first time you read it. But, like a good teacher, I provide all the tools possible for you to learn: examples, **key terms in boldface** that can be looked up in the glossary, and the *opportunity to ask questions which you will do in italics throughout this book.* Also, be warned that **Gary, a sales-obsessed "planner," will appear from time to time in a font similar to this one to express his thoughts.** Part of your education in money management is becoming aware of what his spin might be in certain situations, while determining your own *true* needs.

You: How do I get money?

Gary: I can get you some. If you give me $1,000 now, I guarantee you $5,000 in five years.

Some words to the wise: Always be wary of what people *guarantee.* If an offer seems too good to be true, it usually is. There's no such thing as a sure investment that will quintuple your money in five years. Furthermore, never write a check to an advisor. Write it to the nationally known name of the brokerage house or mutual fund the advisor works with. *Your* name should be on the brokerage house's account statements, not the advisor's alone.

Of course, you'd like to know the best way to accumulate more money. One way is to follow comic Steve Martin's savvy advice for becoming a millionaire: "First, get a million dollars." More realistic methods to acquire money include gifts (most people get gifts, large or small, from time to time), inheritances (for some people), and winning the lottery (for one in a zillion, yet this long shot gets the most press. Unfortunately, many people spend too much money trying to achieve instant wealth through this method.). But gifts, inheritances, and the lottery are far less likely sources for your acquiring money than by *working* for it. That conclusion may seem boring and even uninspiring, but the earnings you receive by working are truly the most important source.

If you start making $30,000 annually at age 22 and receive a 3 percent raise each year, by your early sixties you will have earned more than $2.3 million over your career. When you work at a job, you can expect to get paid for your efforts, or at least your time served.[1] This compensation for your work is your **income** and is a major source of money for nearly everyone.

You: Let me rephrase. How do I get a lot of money other than by working?

Ahh. Well, nearly everyone needs a paycheck to first acquire money. It is how you *treat* the money you earn that determines whether you struggle from paycheck to paycheck or ultimately move beyond.

The real answer to your question is to *create wealth*. Many eye-opening examples of how to create wealth appear throughout this book. None are more important than this first one:

THE MIRACLE OF COMPOUNDING INTEREST

Wake up! If your eyes are reading but your brain isn't paying attention, this is one section that can change your life.

What you will learn in this section changed my life. I was fortunate to have been taught at a young age the lesson I am about to share with you. Few people ever learn this lesson. Of those who do, most learn it so late in life that the biggest advantages the opportunity provides have already passed.

Ever hear the phrase "I will gladly pay you Tuesday for a hamburger today"? This was the trademark phrase of the legendary character Wimpy from the *Popeye* comic strip and television cartoons. That phrase may have been your first introduction to a key financial planning concept.

Wimpy, who could pack 'em away, negotiated for food. Rather than pay for the hamburger when he received (and ate) it, he offered payment

---

[1] If going to work feels like "serving time," think about a new job.

next Tuesday. Of course, Tuesday never seemed to arrive. I can't remember Wimpy ever paying for a hamburger. That gimmick may be a big part of the humor for a five-year-old, but the financial lesson, admittedly unintended, is far deeper.

Even though Tuesday comes each week in the real world, it's nevertheless a good financial strategy to pay in the *future* for something you receive *today*. Similarly, it is better to receive money today instead of receiving the same amount in the future.

Let's say I offer you the following two choices:

1. you receive one dollar today, or
2. you receive one dollar tomorrow.

Which choice do you prefer?

You: It doesn't matter to me. It's already 9 PM and I'm not going out anymore tonight. Whatever. You pick.

Although there's neither much money at stake nor a long time to wait in this scenario, the smarter move is to choose to receive the dollar today. After all, you can spend the dollar today instead of waiting for a day. If you're a saver, you can put the dollar in the bank today and earn interest for an additional day.

Since you don't care that much for either of those choices, try this scenario:

1. you receive $1,000 today, or
2. you receive $1,000 in three years.

You: Now we're talking. I'm free in an hour. Where should we meet?

I thought that thousand bucks would sound pretty good right now. Take an extreme example:

1. you receive $1 million today, or
2. you receive $1 million in 30 years.

You: Do I even need to answer?

No. Now the choice is obvious—you'd be a fool to turn down the million dollars today.

As you can see, the more money involved and the longer the delay to receive it, the more difficult waiting becomes. Because *money is worth more today than in the future* (known as the **time value of money**), you always prefer receiving money sooner. Said another way, a dollar will be worth less in the future. It actually *loses value over time.*

You: Why is my money worth less in the future than it is worth today?

One reason is inflation. **Inflation** is the overall trend of rising prices over time. Most items rise in price. Inflation has historically averaged about 3 to 4 percent each year. You might not notice the small yearly increases, but over many years these increases have a tremendous effect.

Remember when Manhattan was purchased for $24?

You: Um, I'm pretty sure that happened way before I was born.

Hey, you're pretty sharp over there. Indeed, that sale did happen a long time ago; 1626 to be precise. Still, 24 bucks doesn't sound like very much, does it? But assuming 4 percent annual inflation over 381 years, $24 in 1626 is worth roughly $74 million in 2007! So you would have definitely preferred to receive $24 in 1626 instead of receiving $24 in 2007.[2]

> The **interest rate** on your savings account is the percentage of your deposit paid to you over a year. If you have $100 in your savings account on January 1 with an interest rate of 5 percent, you will have $105 on December 31.

Another reason to prefer a dollar today rather than a dollar in the future is what you can do with the dollar you have in the interim—you can invest it.

Imagine two young women, Jessica and Grace. Both are 30 years old, earn the same income, and live in neighboring apartments. If it helps you to see them as remarkably similar, yes, they have the same hairstyle.

---

[2] Still, $74 million for all of Manhattan today is a great deal! But proceed cautiously if someone tries to sell Manhattan to you, especially if he offers to "throw in the Brooklyn Bridge" to sweeten the deal.

Grace receives a gift of $1,000 on January 1, 2007 and Jessica receives the same $1,000 gift ten years later, on January 1, 2017. Each earns an 8 percent interest rate on her $1,000.

Look at the following tables, which highlight the impact of receiving the same gift at different times.

Figure 1-1

The Advantage of a Head Start

Grace receives $1,000 on January 1, 2007.		Jessica receives $1,000 on January 1, 2017.
January 1 Balance	Year	January 1 Balance
$ 1,000	2007	$ —
$ 1,469	2012	$ —
$ 2,159	2017	$1,000
$ 3,172	2022	$1,469
$ 4,661	2027	$2,159
$ 6,848	2032	$3,172
$10,063	2037	$4,661
$14,785	2042	$6,848

What stands out? Perhaps most striking is the amount of money Grace will have accumulated by the time Jessica receives her $1,000 in 2017. Grace's original $1,000 will grow to $2,159. Think about it. That $2,159 figure is more than double what she started with just ten years earlier! Meanwhile, Jessica has only $1,000 at the beginning of 2017 because, after all, that is when she receives it.

Now look at the year 2042, when Grace and Jessica turn 65 and (we'll assume) retire. Grace's original $1,000 has been invested for 35 years compared to 25 years for Jessica's money. While both will have been saving a long time, look at the difference in the value of the original $1,000. Jessica's money will grow to nearly $7,000 over those 25 years. But Grace, due solely to her ten-year head start, will have more than double Jessica's total—a shade under $15,000!

Figure 1-2

Motivation in a Graph

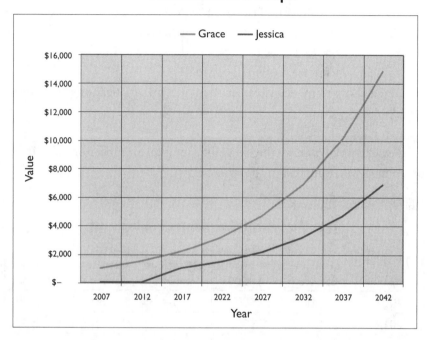

You: *Why does this happen? How can two people each receive exactly $1,000, earn an identical interest rate, and end up with such different amounts of money? Is there more going on here than Grace's head start?*

No, there are no games. The numbers work out this way because of the *miracle of compounding interest.* This miracle is a key factor behind the time value of money.

You: *A miracle? C'mon. The Red Sox beating the Yankees in 2004 was a miracle. TiVo is a miracle. I don't even know what compounding interest is—how could it be a miracle?*

Compounding interest occurs when your money makes money for you. For example, in 2007 Grace earns $80 in interest (calculated as 8 percent or 0.08 x $1,000). The following year she starts with $1,000 *plus* the

$80 of interest earned in 2007. As a result, she earns $86.40 (calculated as 8 percent or 0.08 x $1,080) rather than the $80 earned the year before. The additional $6.40 is a result of the miracle of compounding interest.

You: Big deal. I can barely rent a movie for $6.40.

You're right, it isn't a big deal. Not in the short-term, anyway.

You: So why are we talking about this?

Since short-term decisions have long-term implications, you must simultaneously consider both. It is *your actions in the short term that create your reality in the long term.*

For example, observe the enormous long-term impact of the miracle of compounding interest in the table below:

Figure 1-3

The Miracle of Compounding Interest

Year	January 1 Balance	Interest on the original $1,000	Miracle Interest*	Total Interest Earned	December 31 Balance
2007	$ 1,000	$80	$ –	$ 80	$ 1,080
2012	$ 1,469	$80	$ 38	$ 118	$ 1,587
2017	$ 2,159	$80	$ 93	$ 173	$ 2,332
2022	$ 3,172	$80	$ 174	$ 254	$ 3,426
2027	$ 4,661	$80	$ 293	$ 373	$ 5,034
2032	$ 6,849	$80	$ 468	$ 548	$ 7,396
2037	$10,063	$80	$ 725	$ 805	$10,868
2042	$14,785	$80	$1,103	$1,183	$15,968

*The amount of interest earned on interest previously earned.

Although Grace's original $1,000 earns $80 every year, the total interest she earns increases dramatically. In 2042, she earns $1,183 in interest! That year alone, her interest income is more than her original $1,000 deposit!

You: You've got to be kidding! That is a miracle. Who cares about the Red Sox? Forget TiVo.

Easy does it—I live in New England. But I'm glad you see how powerful compounding interest can be. Have you ever heard the phrase "It takes money to make money"?

You: You bet. Remember, I asked you how to get more money without working.

Compounding interest is a great example of money making money—and it sure beats working. How hard will Grace have to work for the $1,183 of interest she earns in 2042?

You: She doesn't have to work at all for that money.

That's right. Grace's success comes from only two steps and neither one involves going to work. First, she can't spend the original $1,000—she must save it. Second, she must leave the interest earned each year in the account. This allows her money to make more money.

You: Okay, I get it. When I receive $1,000, I should save it and forget I have it. If I leave it alone long enough, I can wind up with big bucks.

You got it.

You: That still leaves one problem, though.

And what is that?

You: I don't have $1,000.

I figured that, and I bet one of the reasons you don't have $1,000 is you didn't know the true implications of saving money at your age. Perhaps your parents told you "saving is important," but before you read this section did you truly understand why it was so important?

You: I guess not.

Of course not—nobody explained this to you, so how could you know? But that just changed. See what awareness of this miracle can do for you? It provides the motivation to save. The strategies for doing so are in Chapter 2.

Look, the lesson here is *not* to emulate Wimpy by buying hamburgers at McDonald's and bargain with the cashier as if you're haggling over jewelry in Cancún on spring break.[3] Rather, find a way to save that $1,000—*or whatever amount you can manage to save*—sooner rather than later. *One thousand dollars a year is less than three bucks a day.*

HOW TO GET MORE MONEY FROM LESS SAVINGS

Allow me to beat what should already be a dead horse but is likely not. Let's understand the implications of adopting a successful savings strategy relatively early in life.[4]

It's time to meet Ben and Henry. They're good friends (some think they must be related) and each will turn 21 in 2008 and begin working full-time. While they earn the same salary, they are quite different with respect to their saving habits:

➤ Ben gets his act together quickly and manages to put $1,000 in his savings account by the end of 2008. He makes saving a priority and continues to save $1,000 each year for ten years ($10,000 in total). After making a $1,000 savings deposit at the end of 2017, he skips the New Year's Eve parties and instead goes to a local park and shouts "I have enough!" four times: once facing North, once South, once East, and once West. Then, in a quieter reflective voice, he vows to neither add nor remove any money from his account until he retires.

➤ Compared to Ben, Henry is neither as committed at age 21 nor as whimsical 10 years later. Henry doesn't save a dime during his first ten working years. "Easy come, easy go" is his mantra. But

---

[3] But if you try, definitely let me know how that works out.
[4] You can pick any point in time. Change the numbers slightly and compare the implications of starting at various ages by visiting *www.totalcandor.com.*

exactly one year after Ben's "moment" in the park, Henry decides to get on the "saving thing." From that point forward, he saves $1,000 a year, and he does so for 35 consecutive years until retirement. He never misses a single year and saves a total of $35,000.

➤ The interest rate on each of their savings accounts is identical: 8 percent every year.

It's now the end of 2052, so both Ben and Henry are 65 years old. Who do you think has more money? Keep in mind Henry saved a total of $35,000 (35 years of $1,000 per year) and Ben saved a total of only $10,000 (ten years of $1,000 per year).

Am I reading your mind? Is the logical side of your brain saying:

"C'mon man. Henry saved over three times what Ben did. Ben didn't have a higher interest rate. Henry has to end up with more money. You can't flake out at age 30 and wind up ahead at the end. There's no way Ben has more, given how much more money Henry saved."

And the cynical side of your brain is saying:

"Look—this guy's trying to prove a point. Why create an example in which the expected and logical answer—Henry having more money—is correct? I guess Ben winds up with a little more money somehow."

Here's what happens.

1. In 2052, Ben has more money than Henry.
2. The totals are *not even close!*

Ben saved less than a third of what Henry saved, yet has 24 percent more than Henry. Let that sink in for a minute. Ben has 24 percent more money available for his retirement though he saved less than one-third the amount Henry saved—and for one simple reason: *Ben started sooner.*

Here's a snapshot of how their respective savings grow over time:

Figure 1-4

Saving Sooner vs. Saving Longer

Balance on December 31 of the Year	Ben	Henry
2008	$ 1,000	$ –
2013	$ 7,336	$ –
2018	$ 15,646	$ 1,000
2023	$ 22,988	$ 7,336
2028	$ 33,777	$ 16,646
2033	$ 49,630	$ 30,324
2038	$ 72,923	$ 50,423
2043	$107,148	$ 79,954
2048	$157,435	$123,346
2052	$214,189	$172,317
Total Saved	$ 10,000	$ 35,000

8% growth rate

Ben saves from 2008 through 2017. After 2017, the increase in Ben's account is completely due to interest.

Henry starts saving in 2018 and continues through 2052.

The miracle of compounding interest is a critical phenomenon to embrace. Now armed with an understanding of the miracle and an appreciation for its benefits, you need to take this knowledge to heart by changing some behaviors. First, you need to start saving right away.

You: But I'm only...

Perhaps. But *you will never be further from retiring than you are right now.* By delaying saving, you choose to waste the opportunity that the miracle of compounding interest provides you. Procrastination has implications. Negative implications.

Another thing: What would the result be if Ben had not had his epiphany in the park? If he kept on saving? Let's look at Lauren, a good friend of Ben and Henry. Like Ben, she started saving at age 21 but kept right on. She saved $1,000 a year for 45 years. Here are the results of Lauren's financial actions:

Figure 1-5

The Result of Long-Term, Consistent Saving

Balance on December 31 of the Year	Ben	Henry	Lauren
2008	$ 1,000	$ –	$ 1,000
2013	$ 7,336	$ –	$ 7,336
2018	$ 15,646	$ 1,000	$ 16,646
2023	$ 22,988	$ 7,336	$ 30,324
2028	$ 33,777	$ 16,646	$ 50,423
2033	$ 49,630	$ 30,324	$ 79,954
2038	$ 72,923	$ 50,423	$123,346
2043	$107,148	$ 79,954	$187,102
2048	$157,435	$123,346	$280,781
2052	$214,189	$172,317	$386,506

Total Saved	$ 10,000	$ 35,000	$ 45,000

8% growth rate

Lauren saves $1,000 annually from 2008 through 2052.

The difference is stunning, isn't it? By saving just $1,000 a year, Lauren has over $385,000! Since saving $1,000 per year is only $3 per day—it *is* achievable. Imagine what her total would look like if she'd been able to save just slightly more, say $5 per day. Or $10!

> emember inflation. A dollar is worth less in the future than it is
> worth today. Lauren's $385,000 in 2052 is actually worth about
> $105,000 in 2008, assuming a 3 percent rate of inflation. Similarly,
> saving $1,000 in the future will be much easier than saving the same
> amount in 2008.

You can retire wealthier by saving a little now than by saving nothing now and saving much more later. Use this miracle, this open secret, as motivation to get going sooner.

Albert Einstein has been credited with saying that compounding interest is the most powerful force in the universe. After you understand these examples, I hope you agree. Besides, are you really prepared to disagree with Albert Einstein? Remember that Wimpy also benefited from the time value of money. So both ends of the intellectual spectrum have weighed in on the importance of taking advantage of this phenomenon. Regardless of who ultimately convinces you, choose to benefit from this miracle. No one gets in trouble for saving too much too soon.

Having money make money, especially for extended periods of time, increases wealth faster and more significantly than any other method. Remember we got on this topic when you asked how to get money other than by working for it. Well, working remains a prerequisite for getting started on the road to wealth, because you need to have savings if you are to take advantage of the miracle. While key savings strategies are in the next chapter, you first need an income to save, so that's where Chapter 2 begins.

Income → Savings → Wealth

CHAPTER 2

Don't Be Cheap, Be Fiscally Responsible

*"Just as soon as people make enough money to live comfortably,
they want to live extravagantly."*
—ANONYMOUS

Most people's primary source of money is income from their jobs. This type of income is **active income.** There is also another key source of income—one fewer people understand—called passive income. **Passive income** is money you receive without working. Obtaining passive income is a crucial component of your long-term personal financial success. While passive income is discussed in Chapter 8, we focus now on active income.

ACTIVE INCOME

Active income is exactly what it sounds like: you have to actively do something (work) to get money. Even if your job demands little more than affixing cover sheets to TPS reports and the careful reading of memos, it is nevertheless work, so the income is considered active.

> **N**ote that the definitions used throughout this book assume you are an employee. Definitions may differ somewhat if you are self-employed.

GROSS INCOME

Your **gross income** is the amount of money you earn. Gross income would also be what you receive if not for tax. Perhaps you can recall working 20 hours during the first week of your first job. Since you were making $6 per hour, you anticipated $120 on payday.

But that's not what happened.

Your *pay stub* did indicate you were paid $120—your gross income. Unfortunately, your *paycheck* was not payable for gross income. The check was for your net income only.

NET INCOME

Net income is what remains after taxes are withheld.[1] Often referred to as **take-home pay,** net income is money you can get your hands on. Net income is society's way of saying "Job well done. You earned $120.00 for all of your hard work. Here's $87.65."

You: That sounds about right. Given that, how do I become wealthy making an income? I have a decent income, but I'm certainly not wealthy.

While income and wealth are not identical concepts, they are more closely related than people like to believe. While there are numerous "get rich quick" books (many with the word "millionaire" displayed prominently on their covers), the most likely road to wealth remains the oldest: You must earn it.

You: That sounds like working. I've tried that and I am not getting anywhere.

---

[1] Subtractions other than taxes might further lower your net income.

You: So how come I'm never paid what I thought I was going to get paid?

The answer to that question is simple: tax. You live in a country that taxes income. If you have income from working, you will pay tax. It doesn't matter if you make minimum wage or work only one hour all year. The taxman always takes his share. This is covered in detail in Chapter 4.

You create wealth in two steps: First, by making an income. This is what you have been doing. Second, by making solid financial decisions that convert your income into wealth over the long term. This is your opportunity.

WEALTH

Wealth is what you own less what you owe. Things you own are **assets.** Amounts you owe are **debts** or **liabilities.** The term **net worth** is a synonym for wealth—the difference between the value of your assets and the value of your debts.

Your assets can include tangible items such as your:

➤ car

➤ house

➤ clothing

➤ DVD collection

When calculating your net worth, however, only include saleable items with a high value. From the list above, those are probably just the car and the house. Nonetheless, if you envision selling some clothes and DVDs for a bunch of cash, you can include those items in your net worth calculation also.

Other important assets might include:

➤ bank checking and savings accounts

➤ retirement plans

➤ cash in your wallet (or between the seats of your car)

Take a few minutes to create a list of your assets and their value by completing the table below.

Figure 2-1

Your Personal Asset Summary

Asset Description	Current Value
Checking account	
Savings account	
Car (if owned)	
Home (if owned)	
401(k) plan	
Individual retirement account	
Other	
Other	
Other	
Other	
Other	
Other	
Other	
Other	
TOTAL:	

On the other hand, your debts might include:

➤ student loan
➤ credit card debt
➤ car loan
➤ home **mortgage**—the amount of the loan still owed on your home purchase
➤ **home equity loan**—the additional amount you borrow against the value of your home
➤ other consumer debt—like when you bought a TV a few months ago with nothing down

Note that neither your apartment lease nor your car lease is listed. That's because both are effectively rentals. If you don't own either your apartment or your car, neither one is your asset. And although you must continue making payments, each installment is an obligation of the lease, not a debt payment.

If you take out a traditional loan to *purchase* your home or car, then a portion of each payment reduces the balance owed before you own the asset outright. This is clearly not how a lease works—at the end of your lease payments, you don't own anything.

Use the following simple formula to calculate your wealth at any given point in time:

Net Worth (Wealth) = Assets − Liabilities

I am a huge believer in the simplification of what many people incorrectly assume must be complex. There are no difficult formulas in any Total Candor℠ books or workshops. Multiplication and addition are all the tools you will ever need to learn personal financial planning.

However rich or poor you feel, the formula is the same.

You: What does this mean for me?

Assuming your goal is to become wealthier...

You: It is. Although, I prefer the word "rich."

...then you are in control. You can become rich simply by creating more assets than debt over time.

You: That sounds easy. It can't be.

Yes it can.

SAVING IS SIMPLE

Creating wealth is easy, but requires effort. The only way to create more assets than debts is to save, and saving requires sacrifice. Sacrifice has always been hard, but in the 2000s seems nearly impossible. Few people today are familiar with **delayed gratification.**

You: I've heard of delayed gratification, but what does it mean?

The concept means making the choice to *not* buy everything you want today. Buying things gives you pleasure...

You: ...making me no different than anyone else.

True, and there's absolutely nothing wrong with enjoying your income. But if you use *all* your income now, you pay a price later. By delaying gratification, you are able to save a portion of your income now. This sacrifice enables you to have additional enjoyable experiences later that would otherwise not be possible.

Making the choice to save means making a lifestyle decision that is admittedly not popular today. However, it is an essential decision to be able to save for the future you want.

You: But how am I supposed to save on my income?

Saving is another extremely simple concept to understand once you see how easy the formula is that defines it:

Your Income – Your Spending = Your Savings

That's it. Think about it for a minute because it is truly powerful. You can pull only two levers to impact your savings level: your income and your spending. With that in mind, do you have control over your income?

You: Heck no. Does anyone?

Very few people control their income, especially in the short term. So we'll say you can't increase your income over the next several months. That leaves only one way to impact the level of your savings: changing your *spending habits.*

Remember we're discussing spending because you want to create wealth (become richer). Here is how your spending decisions have an impact on your net worth:

➤ If you spend more than your income, you lower your net worth.

➤ If you spend less than your income, you increase your net worth.

You: Why?

Imagine yourself in the first category—that you spend more than you make.

You: I don't have to imagine that. Hello? I bought your book.

Fair enough. When you spend more than your income, you must either take money from your existing savings or increase the amount you borrow from others. Here are the implications of each of these actions:

Figure 2-2

The Impact on Net Worth of Spending *More* Than Your Income

Source of Money for Spending	Example	Impact on Asset or Debt	Impact on Your Net Worth
Depleting your existing savings	Withdraw money from your savings account	Decreases the value of your existing assets	**Decreases**
Borrowing from others	Charge on your credit card	Increases debt level	**Decreases**

Whether you spend $50 more than your income or $5,000 more, you decrease your net worth—although much faster in the latter case.

Let's say you are able to alter your spending habits and now spend slightly *less* than your income. With the resulting extra money, you either add to your savings or reduce your existing debt. Here is how your behavior makes a positive impact on your net worth:

Figure 2-3

The Impact on Net Worth of Spending Less Than Your Income

Use of Extra Money	Example	Impact on Asset or Debt	Impact on Your Net Worth
Adding to your savings	Deposit money into your savings account	Increases the value of your existing assets	**Increases**
Reducing your existing borrowing	Pay down balance on your credit card	Decreases debt level	**Increases**

Whatever choice you make for your savings (money earned but not spent), you increase your net worth. You move a step closer to financial success, because you are *creating wealth*. On the other hand, you can *destroy wealth* by spending more than your income. Figure 2-2 demonstrated that. Which road would you rather go down?

You: Seems like creating wealth is an obvious choice. Honestly, none of this is complicated.

That's correct, it isn't difficult. None of this is.

You: Okay—then why aren't most people wealthy?

There are several reasons. One is the lack of knowledge about how easy wealth creation is.

You: And now I have that knowledge.

Indeed you do. But there is also another challenge: you must go against the flow.

You: What?

To develop a successful spending profile and thereby create wealth, you must spend less than you make. As you know, most people do not even consider that today. So, with your new insight into the simplicity of creating wealth, the burden is now on you. You make the choice. You control your financial destiny. That's a fair amount of pressure.

You: I think I can handle the pressure, but I don't want to be cheap.

It's not about being "cheap." *It's about being fiscally responsible. It's about choosing responsibility over insanity.* I purchased my first car, a new Plymouth Neon, in 1994 for $12,800. Selecting an inexpensive car certainly helped me to save, but there were no babes pulling up next to me saying, "Hey, nice bank account."

The external rewards for saving are practically non-existent compared to the high you receive when showing off new expensive shoes, season tickets, or your luxury apartment in the sky. However, it is short-term sacrifice that leads to long-term wealth creation. And there is no better time to take advantage of the miracle of compounding interest than today.

You: So how do I save without becoming cheap?

TEN SIMPLE SAVING STRATEGIES

Here are ten easy strategies to increase your savings level without becoming cheap.

Strategy 1: Don't become emotionally separated from your money.

Remember when a grandparent or special aunt gave you a dollar bill? As a child, you enjoyed simply having the money, looking at it, and even counting it. You knew exactly how much you had and you planned exactly how you were going to use it.

How things have changed! Now your paycheck is direct-deposited and you charge most every expense. You don't have a clue how much money you have in your wallet until you find yourself at a place that doesn't accept credit cards.

This emotional separation from your money makes it much easier for you to spend more. Try using cash instead of credit cards for a while. Keep track for a couple of months and see if your expenses decrease. Handing over six hard-earned twenties is far more difficult than charging $119.40 on a credit card.

Strategy 2: Understand and be honest about expense classifications.

Think of **discretionary expenses** as "wants" and **nondiscretionary expenses** as "needs."

Look at the examples of nondiscretionary expenses on the next page. See how there is little you can do—in the short term—to reduce those expenses? As a result, you need to focus your energy on monitoring your discretionary expenses. But be careful. Frequently, people categorize wants as needs. Incorrectly labeling your expenses limits your ability to take advantage of additional savings opportunities.

Think about decisions you make every day. Are the bulk of your purchases legitimately needs, or do you just view them that way? Eating is a need. Eating out is a want.

Figure 2-4

Expense Classifications

Primarily Non-Discretionary	Primarily Discretionary
Housing (rent or mortgage)	Restaurants/bars
Taxes	Coffee shop visits
Student loans	Premium movie stations
Car payment	Movies/DVD rentals
Insurance premiums	Vacation and travel
Groceries	Charitable contributions
Gasoline	Gifts
Utilities	Concert or sporting event tickets
Commuting expenses (public transportation or parking at the office)	Non-work clothes
Doctor's appointments and medicines	Lunch out while working
Work clothes	Cell phone

Strategy 3: The time to lower your "needs" spending was yesterday.

Despite successful efforts to limit discretionary spending, many people still struggle with saving. Typically, this is because their nondiscretionary expenses are just too high for their income level. The best way to handle this is to avoid the situation in the first place.

It is you who must care enough to review your spending priorities before you make a commitment to an apartment lease, mortgage, or car. *Just because someone will sell you something doesn't mean you can actually afford it.* You determine your nondiscretionary expenses when you sign your name. Keep that point in mind next time. Knowing that additional nondiscretionary expenses could take a significant part of your monthly income for a year or longer just might motivate you to *not* choose the one with "all the extras" for "just a few more bucks a month."

Strategy 4: Enjoy free stuff.

Depending on your interest, you can go on a long hike, sit in a park, talk with a friend, read a book or newspaper, lie on the beach, or play sports with friends without spending a dime. Many people think they can't have a good time unless they spend a fair amount of money. But that belief is based on what has been successful for them in their recent past, not on reality. When you were younger, there were hundreds of days in which you had no money to spend, yet you were as busy and as happy as ever.[2] Can you try just a day or two like that this month?

Strategy 5: Major on the major.

Don't spend much time evaluating minor expenses, such as where to buy pizza. Rather, put major focus on major purchases. A car and a place to live are obviously major expenses. What else is major? Regardless of your age, financial aptitude, or income, a good rule of thumb is to treat anything you can't pay for entirely when you buy it as major. Spend serious time evaluating those purchases to ensure you can afford what you are buying, and you value every feature you'll be paying for over the upcoming months and years.

Strategy 6: Enjoy being with people you like.

Your friends make the evening enjoyable—not the menu design or the lighting where you meet. When a few friends suggest meeting for dinner, it's perfectly fine to suggest a place you loved when you had less money. That place is probably less expensive than the trendy yuppie restaurant that just opened. Many of your friends (but not all) will be thrilled to spend $15 on the evening's food rather than $35. They just lack the courage to propose an alternative to the comparatively free-spending organizers. Don't be surprised if one or two of your friends thank you for your suggestion—in private.

Strategy 7: Don't blow off the recurring minor.

Small *recurring* expenses aren't truly minor. Examples include your cable bill, your cell phone plan, and your morning coffee. Estimate the cost of such expenses for a full year. Are you comfortable with that level of spending?

There is no right or wrong answer here—it's a personal decision. Some people *need* their coffee every morning and it's something they look forward to from the moment they wake up. But other people spend $5 every

---

[2] Maybe happier—you weren't worried about the money you were spending.

weekday morning ($1,300 annually) just to delay getting to the office for another few minutes.

Regardless, don't try to change all your habits at once, but see if you can find at least one minor recurring expense to cut. Perhaps lose the premium cable channel you never actually watch. Or switch to a lower minutes–per-month cell phone plan. Minor expenses aren't really minor if they last a long time.

Figure 2-5

Recurring "Minor" Expenses

- **Home telephone**—Do you even need one or could your cell phone suffice?
- **Dry cleaning**—Can you dry clean half as frequently as you do now?
- **Lunch expenses at work**—Can you bring your lunch at least once per week?
- **Vending machines**—Buy a bunch of candy bars or snacks you like at the grocery store and put them in your desk. You'll need to spend only half as much to satisfy that mid-afternoon craving.
- **Gym membership**—Pay the least for what you value.
- **Bank account fees**—Pay none or get another bank.
- **ATM fees**—Take money out of your bank's ATM and avoid unnecessary fees. Three-dollar's-worth of charges ($1.50 to your bank and $1.50 to the ATM owner) on a $50 withdrawal is like paying a 6 percent tax to get your money. That's expensive. Plan ahead or drive around the corner.

Strategy 8: Spend with comfort on items or experiences you value highly.

As with time management, you cannot prioritize all financial desires as "highly important." Life requires choices. Not prioritizing your spend-ing is itself a choice. Often, the result is giving up control, because you run out of money at an inopportune time.

A better approach is to prioritize your desires. When you know what you truly value, you can spend on those things with no guilt. Enjoy! Sacrifice what is *not* important to you. Few people have enough money for unlimited discretionary expenses, and you are not one of those people. So enjoy whatever you value highly and limit the discretionary expenses you do not.

Strategy 9: You won't spend what you don't see.

Think about a friend with a similar lifestyle who makes 10 percent *more* than you. Seems she should be able to save about 10 percent more of her pay, right?

You: No doubt. We go out together and shop at the same stores. It definitely seems like we spend about the same. I just don't know why she can't save more given she makes more than I do!

Good. The same is true about you because somewhere someone is looking at you in the same way. This person makes 10 percent *less* than you do— and thinks you could save 10 percent of your pay without much effort.

You: Hey!

Suddenly saving this much might seem hard if you don't know what you're spending that "extra" 10 percent on. If your spending is limited only by the money you have available, the money just seems to disappear. The solution is to create a forced savings program,[3] in which a percentage of your income, say 10 percent, is redirected into savings without your ever "seeing it."

If you spend the money you have available (but not more), you quickly learn to spend less. You must, because the missing 10 percent isn't sitting in your checking account. The earlier in your career you participate in a forced savings program, the easier it is to do successfully, so don't delay. When you just start out, any pay is big pay.

Strategy 10: Constant budgeting isn't required.

While some swear by it, I am not a fan of constant budgeting because I find the task too inflexible to deal with life's spontaneity. Still, it is appropriate to prepare a budget when committing to a significant nondiscretionary expense. Evaluate what you can afford based on your income level and spending history. Don't take the salesperson's word that you can afford what he's showing you.

---

[3] Discussed in Chapter 6, a 401(k) plan is a great forced savings program.

However, if you prioritize your values and commence a forced savings program, you will consistently meet any strict budget objectives you would otherwise put together. To me, that's a better way to live.

WALK, THEN RUN

Creating a savings mindset is a required first step to achieving financial success. But don't try to implement all ten of the saving strategies at once. Rather, choose just one[4] or two strategies and note the effect on your bank account over time. As you grow more confident, attempt to implement a few more strategies.

BALANCING ACT

You may need to make several major changes to your spending habits in order to create a successful savings profile. Or, you might only need to pay attention to a few key areas in order to make a major difference in your life. But no matter who you are, don't overdo it.

You: What do you mean?

Don't pay so much attention to your finances that you forget to enjoy the fruits of your labor. While it is clearly important to plan for the future, it is also critical to live in the moment.

You: That seems contradictory. Besides, don't many financial planners suggest saving the most possible?

It may seem contradictory and untraditional to recommend these actions. Yet it is a key to success. It's true that you are unlikely to obtain a second home or take a dream vacation, let alone achieve a comfortable retirement, if you do not plan. But it's also possible that you never reach retirement age. If you had a crystal ball, you could spend your last dollar on your last meal. But you don't. No one knows what tomorrow will bring or if you will be around to see it.

So I advise you plan for both: today and the future.

You: But what does that actually mean?

---

[4] If you are going to try only one strategy, don't choose Strategy 10. That one doesn't work unless it's done along with the others. There are no loopholes, just opportunities.

It means living in balance. It means saving aggressively—beginning today. Doing so clearly implies a fair amount of sacrifice, especially if you have been spending more than your income.

However, do not save everything. Do not sacrifice to the point you become unhappy. Take vacations, although not necessarily those you can't yet afford. Buy new clothes, but not necessarily the top designs at the top stores at their top prices. Do what you want to do, just do so responsibly. Then, every once in a while, do something that might not make any financial sense at all, but that makes you *really* happy. You probably won't be able to do so every day or every month. However, depending on the cost of the treat you so enjoy and the degree to which you otherwise adhere to fiscally responsible strategies, you might be able to afford such special expenses far more often than you previously thought possible.

That's living in balance. I can't imagine a healthier and happier life than one in balance.

YOU ARE WHAT YOU ARE AND YOU DO WHAT YOU DO

You: That sounds good and your strategies make sense, but I'm simply not destined to become rich, I work as a—

I might not know you personally, but I know many people just like you. Perhaps you dreamed of being a radio station shock-jock but wound up hawking contact lenses to eye doctors. Of your childhood friends, Ryan is now a high-powered executive and Jason works for the fire department. Karen became a teacher and Michelle remains a perpetual student.

That's great. Job titles alone do not determine financial destiny. *Many paths* lead to financial success. Although the typical firefighter's salary is not extraordinary, there are wealthy firemen. Similarly, well-paid executives with maxed out credit cards are not to be envied.

A "lower than someone else's" salary is no excuse for failing to make good financial decisions. Don't feel sorry for yourself because you make less money than your boss.

You: But if I just made a few thousand dollars more, it would be so much easier to—

Nonsense. Right now, there are people looking at *you,* wishing for *your* salary. The fact that you can't save is mind-numbing to them.

You: You're not really talking about me. I make only $XX,OOO per year.

This is *not* for a different reader—I am still talking to you. Think about a recent immigrant who makes the minimum wage (maybe), yet still manages to send money home every month. Yes, even at $XX,000, your salary would present many additional opportunities for the immigrant's family.

On the other hand, a high income does not grant anyone the right to spend recklessly and ignore basic financial planning principles. Regardless of salary, folks who spend more than their income are making poor long-term financial choices. Even the well-paid are unexpectedly laid off. Those without a savings cushion find themselves in bigger trouble faster, as their spending habits are much tougher to ratchet down.

Ultimately, your income is important, but your habits are much more so. If you're happy with your chosen profession, congratulations. You've already beaten one set of odds, so enjoy. When you retire, your *savings* determine your lifestyle. The *status* of your former jobs won't even buy you a package of Metamucil.

Though we discussed strategies for saving first, we cannot ignore the opposite of savings: debt. It is critical to understand debt, if for no other reason than you most likely already have some debt. A review of debt, how it affects your financial life, and what you can still do about it are addressed in Chapter 3.

Debt Sucks (Your Money Away)

"Beware of little expenses; a small leak will sink a great ship."
—BENJAMIN FRANKLIN

All debt reduces your net worth; hence, debts are the ultimate destroyer of wealth.

GOOD DEBT, BAD DEBT

Still, not all debt is bad debt. A debt that creates an investment opportunity is a good debt. For example, a mortgage and a student loan each allow you to acquire an asset. When you create mortgage debt, the asset you acquire is your home. Similarly, a student loan allows you to acquire an education, which can lead to a higher-paying job.

On the other hand, consider an expensive pair of shoes or a fancy dinner. If you can't afford such purchases without charging them to a credit card, you create bad debt. That debt, plus its interest payments, continues for months after the shoes go out of style and the meal is digested. No matter how good they make you feel, neither shoes nor a dinner is an investment. Therefore, any debt created as a result of such a purchase should be considered bad debt.

Figure 3-1

Examples of Good Debt and Bad Debt

Good Debt	Bad Debt
Home mortgage	Credit card debt
Student loan	Retail store debt

You: I have good news and bad news.

Yes?

You: I have good debt and bad debt.

You are not alone. Today, people frequently spend more than they earn. As we discuss in Chapter 2, the only way to spend more than you earn is by borrowing. Borrowing creates debt, lowering your net worth.

While I hope we have this conversation *before* you acquire significant debt, there's a good chance it's already too late. So, let's look at the strategies for treating your current debt.

You: Do I treat good debt and bad debt differently?

That depends on when you are "treating" it. Going forward, always carefully evaluate any borrowing that would qualify as bad debt. Your best *bad* debt strategy is to avoid *creating* it in the first place—you won't have to rid yourself of bad debt later if you have none to begin with. If you already have debt, however, there are many key debt reduction strategies. The first is to prioritize which debts to eliminate. This decision is based neither on the type of debt nor the amount of debt. Rather, make your decision based on the *cost* of the debt.

PRIORITIZING DEBT

You: The cost of the debt? Doesn't debt cost what I borrow?

No, because you pay back *more* than you borrow. In addition to repaying the amount you borrowed (**principal**), you pay interest. The interest rate charged is the **cost of the debt.** You must pay back both principal and interest.

You: So which debt should I pay off first?

Get rid of the most expensive debt first. This is the loan with the highest interest rate. Note that this loan might not be the one with the largest principal. Take a look at Craig.

Figure 3-2

Craig's Debts

Loan Description	Current Amount of Debt
Student loans from undergraduate school	$ 40,000
Student loans from graduate school	$ 65,000
Home mortgage	$ 325,000
Car loan on first car	$ 20,000
Car loan on second car	$ 12,000
Credit card #1 debt	$ 7,000
Credit card #2 debt	$ 5,500
Craig's total debt	$ 474,500

Craig has a mountain of debt, but it's not too uncommon, especially for those who have gone to graduate school, gotten married, and bought a house. But Craig's Grandma has unexpectedly sent him a check for $5,000—perhaps because he's been such a good boy. Craig makes a wise decision to use this windfall to reduce his debt. Which debt should he pay down?

You: I don't know.

That's the right answer.

You: What?

Seriously, I don't know either. I have a good guess, but it is impossible to know the correct strategy without additional information. Most importantly, what's the cost of each of Craig's debts? We need to know the interest rates he's paying. As expected, each debt has a different interest rate.

Figure 3-3

Interest Rates on Craig's Debts

Loan Description	Current Interest Rate
Student loans from undergraduate school	4.50%
Student loans from graduate school	5.50%
Home mortgage	5.25%
Car loan on first car	8.00%
Car loan on second car	0.00%
Credit card #1 debt	9.50%
Credit card #2 debt	23.29%

This information makes it crystal clear which debt Craig should pay first—credit card #2. Although credit card #2's principal is the smallest of his debts (only $5,500 out of more than $470,000 owed), this credit card charges him the highest interest rate—and by a wide margin, too. This makes credit card #2 his *most expensive* debt.

You: But he owes so much more on his mortgage. Wouldn't it help more to chop that down?

Absolutely not. Here's how a $5,000 principal payment applied to each debt reduces the interest expense during the next year.

Figure 3-4

First-Year Interest Savings by Paying $5,000 of Principal

Loan Description	Interest Savings
Student loans from undergraduate school	$ 225
Student loans from graduate school	$ 275
Home mortgage	$ 263
Car loan on first car	$ 400
Car loan on second car	$ 0
Credit card #1 debt	$ 475
Credit card #2 debt	$1,165

Many people mistakenly focus on paying off their highest balance debt. That's wrong. Making that error would cost Craig over $900 in one

Not only do Craig's home mortgage and student loans have lower interest rates than his credit cards, but also the interest paid on those good debts might be tax deductible. We'll cover what "tax deductible" means in the next chapter; for now know that deductibility makes the cost of this debt cheaper still. Just another reason to focus on high-rate credit card debt first. Personal credit card interest expense is never tax deductible.

year. That's the difference between a $5,000 payment to his mortgage (resulting in $263 of interest saved) and a $5,000 payment to his credit card ($1,165 of interest savings). Furthermore, this $900 savings can be used to pay down more debt next year.

You: What if I haven't been a good boy? I mean, what if Grandma isn't sending me any $5,000 checks?

Well, you still need to pay your debts. It is important to do everything you can to pay down very expensive debt, such as debt with an interest rate more than 10 percent, as quickly as possible. This may mean some sacrifice. For less pain, try one or two of the "Simple Savings Strategies" in Chapter 2. By spending less, you can allocate more money to reducing your debt. As your debt level decreases, so do your interest payments, freeing up more cash for future spending or saving.

STRATEGIES TO PAY OFF YOUR EXPENSIVE BAD DEBT

Even if you can't come up with any extra cash to pay off your bad debt faster, you have other opportunities to reduce your debt. Taking advantage of these additional strategies increases the likelihood that you will become "bad debt free."

AT LEAST THE MINIMUM

Always make minimum payments on time. Missing a payment or two—even by just a few days—can really hurt you. Credit card companies can charge additional fees, raise your interest rate, and create general financial havoc. When they do, you will have even more difficulty eliminating your credit card debt. Furthermore, missing a payment removes many of the other debt-reduction opportunities I discuss next. Credit card companies don't play nicely with folks who don't at least make minimum payments.

YOUR DEBT IS DESIRABLE TO OTHERS

You: I always make my minimum payments but don't have the dough to pay more than that. Is there something else I can do? I struggle to make these payments, yet I am not making any progress paying the debt off.

Yes, there's more you can do. But first, are you constantly bombarded with credit card offers, including low-rate balance transfer opportunities?

You: I am—but I can't imagine more credit cards are the answer for me.

You're right—they're not. However, that mailbox clutter may give you some bargaining power with your current credit card company. Your credit card debt, now ugly to you, remains very attractive to the company it is owed to. That company is collecting a nice amount of interest from you every month. It doesn't want to give that up. Ideally, you can find a credit card company so eager for your business that they offer you a low interest rate (perhaps as low as zero percent) with no fee to transfer a balance.

So *give your credit card company a call*. Politely tell them you have enjoyed being their customer. Remind them you pay the minimum payments on time and are charged a very high interest rate. Then, inform them you have been offered a new lower rate of (whatever the rate is that you have been offered) by another credit card company. Ask them to match the rate. Don't be surprised if they do. If they don't offer to match the rate, prepare to transfer your balance to a new, lower-rate credit card with no balance transfer fee. Tell your current credit card company of your intention.

Then, put the new card in a safe place and refrain from using it. Remember, the reason you got this new card is not to add more debt; your strategy is to reduce the cost of the debt you already owe so you can actually pay it off. Make the same dollar payment (or higher, when you can) on the new card that you were making on the old card—not the new minimum payment—and you will really see the balance owed decrease.

KEEP YOUR SCORE UP

You: Should I close the old account?

Not necessarily, because closing a credit card account can have a negative impact on your credit score. Your credit score is based on your credit reports. Your **credit report** contains a shocking amount of financial history—virtually all of it. There are three major reporting companies, called **credit bureaus**, which prepare credit reports:

➤ Experian

➤ Equifax

➤ TransUnion

In a perfect world, your credit report from each of the three companies would be identical. But they're usually not. Differences can be caused by different reporting schedules, different sources of information, and outright mistakes. Not surprisingly, many lenders consider multiple credit reports when contemplating lending money to you.

You should check the accuracy of each of these three reports periodically—I suggest annually. One copy of each of your reports is now available, free, at *www.annualcreditreport.com* every 12 months. Countless other web sites and solicitations advertise free credit reports, but read the fine print. Usually, you are simultaneously agreeing to sign up for some other service. If you forget to cancel the service later, you will be charged. That's too much of a nuisance.

Examine each report to make sure there are no errors. If there are, it is important to fix them as they may negatively influence your credit score. Instructions for fixing errors, as well as the contact information to do so, are available at the web sites of the credit bureaus. Their web addresses are included in Appendix B and at *www.totalcandor.com*.

You: How do I calculate my credit score?

You can't. Your **credit score** is the result of sophisticated mathematical calculations not available to the general public. However, the primary factors that influence the score are easy to understand. According to Fair Isaac Corporation, the factors are:

Figure 3-5

What Determines Your Credit Score?

Component	What Helps	What Hurts
How much you owe	You could borrow more on each of your accounts, but you don't.	You consistently borrow nearly the maximum allowed — sometimes more.
Length of credit history	You have several accounts many years old.	You have left-over Chinese food older than most of your credit cards.
Payment history	You consistently make on-time payments.	Oh, that reminds me.
New credit	You have not recently made several new applications for credit.	Over the past few weeks, you applied for many new accounts (for example, to "save 10 percent on today's entire in-store purchase").
Multiple types of credit	Your debts consist of a mortgage, a car loan, and credit cards.	You have store charge cards from each of your favorite 12 stores at the nearest mall and no mortgage.

Since your credit score affects your future borrowing ability and cost, keeping your score high is important. For example, closing down one of your oldest accounts might negatively impact your credit score since your credit history is now shorter. If you are not about to buy a house or a car, apply for a job, or do anything leading others to research your credit, your score decreasing for this reason might not matter too much anyway. But if you are, be careful.

PAY MORE ATTENTION AND LESS INTEREST

Although painful, always read the fine print of a new credit card, because the rate on a new account might be an **introductory rate.** Known as a **teaser rate**—for good reason—this interest rate is in effect for a specific period of time only. Upon its expiration, the new, regular rate is usually much higher. It might even be higher than your current rate. I repeat: be careful.

You: Got it. Be careful with any new cards but be aggressive in lowering my rate. I'll need to haggle a little bit and "play the game."

Exactly—your credit card company is never going to inform you about less-expensive alternatives. That's like a gas station's putting a sign up with directions to a cheaper competitor down the road.

In addition to negotiating your interest rate, *do whatever you can to pay more than the minimum due.* Credit card debt alone can sink an otherwise perfectly healthy financial plan. Take the time to *understand* and *respect* how credit cards affect your net worth. You can do everything else right financially and still struggle if you neglect just your bad debt. Without focusing on eliminating your credit card debt, you'll always have that burden.

DON'T LET ANYONE STEAL YOUR THUNDER

Identity theft, the stealing of another individual's personal information in order to commit illegal financial transactions, is a major problem today. Reviewing your credit reports annually is one way to monitor suspicious activity. In addition, there are other tactics to consider. Some of these tips might seem obvious, but people do make these mistakes and I don't want you to be one of them.

> ➤ Use a crosscut shredder to shred all those credit card solicitations arriving in the mail each day. If you don't, someone can go through your trash (or recyclables) and accept your pre-approved credit card.

> ➤ Choose to receive your current monthly paper statement as an electronic statement instead. This way, no one can find something

valuable in your trash or mailbox, such as a statement with your name, account number, and other useful information. Save the electronic statement on your hard-drive and put a password on your computer.

➤ Be very careful online. Look for the "s" at the end of *https* in the address bar before submitting any confidential information.

➤ Also online, don't respond to emails you receive which ask you to verify account data, such as your name or account number. Such fraudulent contacts are known as phishing. I am unaware of any bank, brokerage house, credit card company, and so forth who asks for your identifying information unsolicited by email. When in doubt about an email correspondence, *call* the financial institution. Don't call the number listed in the potentially phony email; call the one listed on the back of your card or on your last statement. The customer support representative can tell you if the email is legitimate. It won't be.

➤ The last online tip is the most obvious but least taken to heart. Your account passwords shouldn't be your kid's name. Duh. It shouldn't be on a post-it note in your wallet or on the side of the computer either. Double duh. Make your password something not easily figured out and memorize it. If your password looks suspiciously like your email address, it's probably not a good password.

➤ Don't carry your social security card in your wallet. If your wallet is stolen, the thief probably isn't going to have such a high level of integrity as to limit the take to the credit cards and cash in your wallet—the thief is going to apply for more credit in your name. Bigger payday for the thief and an even bigger headache for you.

If you haven't been a victim of identify theft yourself, you probably know someone who has. It's that common. And victims would tell you what an ordeal identity theft is and that it seems to take forever to straighten everything out. It's worth being careful in order to reduce your odds of suffering from the theft of your identity.

THAT MIRACLE CAN BE USED FOR EVIL

Much better than identify theft is the miracle of compounding interest. Remember, it is compounding interest that enables your money to make more money. While my examples so far demonstrate *annual* compounding, there are other possibilities.

The frequency at which your investment **compounds** indicates how often your account receives credit for the interest it earns. *Frequent compounding is better for you if you are receiving interest; worse if you are paying it.*

Let's say you have $1,000 in a savings account earning 5 percent, compounded annually.

You: I'll take it!

Great. At the end of the year, you have $1,050. If your account features monthly compounding, you have more. With monthly compounding, you would receive $4.17 of interest in January—5 percent of $1,000 divided by twelve, the number of months in a year. This $4.17 earns its own interest over the remaining 11 months of the year. Likewise, the interest payment received in February earns interest for the next ten months. As a result, monthly compounding earns you an additional $1.16 of interest on your $1,000 over a year compared to annual compounding.

Here are examples of different compounding frequencies:

Figure 3-6

Effect of Compounding on Stated Interest Rates

	Annual	**Quarterly**	**Monthly**	**Daily**
Original investment	$1,000	$1,000	$1,000	$1,000
Annual interest rate (APR)	5%	5%	5%	5%
Compounding periods per year	1	4	12	365
Effective rate (APY)	5.00%	5.09%	5.12%	5.13%
End-of-year balance	$1,050.00	$1,050.95	$1,051.16	$1,051.27

The different rates have special names. In this example, 5 percent is the **annual percentage rate (APR)** or the **stated** or **nominal** rate. The rate including the impact of compounding is the **effective** rate or **annual percentage yield (APY)**. When comparing different savings options or loans, focus on APY, as it most closely reflects financial reality.

Higher rates and more frequent compounding exacerbate the difference between APR and APY. Credit cards are excellent examples because most use daily compounding. Here is the effect that compounding frequency has on some sample interest rates.

Figure 3-7

Impact of Daily Compounding on High Nominal Interest Rates

Stated interest rate (APR)	15.00%	20.00%	25.00%
Compounding periods per year	365	365	365
Effective interest rate (APY)	16.18%	22.13%	28.39%

Daily compounding means that the true annual cost of a 15 percent stated rate is more than 16 percent. Similarly, a 25 percent APR with daily compounding actually costs more than 28 percent!

You: Wow—those seem pretty high. What does this mean for me?

It means you need to make paying back credit card debt a high priority. For example, look at Jennifer's credit card debt. The following figures are listed prominently in the "account summary" section of the credit card bill she just received:

new balance: $ 7,016

minimum payment: $ 140

If she always makes the minimum payment on time, how long will it take Jennifer to pay off this credit card?

You: I don't know.

Smart fellow. You're right—we can't tell. Not yet. The answer does not appear anywhere on the statement. However, if you look carefully at some of the fine print, you will find the annual percentage yield. This is the interest rate charged. In Jennifer's case, this rate is 17.24 percent. Now, if you are willing to do some math, you can calculate how long it will take Jennifer to pay off her debt by making on-time minimum payments.

You: Well, let's see. If you divide her $7,016 debt by that $140 minimum payment, you get about 50. So 50 payments will cover the principal she owes. But there's also the interest cost. That would probably add another year. So 50 months is a little over 4 years, then add another year. I'd say between 5 and 6 years. Wow, that's a long time.

A well-thought argument.

You: Thanks.

But it's completely wrong. Of Jennifer's first $140 payment, less than $40 is applied to principal. The rest is used just to pay interest. This leads to some serious ugliness: paying only the minimum payment actually means over 45 years of payments for Jennifer. Forty-five years! Over that time, in addition to the $7,016 of debt, she will pay about $17,000 in interest.[1] Can you see why paying only the minimum balance is not a long-term solution to credit card debt?

You: It's as if the miracle of compounding interest is being used against me.

That's exactly what is happening! It is being used for evil. Making only minimum payments is the financial equivalent of endlessly paying interest on items you can no longer remember purchasing. The sooner you accept this, the sooner you will find a way to pay down any credit card balance.

DEBIT CARDS

You: What about debit cards?

Debit cards are entirely different. A debit card is an electronic version of a paper check. When you swipe your debit card, the purchase amount is withdrawn from your bank account. As with checks, you can't spend money you don't have. In other words, you can't borrow with a standard debit card. That's why you never hear about people being in a mountain of debit card debt—it's not possible. That feature alone makes debit cards pretty attractive—it limits your spending to money you actually have.

---

[1] Assuming a fairly standard calculation method of minimum payment: the greater of 2 percent of the balance or $10.

But It's a Debit Card

When I opened a bank account recently, the bank representative told me I could withdraw up to $300 more than my checking account balance and be charged *only* $12. Of course she didn't mention that a $12 charge on $300 is very expensive! (If I paid the money back the next day, I'd owe $312. That's a 4 percent interest charge for *one day,* not one year.) So use debit cards only as intended—as an easier and more convenient option than checks. Make sure you have enough money in your account to avoid overdraft fees. Don't be tempted to use your debit card like a credit card, no matter what the bank representative tells you. Finally, be sure that you will not be charged a fee when using your debit card and entering your PIN at a merchant. Unfortunately, some banks assess a fee for this activity.

MAKE IT GO AWAY?

When you, the debtor, understand the implications of acquiring debt, the ability to borrow can be a good thing. Borrowing allows new businesses to be created and homes to be purchased. When debt is not understood, however, it can have terrible consequences. Take some time to review the debts you already have. Make sure you capture all of them. Then, complete the following table.

Figure 3-8

Your Personal Debt Summary

Debt Description	Current Balance	Current Interest Rate
Credit card #1		
Credit card #2		
Car loan (if financed—not leased)		
Home mortgage		
Home equity loan		
Student loan		
Other		
Other		
Other		
Other		
Other		
Other		
TOTAL:		

Now you know your personal debt situation. Compare the total of your debts to the total of your assets, which you calculate on page 22. Remember, the difference is your net worth. If your total debt is higher than your total assets, you currently have a negative net worth. Although you are "in the hole," you can come out. Just start using the saving and debt strategies I discuss here and in the last chapter. Start by attacking your most expensive debt first. Then go after your next most expensive debt. And so on.

If your net worth is positive, you can nevertheless benefit from using the same strategies. By reducing your debt further, you can grow your assets—and therefore your wealth—even faster!

While eliminating your bad debt is an achievable goal, another undesirable part of your financial life won't ever go away: taxes. Although taxes are quite complicated and specific to each person, there are four facts about you and taxes I can share right now.

1. You will pay taxes.
2. You will pay more taxes than you'd like.
3. You'll learn a lot about taxes in the next chapter.
4. Number 3 won't change anything about numbers 1 and 2.

CHAPTER 4

. . . .

Taxes on Your Taxes Are Taxing (Yet Real)

"Our Founding Fathers objected to taxation without representation.
They should see it today with representation."
—ANONYMOUS

❝❝Who should aspire to be a tax accountant?" That was the question my tax professor at the University of Michigan, Carleton Griffin, posed rhetorically. To the members of a dumbstruck class, each one privately hoping the professor would neither point to nor describe, he continued, "If you're the sort of person who likes to do jigsaw puzzles, the really complicated kinds with thousands of pieces that have no corners and *no pictures on either side,* you might enjoy a career as a tax accountant."[1]

Tax is both confusing and certain. Although there isn't much you can do about your taxes in the short term, you must be aware of your tax situation and understand it. Be forewarned: I don't control tax laws either. When you don't like what you learn, remember: I am only the messenger.

You: Why are there taxes, anyway?

The government collects taxes to provide services to the population. Examples include assisting the less fortunate with social welfare programs,

---

[1] Professor Griffin knows the limits of tax humor: "Students keep telling me we need more jokes in this class. Sorry to say, the only other one is even worse."

building and fixing collapsing tunnels in Boston, granting financial aid to students, employing the friendly people at the Department of Motor Vehicles, maintaining nuclear weapons, and, perhaps most importantly, funding the Swine Odor and Manure Management Research Unit. You pay tax regardless of whether you personally benefit from the services— although you do gain from knowing you live in a society that takes care of its people who need help and that genuinely understands the odors coming from its pigs. You pay when the services are poor. You pay regardless of your opinion on governmental spending priorities. Even if you have no income, you pay tax. Get the theme?

> *You: I'm paying tax.*

You bet.

The reason I am so confident you pay tax is because there are many ways to pay tax. Common taxes are:

- ➤ sales tax (page 53)
- ➤ property tax (page 56)
- ➤ income taxes (page 57)
- ➤ payroll taxes (page 76)
- ➤ gasoline tax
- ➤ and on, and on, and on...

> *You: Where does all this come from?*
>
> The **Internal Revenue Code (IRC)**, which defines taxation, is both infamously lengthy and confusing. The volumes containing the IRC were already heavy when I first consulted them years ago.[2] Since then, the IRC has grown further. Today, it's well over 5,000 pages set in a font much smaller than the one you are reading now. (Review pages 54 and 55 to get a sense for this magnificent literary work.) In the real version, the paper is so thin it is nearly transparent. Despite its enormous size, the IRC doesn't deal with taxes collected by state and local governments.

---

[2] Accountants are not typically gym hounds. Accountant nicknames include "Audit Man" and "Chuck." Not too many CPAs go by "Muscles" or "Big Dog."

You: How much tax do I have to pay?

Despite all the complexity about tax, the answer to that question is simple. Calculating a tax is based on just two components:

➤ tax rate

➤ value taxed

You: What is a tax rate?

A **tax rate** is just a percentage. Multiply the tax rate by the value of the item taxed to calculate tax owed. The higher the tax rate, the greater the tax owed:

> tax rate   x   value taxed   =   tax

You: What's the value taxed?

Sometimes the value taxed is easy to define, as when sales tax is calculated. When you purchase something labeled $1.99, the value taxed is $1.99. But other times the value taxed is far less clear. As a result, there are thousands of professionals, such as those employed by accounting and law firms, who are well paid to calculate the value taxed.

SALES TAX

Sales tax is collected on many of the items you purchase. When you bought your first pack of baseball cards, a toy, or a CD, you became a taxpayer for the first time.

With great anticipation, you went to the store with your $5 bill and found something cool for $4.79. Gee, you'd have money left over for next time! Yet there was no change coming to you. Instead, Mom or Dad needed to throw in an extra few cents to satisfy the cashier.

To explain why, remember the formula from above:

> tax rate   x   value taxed   =   tax

Assume the sales tax rate is 8 percent. Because your toy cost $4.79, that's the value taxed.

$$8 \text{ percent} \quad x \quad \$4.79 \quad = \quad \$0.38$$

Figure 4-1

Is This Any Way to Treat a Secretary?
Sample Internal Revenue Code Pages

(8) TREATMENT OF LEASEHOLD IMPROVEMENTS.—

(A) IN GENERAL.—In the case of any building erected (or improvements made) on leased property, if such building or improvement i[...] section applies, the depreciation deduction shall be determined un[...] section.

This clause has nothing to do with animal rights.

(B) TREATMENT OF LESSOR IMPROVEMENTS W[...] [TER]MINATION OF LEASE.—An improvement—

(i) which is made by the lessor of le[...] [less]ee of such property, and

(ii) which is irrevocably disposed of or abandoned by the lessor at the termination [of the lease with respect to such less]ee,

That's right—the IRS provides rules about what's normal.

sh[...] [purpo]ses of determining gain or loss under this title as disposed of by th[...] [dispos]ed of or abandoned.

[...] f qualified long-term real property constructed or improved in connection with cash or rent reduction from lessor to lessee, see section 110(b).

(9) NORMALIZATION RULES.—

(A) IN GENERAL.—In order to use a normalization method of accounting with respect to any public utility property for purposes of subsection (f)(2)—

(i) the taxpayer must, in computing its tax expense for purposes of establishing its cost of service for ratemaking purposes and reflecting operating results in its regulated books of account, use a method of depreciation with respect to such property that is the same as, and a depreciation period for such property that is no shorter than, the method and period used to compute its depreciation expense for such purposes; and

(ii) if the amount allowable as a deduction under this section with respect to such property differs from the amoun[...] [a]s a deduction under section 167 using the method (including *Believe it or not, the* [...] [y]ear convention, and salvage value) used to compute regulate *clause above is only* (i), the taxpayer must make adjustments to a reserve to refle *part of a sentence.* [...]ing from such difference.

(B) USE OF INCONSISTENT ESTIMATE[...]

(i) IN GENERAL.—One way in which the requirements of subparagraph (A) are not met is if the taxpayer, for ratemaking purposes, uses a procedure or adjustment which is inconsistent with the requirements of subparagraph (A).

(ii) USE OF INCONSISTENT ESTIMATES AND PROJECTIONS.—The procedures and adjustments which are to be treated as inconsistent for purposes of clause (i) shall include any procedure or adjustment for ratemaking purposes which uses an estimate or projection of the taxpayer's tax expense, depreciation expense, or reserve for deferred taxes under subparagraph (A)(ii) unless such estimate or projection is also used, for ratemaking purposes, with respect to the other 2 such items and with respect to the rate base.

(iii) REGULATORY AUTHORITY.—The Secretary may by regulations prescribe procedures and adjustments (in addition to those specified in clause (ii)) which are to be treated as inconsistent for purposes of clause (i).

(C) PUBLIC UTILITY PROPERTY WHICH DOES NOT MEE[...] *Secretaries have* [...] the case of any public utility property to which this section d *enough to do* [...] [o]f subsection (f)(2), the allowance for depreciation under section *without having all of* [...] [no]t computed using the method and period referred to in subparag *this thrown at them.*

(10) PUBLIC UTILITY PROPERTY.—The term "public ut[...] [pr]operty used predominantly in the trade or business of the furnishing o[...]

(A) electrical energy, water, or sewage disposal services,

(B) gas or steam through a local distribution system,

(C) telephone services, or other communication services if furnished or sold by the Communications Satellite Corporation for purposes authorized by the Communications Satellite Act of 1962 (47 U.S.C. 701), or

(D) transportation of gas or steam by pipeline,

if the rates for such furnishing or sale, as the case may be, have been established or approved by a State or political subdivision thereof, by any agency or instrumentality of the United States, or by a public service or public utility commission or other similar body of any State or political subdivision thereof.

(11) RESEARCH AND EXPERIMENTATION.—The term "researc[...] *This might refer to* [...] has the same meaning as the term research and experimental has unde *a bugle, but I don't* [...]

(12) SECTION 1245 AND 1250 PROPERTY.—The terms "section *really know.* [...] [sect]ion 1250 property" have the meanings given such terms by sections 1245(a)(3) and 1250(c), respectively.

Internal Revenue Code   **Sec. 168(i)(12)**

• 1976, [...] 76 (P.L. 94-455)
P.L. 94-4[...]
Amend[...] uting "Secretary" for "Sec-retary or [...] ace it appeared. **Effective** 2-1-77.

Want more proof they've thought of everything?

[Sec. 5054(b)]

(b) TAX ON RETURNED BEER.—Beer which has been removed for consumption or sale and is thereafter returned to the brewery shall be subject to all provisions of this chapter relating to beer prior to removal for consumption or sale, including the tax imposed by section 5051. The tax on any such returned beer which is again removed for consumption or sale shall be determined and paid without respect to the tax which was determined at the time of prior removal of the beer for consumption or sale.

[Sec. 5054(c)]

(c) APPLICABILITY OF OTHER PROVISIONS OF LAW.—All administrative and penal provisions of this title, insofar as applicable, shall apply to any tax imposed by section 5051.

Amendments

• 1976, Tax Reform Act of 1976 (P.L. 94-455)

P.L. 94-455, § 1905(a)(5):

Struck out former Code Sec. 5054(c) (see below) and redesignated former Code Sec. 5054(d) as Code Sec. 5054(c). **Effective** 2-1-77. Prior to striking, former Code Sec. 5054(c) read as follows:

(c) STAMPS OR OTHER DEVICES AS EVIDENCE OF PAYMENT OF TAX.—When the Secretary or his delegate finds it necessary for the protection of the revenue, he may require stamps, or other devices, evidencing the tax or indicating a compliance with the provisions of this chapter, to be affixed to hogs-heads, barrels, or kegs of beer at the time of removal. The Secretary or his delegate shall by regulations prescribe the manner by which such stamps or other devices shall be supplied, affixed, and accounted for.

Smaller font sizes not easily found.

[Sec. 5055]

SEC. 5055. DRAWBACK OF TAX.

On the exportation of beer, brewed or produced in the United States, the brewer thereof shall be allowed a drawback equal in amount to the tax paid on such beer if there is such proof of exportation as the Secretary may by regulations require. For the purpose of this section, exportation shall include delivery for use as supplies on the vessels and aircraft described in section 309 of the Tariff Act of [...]9 U. S. C. 1309).

More work dumped on the Secretary.

Amendments

• [...] ief Act of 1997 (P.L. 105-34)

[...]055 by striking "found to have been paid" and all that follows in the first sentence and inserting "paid on such beer if there is such proof of exportation as the Secretary may by regulations require.". **Effective** on the 1st day of the 1st calendar quarter that begins at least 180 days after 8-5-97. Prior to amendment, Code Sec. 5055 read as follows:

SEC. 5055. DRAWBACK OF TAX.

On the exportation of beer, brewed or produced in the United States, the brewer thereof shall be allowed a draw-back equal in amount to the tax found to have been paid on such beer, to be paid on submission of such evidence, records and certificates indicating exportation, as the Secretary may by regulations prescribe. For the purpose of this section, exportation shall include delivery for use as supplies on the vessels and aircraft described in section 309 of the Tariff Act of 1930 as amended (19 U. S. C. 1309).

• 1976, Tax Refo[rm ...] 55)

P.L. 94-455, § 1906[...]

Amended 1954 C[...] [...]ry" for "Sec-retary or his deleg[...] [...]d. **Effective** 2-1-77.

Remember this one from social studies?

[Sec. 5056]

SEC. 5056. REFUND AND CREDIT OF TAX, OR RELIEF FROM LIABILITY.

[Sec. 5056(a)]

(a) BEER RETURNED OR VOLUNTARILY DESTROYED.—Any tax paid by any brewer on beer removed for consumption or sale may be refunded or credited to the brewer, without interest, or if the tax has not been paid, the [...] liability therefor, under such regulations as the Secretary may prescribe, [...] o any brewery of the brewer or is destroyed under the supervision req[...] n determining the amount of tax due on beer removed on any day, the q[...] the same brewery from which removed shall be allowed, under such reg[...] y prescribe, as an offset against or deduction from the total quantity of beer removed from that brewery on the day of such return.

No wonder why the IRS office parties are so much fun.

Amendments

• 1998, IRS Restructuring and Reform Act of 1998 (P.L. 105-206)

P.L. 105-206, § 6014(a)(3):

Amended Code Sec. 5056 by striking "produced in the United States" and inserting "removed for consumption or sale". **Effective** as if included in the provision of P.L. 105-34 to which it relates [effective 4-1-98.—CCH].

• 1976, Tax Reform Act of 1976 (P.L. 94-455)

P.L. 94-455, § 1906(b)(13)(A):

Amended 1954 Code by substituting "Secretary" for "Secretary or his delegate" each place it appeared. **Effective** 2-1-77.

• 1971 (P.L. 91-673)

P.L. 91-673, § 1(a):

Amended Code Sec. 5056(a). **Effective** 5-1-71. Prior to amendment, the section read as follows.

(a) BEER REMOVED FROM MARKET.—Any tax paid by any brewer on beer produced in the United States may be refunded [...] er, without interest, or if the tax has [...] er may be relieved of liability therefor [...] ns as the Secretary or his delegate [...] n beer is removed from the market [...] ewery or is destroyed under the supe[...] h regulations.

It appears there was once a tax on shoplifting.

Internal Revenue Code

Sec. 5056(a)

Although store owners collect more money due to the sales tax, owners usually don't like it. Of the $5.17 the store owner collects, he or she keeps only $4.79; 38 cents of sales tax must be paid to the government. If customers paid no sales tax, they'd have more money to spend, possibly increasing the store owner's income.

You owe sales tax of 38 cents on your purchase. Add 38 cents to the $4.79 cost of the toy, and the cashier says:

"Five dollars and seventeen cents, please."

Sales tax increases the cost of most items you buy.[3] For a big-ticket item such as a car, a refrigerator, or an engagement ring, sales tax can be a major expense. All sales taxes are paid to the state government, local government, or both—there is no national sales tax. Fair warning: a national sales tax is periodically discussed in Congress. In addition, sales taxes may be charged on all Internet purchases one day. Currently, only some web sites collect sales taxes.

You: Okay—got it. Sales tax is pretty simple and I've paid it my whole life. Plus, like you said, there isn't much I can do about it anyway.

So let's keep going, and gradually increase the complexity of our conversation.

PROPERTY TAX

Property tax is another tax we pay. Like sales tax, there is no national property tax, so all property taxes are paid to the state government, local government, or both. A frequent major use of property tax is public education.

Not surprisingly, **property tax** is paid on property owned. Although some states collect property taxes on automobiles, the most common type

---

[3] I say "most" for two reasons: First, some states have no sales tax. Second, many states do not charge sales tax on certain items, such as fruits and vegetables purchased at a grocery store.

of property taxed is a home. But if you don't *own* property, you don't pay property tax—directly. If you rent your residence, you do not receive a property tax bill. However, your landlord does, and considers this cost when determining the rent to charge you.

Usually, the value taxed is not the property's true value. Rather, the value taxed is the **assessed value.** The assessed value is what the government—for purposes of the property tax only—determines your home is worth. In some places, the assessed value is close to the home's true worth. Elsewhere, the two values are quite different.

To determine property tax, take the value taxed (assessed value) and multiply it by the tax rate. For example:

Your house is worth:	$200,000
Assessed Value:	$150,000
Tax Rate:	5 mills[4] or 0.005

Tax Rate	x	Assessed Value	=	Annual Property Tax bill
0.005	x	150,000	=	$750

You'll never need to make this calculation yourself. If you are considering buying a house, ask the seller to share the amount of the property tax. However, it is important to understand the relationship between the assessed value and the purchase price. In *some* places, a big difference between the two leads to significant property tax increases when the property's sale triggers a reassessment.

INCOME TAXES

Income taxes are paid to the federal government and some state governments based on—and here's a shocker—your gross income. You certainly notice a good chunk of your paycheck withheld for income taxes.

You: There's nothing "good" about it.

I feel your pain.

---

[4] One mill is one one-thousandth or 0.001.

WITHHOLDING

However strong your morality, withholdings from your first paycheck probably caused you to shout several "unprintables." On payday, you can see people holding their pay stubs and shaking their heads or making wild animated gestures. **Withholdings** are taxes paid directly from your paycheck. The term "withholding" is used because money is, literally, withheld from your take-home paycheck. When you earn $1,000 in salary but receive only $693.27 in your paycheck, that's the phenomenon of withholding. The $306.73 you earn but never receive is withheld from you.

You: Why is there withholding?

Withholding ensures that the government is paid. Your employer is required to divert a portion of your earned income to the government before you can possibly spend it and, perhaps, be unable to come up with the tax money later. From the government's perspective, it's a smart idea. How often do you fail to have money for things you want?

You: Too often.

How high do you prioritize tax when making spending choices?

You: Not so high.

Withholding guarantees that taxes are always your highest priority.

FEDERAL INCOME TAX

This is the big one. **Federal income tax** (often abbreviated FED or FIT on your pay stub) is paid to the national government, and receives plenty of political and media attention. To understand federal income tax, start with income.

Many people are surprised to learn they have control over the amount of tax withheld from their paychecks. Your withholding amount is determined by **Form W-4.** Don't remember filling out Form W-4? It was one of the many forms you filled out on your first day of work. (We'll cover how this form works later in the chapter.)

You: We covered income already.

True enough, back in Chapter 2. However, the definition used then was a personal finance definition, not an income tax definition. Those two definitions differ. For tax purposes, every dollar you receive from any source is income. Then, there is a list of exceptions. Two exceptions are gifts and inheritances. Although money you receive as a gift or an inheritance is income, it is not **income subject to tax**.

You might think **taxable income** is the same as income subject to tax. While that makes sense, it's wrong. To calculate taxable income, subtract tax deductions from income subject to tax.

DEDUCTIONS (AKA WRITE-OFFS)

> **From the "Seinfeld" episode "The Package"**
>
> Jerry: Hey, what happened to my stereo? It's all smashed up.
>
> Kramer: That's right. Now it looks like it was broken during shipping, and I insured it for $400.
>
> Jerry: But you were supposed to get me a refund.
>
> Kramer: You can't get a refund. Your warranty expired two years ago.
>
> Jerry: So we're going to make the Post Office pay for my new stereo now?
>
> Kramer: It's a write-off for them.
>
> Jerry: How is it a write-off?
>
> Kramer: They just write it off.
>
> Jerry: Write it off what?
>
> Kramer: Jerry, all these big companies, they write off everything.
>
> Jerry: You don't even know what a write-off is.
>
> Kramer: Do you?
>
> Jerry: No, I don't.
>
> Kramer: But they do and they're the ones writing it off.
>
> Jerry: I wish I had the last twenty seconds of my life back.

Deductions are expenses you subtract (that is, deduct) to determine taxable income. Deductions are also referred to as write-offs. There are dozens of possible deductions, ranging from the obvious and rational to the obscure and … well, I don't want to be audited. Here are examples of expenses that may qualify as legitimate deductions:

➤ state income taxes
➤ charitable contributions
➤ IRA contributions
➤ education expenses
➤ moving expenses
➤ student loan interest
➤ reforestation amortization
➤ business expenses

You: How do I deduct all these? I have to pay state income tax too? Who is Ira and why do I have to give him money?

Don't panic! Yes, you probably pay state income tax, but we get to that on page 75. Wondering who Ira is? No worries, that's on page 140. On the other hand, even if you plant trees on Arbor Day, you're not qualifying for the reforestation amortization deduction. So that's not covered anywhere in this book.

Of course, you won't incur every expense on this list and you typically cannot deduct expenses you don't pay. But even if you pay a specific deductible expense, it still might not be deductible—for you.

You: Huh?

I know—that one confuses people. Some expenses are deductible only for certain types of people.

You: Well, aren't they special? How does that work?

Not all deductions are treated alike. Some expenses virtually anyone can deduct. For those write-offs, the level of income and amount of other deductions do not matter.

An example is moving expenses. You qualify for the moving expense deduction as long as you meet two simple requirements: (a) move far enough and (b) work in your new location. Basically, as long as you move far enough that your TV stations change and you have a job in your new city, you'll be able to deduct certain moving expenses. This is true for a business executive with three children as well as a 21-year-old student moving from college for her first job.

Although the moving expense deduction is available regardless of other deductions or income level, other write-offs are not. Take the state income tax deduction, for example. Most workers pay state income tax because most states tax wages. However, many workers do not benefit from the state income tax deduction because of the standard deduction.

You: The what?

The standard deduction. When calculating taxable income, people choose either a **standard deduction** or the total of their itemized deductions to subtract. Whichever deduction amount is higher, they choose that amount to lower the tax they have to pay.

You: How much can I deduct?

The standard deduction amount is based on the tax year and filing status. In 2007, a single individual is entitled to a standard deduction of $5,350, while those married filing jointly receive a $10,700 standard deduction.

FILING STATUS

Filing status is a classification affecting tax rates and deductions. Selecting a filing status is usually simple. Most people not married on December 31 of the year for which tax is due choose **single.** If you are married and you and your spouse file one return together, your filing status is **married filing jointly (MFJ).** A less common choice is for each spouse to file his/her own return. In this case, each spouse selects the **married filing separately (MFS)** option.

Two remaining choices are **head of household (HOH)** and **qualifying widow(er) (QW).** Determining if you qualify for either status is somewhat complicated and best left to a tax advisor. If you use QW or HOH, you usually pay less tax than if you select "single."

The total of your itemized deductions can be either less or more than your standard deduction. Some important **itemized deductions** are:

➤ state income tax

➤ charitable contributions

➤ home mortgage interest

➤ property tax

➤ medical expenses

Generally speaking, if you don't own your home or have a sizable income (well over $100,000), your itemized deductions are lower than your standard deduction. Since you prefer to pay less tax…

You: That is certainly my preference.

…then you select the standard deduction. As a result, a non-homeowner with an average income does not receive a tax benefit from any expense that is deductible only as an itemized deduction.

You: That's still a mouthful.

Precisely. An example is in order:

Consider someone named Sumit[5]:

S ome people are able to deduct business expenses. For employees, this is not common. For a worker to be able to deduct such expenses, these must exceed a set percentage of the worker's income. This percentage is typically too high of a hurdle, preventing any tax benefit from these expenses.

---

[5] There are few personal finance books with examples using Indian-American names. Maybe this will start a trend. But probably not.

Figure 4-2

Itemized Deductions Aren't Helpful to Everyone

Sumit's itemized deductions:

State income taxes	$ 1,500	
Charitable contributions	$ 175	
Home mortgage and real estate taxes	$ –	Note: Sumit rents.
Business expenses	$ –	
Total itemized deductions	$ 1,675	

Sumit's standard deduction

filing single for the year 2007 $ 5,350

Sumit wants to keep his tax as low as legally possible. Since his $5,350 standard deduction is far greater than the $1,675 total of his itemized deductions, Sumit chooses the standard deduction—which means he doesn't **itemize**. If Sumit's itemized deductions did amount to more than his standard deduction, he would itemize.

You: So if I don't itemize, I don't save any tax when I make charitable contributions? But the charity said my donation was tax deductible!

Look at you, correctly using "itemize" in a sentence! Good for you. You are right—if you do not itemize, you do *not* save money on tax by making charitable contributions.[6] That's why your donation receipt probably said your donation "*may* be tax deductible."

EXEMPTIONS

Exemptions are similar to deductions—both reduce the amount of tax you pay. Exemptions are a special kind of deduction. There is an **exemption** for every U.S. citizen. The individual who provides more than

---

[6] Of course, there are many non-financial benefits of charitable giving.

half the financial support of the person with the exemption usually claims the exemption. Some examples:

➤ If you are single and support yourself, you claim your own exemption.

➤ If you're married, together you have two exemptions you can claim.

➤ Have a kid? Congratulations—that's another exemption.

➤ Are you a teenager living at home who has an after-school job? Congratulations on your work ethic and your desire to learn financial planning at an early age. But sorry, no exemption for you—so long as your parents provide more than half of what it takes to keep you on this planet. Your parents claim your exemption.

Each exemption is worth $3,400 (a 2007 figure). A typical family of three has $10,200 of exemptions they subtract to calculate their taxable income.[7]

You: I think it's time for another example.

Indeed.

➤ Imagine a single woman, Tamara, who has $50,000 of income during 2007.

➤ Because $500 of Tamara's income is from gifts, and because gifts are not taxable, her income subject to tax is $49,500.

➤ Tamara has $10,000 in deductions (her $5,350 standard deduction and $4,650 of moving expenses).[8]

➤ Tamara can claim her $3,400 personal exemption because she completely supports herself.

This is how we calculate Tamara's taxable income:

Income subject to tax:	$49,500
Less: deductions:	− 10,000
Less: exemption:	− 3,400
Taxable income:	$36,100

---

[7] People with very high incomes may not receive a tax benefit for their exemptions.

[8] Remember that moving expenses are not an itemized deduction. Regardless of whether Tamara itemizes, she can deduct qualified moving expenses.

You: Okay, she has $36,100 in taxable income. How much tax will she pay?

Gary: I can answer that. I can make her income and yours "disappear." If you buy my book "No Tax, No Tax, No Tax," you'll never have to pay a dime of income tax again.

Gary, that's ridiculous. Besides, I thought you left us.

Gary: No way. I just pick my spots. Now that the reader is beginning to stress over taxes, I sense a sales opportunity. Time to move in, you know?

No, I don't. And I really wish you wouldn't.

Gary: Michael, this is nothing. Just wait until we get to insurance and investing.

I know your kind and I'll be ready for you.

Gary: Yeah, well, my golf game is way better than yours.

You: Excuse me. Am I interrupting something here?

Sorry. As you become more financially sophisticated, you might be presented with strategies enabling you to reduce your income taxes. However, most working people pay income tax. Furthermore, those working as employees have comparatively fewer options to legally reduce their taxes than do the self-employed.

Don't give money to anyone who promises more than help in planning and completing your taxes lawfully. Take advantage of every deduction you are entitled to—there is no reason to pay more in tax than you are obligated to. But don't go overboard and try schemes that don't sit well in your gut. After all, while pigs get fat, hogs get slaughtered.

You: Okay, I hear you, but how much tax will Tamara have to pay?

INCOME TAX RATES

If income tax rates were like sales tax rates, this section would be nearly over.

You: Wouldn't that be nice?

Watch it. If Tamara had a 10 percent income tax rate, she'd owe $3,610 on her $36,100 of taxable income. But the federal income tax doesn't work that way. The federal income tax is progressive. With a **progressive tax**, your tax rate increases as your taxable income increases.

That's a mouthful, so here's a detailed example comparing two single taxpayers, Paul and Dennis.

You: What about Tamara?

She'll be back.

Paul's gross income is $38,750 and his taxable income is $30,000. Based on 2007 tax rates, he'll pay $4,109 in federal tax. This means Paul's **average tax rate** (his total tax paid divided by his total income) is 10.6 percent ($4,109 divided by $38,750).

Dennis's gross income is $58,750 and his taxable income is $50,000. If the income tax rates worked like sales tax, in which everyone pays the *same rate*, Dennis would also pay 10.6 percent, or $6,228. But since the federal income tax is progressive, Dennis's tax is actually $8,924—over 15.1 percent of his gross income.

If your income increases significantly, you will notice the effects of a progressive tax. Dennis's income is *less* than double what Paul's is ($58,750 vs. $38,750). Yet Dennis's tax is *more* than double what Paul's tax is ($8,924 vs. $4,109). Not only is Dennis's *tax* higher than Paul's, so is Dennis's *tax rate*.

There is a different schedule of tax rates for each filing status. The **tax schedules** corresponding to the two most commonly used filing statuses (single and married filing jointly) are on the following page. If you file using a different filing status and wish to see your tax schedule, visit *www.totalcandor.com*.

To determine your tax bracket, find the appropriate tax schedule. Within each schedule are several rows. Each represents a **tax bracket**. Find the row you fit into based on your taxable income.[9] Then, read across to see the top rate at which your income is taxed. *This percentage is your tax bracket.* You might be in the 10 percent bracket, the 15 percent bracket, the 25 percent bracket, and so forth. The progressive tax rate structure is clearly demonstrated by the increases in tax rate shown alongside rising income levels.

---

[9] Remember, your salary does not equal your taxable income. Don't forget to subtract your exemption(s) and deductions.

Figure 4-3

Single 2007 Tax Schedule

If taxable income is over:	but not over:	the tax is:
$0	$7,825	10 percent of the amount over $0
$7,825	$31,850	$782.50 plus 15 percent of the amount over $7,825
$31,850	$77,100	$4,386.25 plus 25 percent of the amount over $31,850
$77,100	$160,850	$15,698.75 plus 28 percent of the amount over $77,100
$160,850	$349,700	$39,148.75 plus 33 percent of the amount over $160,850
$349,700	no limit	$101,469.25 plus 35 percent of the amount over $349,700

Figure 4-4

Married Filing Jointly 2007 Tax Schedule

If taxable income is over:	but not over:	the tax is:
$0	$15,650	10 percent of the amount over $0
$15,650	$63,700	$1,565.00 plus 15 percent of the amount over $15,650
$63,700	$128,500	$8,772.50 plus 25 percent of the amount over $63,700
$128,500	$195,850	$24,972.50 plus 28 percent of the amount over $128,500
$195,850	$349,700	$43,830.50 plus 33 percent of the amount over $195,850
$349,700	no limit	$94,601.00 plus 35 percent of the amount over $349,700

> I n addition to progressive taxes, there are also flat and regressive taxes. **Flat taxes** are taxes for which the rates don't change regardless of income. The sales tax is a flat tax. **Regressive taxes** are those for which the rate goes down as income increases.

Only those in the lowest tax bracket have their entire income taxed at one rate. All others have income taxed at more than one rate. The highest of these rates you pay is called your **top tax rate** or **marginal tax rate.** Let's take Bradley as an example.

You: Does he know Tamara?

No, he lives in New Mexico. Tamara lives in New Jersey. What a shame—I know. I promise I'll get back to Tamara in a minute.

Bradley is single and has taxable income of $40,000. By reviewing the tax schedule, you determine he is in the 25 percent tax bracket. (His taxable income is between $31,850 and $77,100.) To figure Bradley's tax, first calculate the amount by which his taxable income exceeds $31,850. This is $8,150 ($40,000 minus $31,850). Multiply this $8,150 by 25 percent, which equals $2,037.50. Add $2,037.50 to $4,386.25, as the schedule indicates, for a total tax of $6,423.75.

While Bradley's tax bracket is 25 percent, only his last $8,150 of taxable income is actually taxed at 25 percent. This makes 25 percent Bradley's top tax rate. In fact, the first $7,825 of Bradley's (and every single individual's) taxable income is taxed at only 10 percent.

FAQS AND IAQS ON TAXES COVERED SO FAR

Some of the following questions are asked frequently, so they are called FAQs. Others are asked only infrequently (IAQs) because people think they already understand taxes. But sometimes people are wrong. Ask away, and you can impress your friends with your new tax knowledge.

You: How 'bout you and I just keep my "new tax knowledge" a secret?
Your call.

You: Okay. My show-off boss tells me he recently finished building a vacation home in the mountains. However, he just learned that the property tax on his nice, new, and expensive home is very high. But boss man says he doesn't care about the property tax because he just writes it off. Whoa! Does that mean he basically pays no property tax since he gets it all back as a deduction on his tax return? That's not fair.

I agree—it's not fair. Also, it's not true.

It's a common misconception that a deduction, such as the one for property tax, reduces your income tax by the amount of the deduction. False! Take your boss's tax situation:

Property tax on mountain home:	$10,000
Top income tax rate:	28 percent
Taxable income prior to new mountain home:	$150,000

Let's see what changes as a result of his new property tax deduction. To determine his new taxable income of $140,000, subtract the $10,000 property tax write-off from his $150,000 of taxable income. Make sense?

You: So far.

Let's keep going. Before the home, he and his wife's tax bill was $30,992.50. This is calculated using the tax schedule on page 67. After he purchases this home, what is his new income tax bill?

You: Umm—

It's $28,192.50.

You: How did you figure that out so fast?

Well, first off, this is a book so the calculation could have taken me days and you wouldn't know it. However, this is a really simple calculation that can be made quickly: take the new $10,000 income tax deduction and multiply it by your boss's top income tax rate of 28 percent.[10] That's a $2,800 tax savings. Then, subtract $2,800 from the previous tax amount and voila, $30,992.50 − $2,800 = $28,192.50. You can also compute the new tax amount using the tax schedule for taxable income of $140,000 ($150,000 taxable income prior to the new property tax deduction minus the new $10,000 property tax deduction).

---

[10] Note that this shortcut works only if the individual isn't close to being in another tax bracket.

Next, compare your boss's combined expenses for income tax and property tax:

Before the vacation home:
$30,992.50 Income tax

After the vacation home:
$28,192.50 Income tax
+ $10,000.00 Property tax
$38,192.50 Total tax

His total tax expenses increased by $7,200. If he thought his write-off made his new property tax expense essentially free, he was wrong. There are definite savings from tax-deductible expenses—in this case $2,800—but they are not dollar-for-dollar savings. A write-off does not make an expense free.

Next question?

You: I should have asked this first: What the hell happened to Tamara?

She's been real busy, but we can finish her example now. Tamara was the person on page 64 with taxable income of $36,100. By reviewing the tax schedule on page 67, you can calculate her tax as $5,449.

What else is on your mind?

You: All this tax stuff goes against what I thought I learned growing up: Our forefathers were angry about tax when we fought England. I can't find income tax anywhere in the Constitution. (Yes, I looked.) Where does the government get the right to take my income? This is ridiculous. Is this really what we want?

That's quite an impassioned question.

You: Today was payday and I'm sick of FICA taking all my money.

That explains your animated gestures as well. Well, it turns out there was no income tax originally. So don't blame your forefathers. That's right—the Constitution specifically prohibited direct taxation upon the population. And that's how it read for about 126 years. But if you read the

16th Amendment, passed in 1913, you see thirty little words legalizing an income tax and changing the course of history—or, at least, the amount of your paycheck.

FORM W-4: WITHHOLDING ALLOWANCES

Withholding allowances are among the most unnecessarily complicated ways the government treats ordinary people. Think I overstate the case? Don't take my word for it. Read this paragraph, from a high traffic web site:

Withholding Calculator

The purpose of this application is to help employees to ensure that they do not have too much or too little income tax withheld from their pay. It is not a replacement for Form W-4, *but most people will find it more accurate and easier to use than the worksheets that accompany Form W-4.* You may use the results of this program to help you complete a new Form W-4, which you will submit to your employer. (Emphasis added.)

The web site you'll find this on? How about *www.irs.gov?*[11] That's right—the **Internal Revenue Service,** the government agency responsible for collecting the tax and *creating the forms,* had that to say about Form W-4.

The good news is that the only time you encounter withholding allowances is when you complete Form W-4. The number on line 5 of page 1 of your W-4 (total allowances) is entered in your employer's payroll system, resulting in the amount withheld from your paycheck.

---

[11] To find this specific paragraph, try typing "withholding calculator" in the search box at the top of the IRS home page.

For some people an easy relationship exists between the number of exemptions claimed and the number of allowances. However, for many others, the appropriate number of allowances is complicated by other factors, including:

➤ whether both spouses work,

➤ what their income levels are—both together and individually, and

➤ the amount of their deductions.

You: Okay, but what's an allowance? You still haven't told me.

You're absolutely right and that's because I don't know. And I don't know anyone who does. But I do know how allowances work, and that's what you need to understand:

➤ The more allowances claimed on Form W-4, the less tax withheld from your paycheck.

➤ The fewer allowances claimed on Form W-4, the more tax withheld from your paycheck.

You: Why does it matter?

Because the amount withheld determines if you overpay your tax and receive a refund or underpay your tax and owe an additional amount when you file your income tax return. Furthermore, if you underpay your tax during the year, it's possible you'll owe interest and penalties when you file your return the following April. And, as we'll discuss, getting a huge refund isn't a great financial strategy either.

You: So you're telling me that this Form W-4—which I don't even remember completing, let alone what I wrote on it—helps determine whether I receive an income tax refund?

Yes.

You: How do I know if I completed the W-4 properly?

I thought you'd ask. Keep reading.

INCOME TAX RETURN

You: Ugh. Gross income, deductions, exemptions, withholding, and allowances—when and how does the government do all these calculations for me?

The government does not do these calculations for you. *You* must do them for the government!

You: Oh this is crazy. I don't have time for this.

You can hire someone, such as an accountant, to do it for you. These computations are done once a year—when you file your income tax return. In fact, the only thing the **income tax return** actually does is iron out all those calculations. By April 15 of each year, you tell the government all of your numbers for the previous year. That date gives you three and a half months after the end of the year to figure it out.

When you file your tax return, you either owe money or receive a refund. You might wonder why some people owe and others get a refund. If the amount withheld during the year is *less* than the total tax bill, you owe the difference. *So, your total tax is not what you owe on April 15, but any amount due with your return plus all the withholdings you paid during the year.*

On the other hand, if the amount withheld during the previous year is *more* than your total tax bill, the difference is refunded to you. *Note: this is not the government giving you some money. It is the government giving you back your own money!*

You: But it's still better to get a refund, right?

No! Remember, the refund is your own money that you overpaid by having higher than necessary withholding. Imagine that you get a great deal on a $1,000 appliance. You don't need to use it right away so you put it in the attic. A year later, you remember you still have the appliance and ought to take it back to the store. Because the store has a great return policy, they give you a full $1,000 refund.

Do you consider the $1,000 "free money?" Is it a windfall? Is the store giving you its money? Do you feel good about how you managed your finances?

You: No, of course not.

Why?

You: Because it's my money. By not returning the appliance sooner, I was just being lazy. I could have gone to the store any time and gotten my refund.

Exactly—that $1,000 is yours! All you had to do was go ask for it. Instead, you lent the cash to a store. And guess who made interest on that $1,000 all year long? Hint: It wasn't you.

You: Where is this going?

A returnable appliance resting in the attic is no different than an income tax refund. By receiving a refund, you allow the government to hold your money for a year before they give it back to you. A portion of that refund should have been in each of your paychecks all along, letting you spend it—or save it—earlier. If you save it, you earn interest for an additional year.

When you get your money back from the government, you are not paid interest. In essence, a tax refund means you made an **interest free loan** to the government. Don't congratulate yourself for receiving an income tax refund. If you consistently receive a sizable refund, use the withholding calculator at the IRS web site to determine the right number of allowances. Then complete a new Form W-4 and submit it to your payroll department. This should *increase your paychecks* from then on. In effect, you are giving yourself a raise! Enjoy your money as you earn it, not when the government gives it to you next April or May.

You: Speaking of taxes and refunds, I remember seeing advertisements last spring for faster refunds. Is that a good idea?

How can I say this in the clearest way possible? Hmm. Here are some possible answers:

➤ Absolutely not.
➤ Please don't do this.
➤ Thumbs down.
➤ Nope.
➤ I would be happier if you were to go to the ATM, withdraw $50, and light it on fire.

You: So, "No," huh?

NO!

You: Are you upset?

Yes. Called **refund anticipation loans**, these loans are often made possible by the company preparing your income tax return. A typical arrangement is for you to receive your refund immediately rather than when the IRS has it for you.

You: Why are these loans so bad?

First, by including your direct deposit information on your tax return, you might get your tax refund from the IRS in just a week or two. So, it's not as though you typically have to wait months for your tax refund. But the real clincher is the cost to you of receiving your refund a little quicker. In fact, the lender frequently charges an interest rate that could make a credit card company jealous. When you add in other charges related to the loan, the total interest and fees can equate to an interest rate of more than 100 or even 1,000 percent. Such greed is embarrassing to the human race. That's why I am so upset.

You: But are you okay now?

Telling you this makes me feel much better. Thanks.

You: Okay, I got it. Stay away from refund anticipation loans. Plus, no more high-fiving refund checks. I'll give myself a raise by getting this W-4 thing right. What's next?

Well, there are other taxes you pay.

You: MORE TAXES?

Plenty.

You: [Expletive deleted.]

STATE INCOME TAXES

To start with, you most likely pay income tax to the state you live in. Only nine states do not tax wages:

➤ Alaska
➤ Florida
➤ Nevada
➤ New Hampshire

> South Dakota
> Tennessee
> Texas
> Washington
> Wyoming

If you live in one state and work in a different state, you pay an amount approximately equal to the higher of the two states' tax rates. Isn't that great?

You: No. It sucks.

I hear you. Some states have a progressive income tax and others have a flat income tax. Remember, a flat tax means the tax rate is the same on all dollars of income. Illinois has a flat income tax of 3 percent, so if you have $20,000 of taxable income in Illinois, you'll pay $600. If you have $200,000 in taxable Illinois income (ten times as much), you'll pay $6,000 (ten times as much). States such as New York and California have progressive income tax rates. Like the federal income tax, tax rates in these states increase as taxable income increases.

Note that state taxes are not the same as *estate* taxes. Your heirs may pay those some day—but not while you're alive. More on those later.

LOCAL INCOME TAXES

Some municipalities collect a **local income tax.** From New York City to Jackson, Michigan, these taxes are collected in a similar manner to the state income tax. Sometimes you must pay local tax if you only work in a taxing location but don't live there.

PAYROLL TAXES: SOCIAL SECURITY AND MEDICARE

Like income taxes, payroll taxes are collected on income. However, the payroll taxes are in addition to and separate from the income tax. Furthermore, the **payroll taxes** are composed of two different taxes: **FICA,**[12] which is also known as **Social Security**, and **Medicare.** Payroll

---

[12] FICA stands for Federal Insurance Contributions Act. Nowhere is this knowledge useful except if you watch Jeopardy!™.

taxes are charged only on compensation from working, not on interest or other investment income. Social Security provides many benefits, including monthly payments to current retirees, the disabled, and the widowed. Medicare pays many of the health care expenses of qualifying older Americans and those with disabilities. The tax rates for Social Security and Medicare are the same for everyone. The FICA rate is 12.4 percent and the Medicare rate is 2.9 percent, for a combined 15.3 percent payroll tax.

You: And this is on top of my income tax?

Yes.

You: That sounds like a lot.

It *is* a lot.

You: This is crazy. I thought my employer paid half of those payroll tax amounts.

In fact, they do. Withholding from your paycheck for payroll taxes therefore consists of 6.2 percent for FICA and 1.45 percent for Medicare.

You: What about self-employed people?

Since self-employed people are their own employers, they must pay both halves (the employee portion and the employer portion) of the payroll taxes. In other words, the payroll taxes they must pay are 12.4 percent of their income from self-employment.

You: So they don't get out of this either?

Nope.

You: You make good points, but I must tell you I do not like most of the conclusions.

That's fair. Taxes are certainly not the most enjoyable part of personal finance. Regardless, you can really benefit by understanding how they impact your financial life now and in the future.

For example, did you know that it is only the first $97,500 of wages paid in 2007 that is subject to FICA tax?

You: No—that's trivia.

Perhaps. But it has some interesting consequences. Because of this "cap," the most an individual sees subtracted from his or her pay stub is $6,045, or 6.2 percent of $97,500.

The following five people demonstrate how the Social Security tax is withheld:

Figure 4-5

Social Security Tax by Wage Level: 2007

	Holly	Doug	Jonathan	Lisa	Todd
Gross income from wages	$30,000	$60,000	$90,000	$120,000	$500,000
Amount subject to Social Security tax	$30,000	$60,000	$90,000	$ 97,500	$ 97,500
Social Security tax rate	6.20%	6.20%	6.20%	6.20%	6.20%
Social Security tax	$ 1,860	$ 3,720	$ 5,580	$ 6,045	$ 6,045
Effective Social Security tax rate	6.2%	6.2%	6.2%	5.0%	1.2%

If you make up to $97,500, the FICA tax is effectively flat, since everyone pays the same 6.2 percent tax rate from his or her paycheck. If you earn more than $97,500, your total tax is capped. Paychecks you receive after you earn $97,500 have no Social Security tax withheld. As a result, people with extremely high incomes have low effective Social Security tax rates: Todd pays a rate of little more than 1 percent on his half-million of wages while Holly pays 6.2 percent on her $30,000.

You: Argh. Is this how the Medicare tax works too?

No, unlike the Social Security tax, the Medicare tax has no income limit. Therefore, Todd has 1.45 percent subtracted from his entire $500,000 wage income, not just 1.45 percent on the first $97,500. As a result, he pays more in Medicare tax (1.45 percent x $500,000 equals $7,250) than in Social Security tax ($6,045).

You: But if I make less than $97,500, I pay 6.2 percent FICA and 1.45 percent Medicare on all my income right?

Close. Only on all your wages. Any bank interest or investment income is not subject to the payroll taxes. Ready to move on to—

You: Hold on there, cowboy. Payroll taxes are not on your list of deductible items. State income and property taxes are, but not payroll taxes. Did you just leave it out or are payroll taxes really not deductible?

Payroll taxes withheld from your paycheck are not deductible from your federal income tax. Remember, the federal income tax and the payroll tax are completely separate taxes.

You: What's the impact of payroll taxes not being deductible? (I doubt I'm going to like the answer to this one.)

Well, since the payroll taxes you pay can't be deducted from your federal taxable income, you pay federal income tax on your payroll taxes. Take Erin, for example.

Figure 4-6

Payroll Taxes are Not Deductible

Salary		$40,000
Social Security tax (6.2%)	$ 2,480	
Medicare tax (1.45%)	$ 580	
Total payroll taxes		$ 3,060
Pay before income taxes		$36,940

Erin can't deduct her payroll taxes when calculating her federal income tax. This means the $3,060 of payroll taxes withheld from her paycheck cannot be subtracted on her income tax return. Therefore, Erin's federal income tax withholding is based on her full $40,000 salary. Not only does she not receive the $3,060 she earns (withheld for payroll taxes), but she also *owes federal income tax on the money she never receives!* She pays approximately $765 of *tax on a tax* if she is in the 25 percent tax bracket!

You: It can't be fair to have to pay tax on a tax.

I agree with you.

You: This is outrageous! How come people don't complain?

Good question. I have only one guess: There hasn't been much pressure on the government to change the system because most people don't realize this is how it works. Plus, the government would have to give up significant tax revenue if it removed the "tax on tax," and we have a national debt you may have heard about …

ESTATE TAX

When you die, everything you leave behind for others, including leftovers in the refrigerator, becomes your **estate**. The estate tax is not something you pay while you are alive; it is a tax your heirs might pay if they inherit significant money from your estate. The estate planning rules are constantly changing due to Congressional activity, as well as the lack thereof. But if you die with an estate of less than $1 million, there's probably no estate tax for your heirs to worry about. For most people, taking care of basic estate planning is far more important than anticipating the estate tax. Chapter 9 discusses estate planning.

CONCLUDING THOUGHTS ON TAXES

If you get into a high level of detail, taxes can be very confusing. Many experts believe it is impossible to learn tax without dedicating your life to it.[13] But you now understand the most important part of taxes: those that affect your life. For example, you comprehend the difference between gross income and taxable income and what it *really* means to write something off.

Most people do not have complicated tax situations. If the tax forms you receive are limited to a W-2 from your employer, interest income from a bank, some home mortgage interest, and property tax, you should *at least try* to do your own tax return next year.

You: You really are crazy.

Perhaps, but I don't think so.

Consider this "Part Two" of your basic personal tax training. There's no better way to learn than by doing. If you are nervous, you can always— and probably should—go to your accountant after you complete your return and before you file it. See how it changes (or does not) after your

---

[13] I disagree. To become a true tax expert, a human's average lifetime is not nearly long enough.

accountant reviews it. Have a discussion about your income taxes with your accountant. Doing all this takes some time, but not money—and it might save you some. You will certainly learn a thing or two about *your* taxes in the process.

So that's the news on tax. As I said previously, taxes are not the world's most enjoyable topic and there isn't a whole lot you can do about them. You might already long for your days of tax apathy.

You: You have taken my innocence.

And perhaps your ignorance too. But now you know what's going on with your paycheck. You are now knowledgeable in an area most are not. Of course, there's always the risk you don't recall the fact that *I am only the messenger.* Is that why I have life insurance? Find out in the next chapter.

CHAPTER 5

Use Protection: Insurance

"The greatest misfortune of all is not to be able to bear misfortune."
—Bias

You would not like a world without insurance. Insurance allows society to function by protecting people from the full impact of random and devastating events.

A fire is an example of such a random and devastating event. The odds are extremely small[1] of your home burning down in a fire—whether that home is an apartment, condo, house, or houseboat. We no longer build cities from wood, and we have fire extinguishers, smoke alarms, and sprinkler systems. Still, if your home burns down in a world without insurance, you are devastated. And while the emotional devastation passes in time, the financial devastation can be permanent.

➤ Where do you and your family live once your home is destroyed?

➤ When you find a new home, how do you afford the old mortgage and the new one simultaneously?

---

[1] Please do NOT prove me wrong. **Arson** is not defined here for a reason.

➤ What about the things that burned, such as your clothes, your appliances, your Joan Jett albums, and your furniture? How do you replace all your stuff?

Fortunately, insurance reduces the financial devastation caused by an uncontrollable and unlikely event.

You: But how does insurance actually work?

From fires to hurricanes, from car accidents to premature death, insurance works the same way. People who want insurance put a small amount of money into a "shared fund." The amount each person contributes to the fund is based on (1) the likelihood a loss will occur and (2) its severity.

Of those who participate in an insurance program, a very small number of (pretty unlucky) people will experience fire damage. To assist with their misfortune, they receive money from the shared fund. The amount of money received is usually slightly less than the cost of damages suffered.

Those who have no fire damage (the overwhelming majority) receive nothing—other than peace of mind. Ideally, the shared fund pays less to victims than the total amount it receives from all the folks that pay into the fund.

If you do not participate in an insurance program, you do not pay into the shared fund. Accordingly, you receive no money from the fund if you suffer a loss because of a fire. Such a combination—a significant loss, but no insurance—would likely bring about the very financial devastation that insurance is designed to prevent.

You: That seems relatively simple, but you didn't use any words I don't know. Whenever I call my insurance guy, he always uses terms I don't know.

Insurance has its own language, but you can learn it. We'll use car insurance to introduce the insurance vocabulary. Let's say you are in an automobile accident.

You: Been there—more than once, too.

Were you talking on the cell phone this time?

You: Well, sort of. I'm about to call Bryan, but Bryan isn't on my speed dial, so I look down to scroll through the pictures I saved. There was a curve, a tree, and—

I get it. Luckily, you had insurance because you previously purchased an **insurance policy**, a written description of the key conditions. The policy states the who, what, when, where, how, and why of your insurance.

Your insurance policy exists for a limited amount of time. It does not last forever. The time period you have insurance for is known as the policy **term**. An example of a term is one year, starting on the date the policy is purchased. Six-month policies are also common, especially for automobile insurance.

Because a car accident is a **covered event** in standard automobile insurance policies, you have **coverage** for your accident. In order to receive money to help pay for the financial damages you suffer (such as expensive auto-body repair), you **make a claim** by contacting your insurance company and telling them about your accident.

You acquire car insurance by paying **premiums.** Premiums are money you pay to the shared fund in exchange for some protection from financial losses due to covered events. When you pay premiums, your car is **insured**.

The entity that collects and distributes the shared fund of money is the **insurance company,** to which you pay premiums and make any claims. The insurance company administers the fund and makes payments to victims of covered events. They also attempt to make a profit from their work.

You: How much money do I receive if I have an accident?

Here are some factors that affect how much money you receive when you file your claim:

➤ money lost
➤ deductible amount
➤ coverage limit

First, the insurance company needs to estimate the extent of your financial loss. When you call your insurance company to report a claim, the agent is likely to either direct you to a repair shop for an estimate or to send an **insurance adjuster** to estimate the damage to your car.

The **deductible** is the amount *you* pay before the insurance company pays anything. (You select a deductible level when you purchase a policy.) Your deductible is subtracted from the amount of loss estimated. Therefore, you receive a check for *the amount of the loss minus the deductible.*

However, if this amount is greater than the policy **coverage limit**, your check is reduced. The coverage limit is the maximum amount the insurance company pays for any claim.

So how smart do you feel now about insurance?

You: Let's see. In order to have car insurance that allows me to make a claim if there is a covered event during the policy term, I must purchase an insurance policy, choose a deductible level, and make premium payments to the insurance company.

Bravo!

TYPES OF INSURANCE

There are many types of insurance. They work the same basic way—those who choose to participate pay premiums to an insurance company, which pools this money and pays claims, while trying to make a profit.

You will probably consider the following insurance policies at some point in your life:

Insurance Not Typically Offered Through an Employer

> auto
> homeowner's or renter's
> life
> long-term care
> umbrella

Insurance Frequently Available Through Your Employer

> health (medical)
> life
> disability
> dental
> accidental death and dismemberment (AD&D)

You: Is this last one a joke?

Gary: No, it's a "must have." People die in accidents every day. AD&D pays a high benefit, yet costs very little. It's an amazing deal, and I can get you an even better arrangement if you purchase a policy from me.

For my thoughts on AD&D, read page 109. I say stay away.

You: Why is life insurance on both lists?

Although many people will find life insurance available at work, some will not. Besides, even those that have life insurance available at work should understand the privately purchased option.

There are other forms of insurance but, for the majority of people, the above are the most important. We go through them one at a time so you can understand each one.

AUTOMOBILE INSURANCE

Not surprisingly, auto insurance is for your vehicle. If you haven't purchased auto insurance before, it's probably because you're still on your parents' policy, don't have your own car, or are "a person of interest" in the eyes of state troopers from Wisconsin, Texas, and Mississippi. If you have a car, you are required by law to have car insurance in most states. New Hampshire, where I live, is a rare exception.

You: Really?

Yes. Live Free or Die.

You: Excuse me?

It's the New Hampshire state motto.

You: Oh. I guess I choose to live free.

Thanks, but I wasn't asking you a question. I'm sure glad you opted for the non-death option. Especially before our life insurance discussion.

You: That wasn't the only reason I made that choice.

Phew. Financial planning is important, but it's not life or death.

You: Okay, getting back to car insurance—so you're not required to have car insurance where you live?

That's correct.

You: But you have it anyway, right?

You bet. It's much too risky to drive around without car insurance. And I'd feel that way even if we didn't have all those traffic circles.

You: Didn't you find car insurance confusing to purchase?

Maybe the first time. But people often make car insurance more difficult than it needs to be. I'll simplify it here. Again, the purpose of insurance is to protect you financially if something bad and unexpected happens.

Your odds of being in a car accident are far higher than your house being damaged from a tornado—even in Kansas. That's one reason auto insurance is much more expensive than other types of insurance.

Here are three important components of auto insurance:

1. **Collision**—Covers damages as a result of an accident.
2. **Comprehensive**—Covers you for most non–accident-related damage. Examples include vandalism, a tree falling on your car, and theft.
3. **Liability**—Provides you with coverage—and often a lawyer to represent you—in case you are sued as a result of an accident. This includes injuring or killing somebody.

You: I had many choices when I purchased car insurance. How do I know if I made the right choices?

Consider the following general guidelines when purchasing car insurance. You can usually change your car insurance coverage options at any time—you typically don't need to wait until the end of the term.

HIGH DEDUCTIBLES SAVE YOU MONEY

Remember, the insurance company is in this game to make money. If you select a low deductible (say $100), you can make a claim for a measly $200 accident. In addition to paying you for your small loss, the insurance company also assigns a representative to your claim and incurs other related costs. In order for the insurance company to compensate for its expected more frequent dealings and payments to you, it charges you a higher premium.

A better choice might be a high deductible. For example, raising your deductible to $500 might save you a couple of hundred dollars each year in premiums. You'll probably be better off with a higher deductible even if you have accidents every couple of years. Although with that kind of driving record, your rates are probably going to be extremely high no matter what your deductible is.

Of course, a $500 deductible means that an accident costs *you* up to $500. But if you have an **emergency fund** (readily available money for just such an occasion, discussed in Chapter 7), you have cash available for such an unfortunate event.

COVERAGE LIMITS

Typically, there are state-mandated minimum coverage limits for your automobile policy. These minimums might be too low to provide adequate protection if you have significant assets or earning potential. If so, consider a coverage level of at least $100,000/$300,000. (The two figures represent per person/per incident.) The cost for you to increase your limits is usually minor, especially if they are increased simultaneously with the raising of your deductibles.

You: My insurance is so expensive. Besides a higher deductible, how else can I keep my rates in check?

In most states, your rates are largely determined by the insurance company's perception of the likelihood of your filing a claim. If you have a long driving history, the insurance company examines it to determine your premiums. Someone with a good driving record—relatively few accidents and speeding tickets—is a lower risk than someone whose driving record indicates he views most stop signs as optional. The difference in rates between a safe driver and one with a history of many claims is tremendous, because the difference in risk to the insurance company is even greater.

When you are in your early twenties, you won't have a significant driving history. The insurance company can't look back at a multi-decade driving history. However, they might profile you. Statistics show that a young, single male is more likely to be in an accident than a young married female. So, even if the young married female and her unmarried single male co-worker have identical driving histories, she will usually pay less in car insurance premiums.

You: Are you suggesting I get married to decrease my car insurance rates?

No, and I am not advocating a sex-change operation for men, either. Lower auto insurance premiums are a nice side-benefit of marriage. Still, there are other things you can do to keep your rates in check:

> *Keep your accidents and moving violations to a minimum.* While important at every age, it is especially critical while you are in your twenties. Your limited driving history and the unfavorable driving statistics of young folks are already working against you.

Add an accident or a speeding ticket to the mix and your high rates might just go higher. One small piece of good news: parking tickets don't affect your insurance rates.

➤ Statistics show that certain vehicles are more likely to be involved in accidents. Some vehicles are more likely to be in *expensive* accidents. And some cars are more likely to be in both more frequent and more expensive accidents.

When you are car shopping and narrow your selection to a few models, call two or more insurance companies to ask for rate quotes for each car you are considering. Don't be surprised if one of these cars costs much more (or much less) to insure than the others. *Consider the insurance cost when purchasing a car.* There isn't much you can do about that cost after you've already purchased the car.

➤ All else being equal, *a more expensive car costs more to insure.* After all, if your car is totaled, the insurance company is on the hook for much more dough when it's a high-end luxury car rather than a clunker.

➤ Take advantage of any professional associations or clubs you belong to. Although the relevance of this strategy varies by organization and by state, sometimes membership discounts can be significant. It's worth investigating. Ask the agent what group discounts are available.

➤ Finally, if you obtain your auto insurance from the same insurance company as your homeowner's or renter's policy, you might receive a discount.

HOMEOWNER'S OR RENTER'S INSURANCE

You can have either homeowner's or renter's insurance for the place where you live, but not both. Which one is determined solely by your ownership status. If you own your home, you buy homeowner's and if you rent your friendly abode, you purchase renter's. See? Not too hard.

If you own your home and have a mortgage, the bank probably requires you to purchase homeowner's insurance. A homeowner's policy covers your home, its contents, and personal liability. If you rent—

You: Why would I get insurance if I don't own the place? Doesn't the guy who owns the building have to get insurance?

Whoever owns the building where you rent probably has insurance covering the building. However, the landlord's insurance does not cover your belongings. Renter's insurance covers personal liability and your possessions. Say you buy an expensive new TV that melts in a fire caused by the guy in the apartment below you who "meant to put the cigarette out." If you don't have renter's insurance, you are probably out of luck.

Renter's insurance is inexpensive, often less than $20 per month. If you are renting, you'll seldom be legally required to have renter's insurance—but you should still get it.

You: Is it confusing?

Gary: It can be. Come into the back. I'll do my best to explain it to you. Can I get you some coffee?

You: I don't think so.

Good answer. I'd like you to keep a few key things in mind when purchasing renter's insurance:

➤ *Coverage limits.* Remember, the coverage limit is the maximum amount the insurance company pays on a claim. Many people simply choose the minimum coverage option (usually $10,000 or $15,000). If the value of your possessions is that amount or less, the minimum is fine. However, *determine what it would cost to replace everything you own if you suddenly lost it all.* A friend of mine assumed she didn't own anywhere near the $15,000 minimum insurance coverage limit she purchased. But when there was a fire in her building, she learned—the hard way—that it cost significantly more than $15,000 to replace her possessions.

➤ *Choose* **replacement cost coverage.** This option means you receive payment for the cost to *replace* what is destroyed. An alternative is an **actual value** policy in which the payment you receive is for the value lost. Take, for instance, your two-year-old business suit. It might be worth only $50 on eBay, but you use it and it fits your needs. If you had to replace it with a new suit, you would spend far more than $50. Therefore, you are better off with replacement cost coverage.

➤ *Understand specific limitations.* Most policies limit the amount you can claim of specific types of losses, such as cash or jewelry. But you can insure your engagement ring, for example, by adding a rider to your policy. A **rider** is a supplement to an insurance policy that provides additional coverage for an additional fee. Don't be surprised if the rider for an expensive engagement ring doubles the price of the policy. Of course, imagine the conversation with your spouse or fiancé if you lose the ring and don't have insurance.[2]

LIFE INSURANCE

Life insurance should be one of the easiest types of insurance to understand. If you die while covered by a standard life insurance policy, your beneficiary receives money from the life insurance company. The money your beneficiary receives is the **net death benefit.** That's all there is to it.

Gary: Actually, there's plenty more—

—that you can do to confuse people.

Gary: That's not what I was going to say.

Of course not. Look, please keep your shtick to yourself for the moment. We'll have that discussion later.

As I started to say, your designated **beneficiary** is the person who receives the money from your life insurance policy when you die. You choose your beneficiary in advance. If you are married, you typically choose your spouse. If you have no spouse, partner, or children, another relative, such as a sibling or parent, is frequently selected. Others might prefer to leave part or all of the money to a charitable organization, such as a religious institution or a university.

You can choose any person to be your beneficiary. However, if you are married and select someone other than your spouse, your spouse is often required to agree—in writing. Regardless of the person you choose, make sure your beneficiary likes you…alive.

---

[2] It ends with "No, I don't know how. I'm really, really, really, sorry. I love you too."

You: Should I get life insurance?

That depends.

You: On?

On who relies on you or your income. Ask yourself the following question:

Who would be harmed *financially* by your untimely demise?

Does your answer include a spouse, children, or other loved ones? Or merely the local coffee shop and the late-night taco stand?

Your answer forces you to consider how your death causes *financial harm to others*. Only those people relying on you or your income need the protection life insurance provides. If you have a spouse, child, or parent depending on your income to maintain their lifestyle, you probably need life insurance.

You: So if I am a stay-at-home parent, I don't need life insurance, right?

Actually, you probably do. It is not only those making an income who need to be insured. Even if you work full-time in the home and receive no salary, there is a tremendous financial cost to the survivors resulting from your early death. As you told your spouse during your last argument, it would cost big bucks to replace the childcare, cleaning, and personal chef responsibilities—in addition to everything else you do.

How would your surviving spouse be able to keep his/her job and perform all your responsibilities if you were gone? Quite likely, it would be impossible. Life insurance on the homemaker spouse enables the surviving spouse to keep the job he/she has and afford to hire others to help with the tasks formerly performed by the homemaker spouse.

You: What if I am unmarried without children?

If you can't identify anyone negatively affected *financially* by your death, you probably don't need life insurance. For example, an unmarried 30-year-old with no kids or other dependents almost certainly has no reason to purchase life insurance. Even someone who is married but whose spouse also works might not need life insurance.

You: Why not?

After a grieving period following your death, your surviving spouse likely goes back to work. If your spouse was living on his or her share of your combined income, he or she can continue to do so. No children or other dependents exist so none are affected. On the other hand, if your mortgage is based on your combined incomes and you would want your spouse to be able to continue to live in your home after you are gone, you will likely need to purchase life insurance to increase the chance your current home remains affordable when you are gone.

You: How much insurance should I purchase?

The basic goal is to satisfy your survivor's needs for a specific period of time. For example, you might purchase enough insurance so that your spouse would not have to work for the rest of the time your children were expected to live in the home. You might further choose to purchase enough to pay for your children's expected college expenses. If you also purchased enough insurance so that your spouse would never have to work again and could afford to purchase most of the north shore of the Hawaiian island of Oahu, you've probably purchased too much insurance. Take advantage of the tools available to assist you to estimate the appropriate amount of insurance to purchase at *www.totalcandor.com*.

You: What kind of insurance should I get?

Gary: I love this question.

I can't tell you exactly what to do. But I can provide you with some background and tell you what to be most cautious of. With that information, you will probably know what makes the most sense for your situation.

You: I hope so.

Trust me, you'll get it. Broadly speaking, there are two types of life insurance you can choose to buy: whole life insurance and term life insurance. Whole life insurance is further divided into a bunch of other types of policies with buzzwords such as universal, variable, and single premium. Gary will quickly discuss the merits of whole life insurance policies in Chapter 7. I'll, of course, be there too to defuse much of his spin.

Term insurance, on the other hand, is the purest kind of insurance. You pay premiums for the specific length of time (the term) the policy covers. Possible terms might include 10 years and 20 years. If you pay your premiums and die during the term of the policy, your beneficiary receives the full amount of life insurance proceeds. If you do not die during the term of the policy, you get nothing. It is very simple.

You: That is simple.

Partly due to this simplicity, it is relatively easy to compare policies among the various companies selling term life insurance. There just aren't as many numbers (especially when compared to the many variations of whole life insurance policies) to confuse you. Once you identify how much insurance you want and for what period of time, the most important considerations remaining are the strength of the company selling you the policy and the price of the policy.

You: I get the price thing. What do you mean by the "strength of the company?"

Since it's possible you might die many years subsequent to your purchase of a life insurance policy, you want to be confident the company you've paid premiums to will be able to pay the death benefit to your beneficiary. The stronger, financially speaking, your life insurance company, the higher the chances your death benefit will be paid. There are many rating services that assess the financial strength of life insurance companies. The rating services have scales with grades, usually some variation of AA or A+ and so on. (An F is never a good grade, even in life insurance ratings.)

Most of the top insurance companies have very strong ratings. I only mention the ratings to make sure you don't rely solely on price. If you receive a term life insurance quote that is significantly less than the other term life quotes, just be sure that it has the financial strength you'd expect before purchasing the policy.

Finally, some level of life insurance may be offered to you as part of your corporate benefits program. This possibility is discussed in Chapter 6.

LONG-TERM CARE INSURANCE

Long-term care insurance pays a portion of the cost of nursing home care. This is typically not something that makes sense to purchase for yourself if you are under age 50. It might be something for your parents or grandparents to consider, however.

You: Okay, but I am trying to get my own situation in order first.

As well you should. However, the long-term care situation of your older relatives may very well affect your financial future.

You: How?

Not only the amount but also the very existence of an inheritance might be dramatically impacted by how your older relatives handle—or do not handle—this part of their financial lives.

You: Oh, c'mon!

It's admittedly not where you should start your financial planning life. But once you've got a handle on your personal affairs, it might be worth your time to have some heart-to-heart conversations with your elder relatives.

You: So much to look forward to.

But think about how you'll feel knowing you might have made a significant impact to your financial situation, as well as, potentially, that of your parents and siblings.

UMBRELLA INSURANCE

This protects you in case it rains on your birthday.

You: Cool. The insurance industry sells everything.

Not quite. **Umbrella insurance** protects you if (and *only* if) you suffer a loss that exceeds the coverage level of one of your other policies. Let's say you have a $500,000 coverage limit for liability on your automobile policy. You get into an accident, are found to be at fault, and are successfully sued for $800,000. If you have a $1 million umbrella insurance policy, your auto policy pays the first $500,000 (minus your deductible) and your umbrella insurance policy pays the remaining $300,000. Until you have significant wealth or earning potential that exceeds the coverage limits of your policies, it is seldom necessary to purchase an umbrella policy.

However, if you do have significant assets or earning potential, umbrella insurance is an extremely affordable insurance you should consider. For just a couple of hundred dollars annually, you can typically afford to add an additional $1 million of protection by purchasing an umbrella policy. That can help you sleep better at night.

SOME INSURANCE IS STUPID

The primary purpose of any insurance *should be* to protect you from significant and negative financial repercussions caused by unexpected events. Insurance is not a great idea for anything else. A stain that won't come out of your couch does not qualify as significant. Neither does your television breaking. Even if both events occur during the pre-game show of the Super Bowl.

Still, insurance—in the form of an extended warranty plan—is sold for just such contingencies. But considering the likelihood of needing a repair or replacement, and its cost, it is rarely a good idea to buy the warranty. As insurance goes, it is not cheap.

If someone offers you a two-year extended warranty for $40 on a $100 printer, think about it. But only for as long as it takes to politely say, "No thank you."

You: Why?

Well, for one thing, the odds are low that your printer breaks during the warranty period, and lower still that it breaks for a reason actually covered. (If you know differently, purchase a different printer.) Even if your printer does break for the right reason at the right time, buying a similar one would also cost about $100. By participating in an extended warranty program, you are saying you don't want a new printer for $100. Rather, you prefer to pre-pay $40 (a couple of years in advance, no less) to repair a two-year-old printer.

You are further saying that you have plenty of free time so you don't mind spending it waiting for the repair or engaging in correspondence with the repair company, not to mention a possible shipping expense, and so on. *Don't spend your hard-earned money insuring against minor chances of future small-dollar expenses.* That's not what insurance is for.

Several additional insurance programs are discussed in the chapter on corporate benefits that follows. Employer-provided benefits are also usually, *but not always*, the most economical source for acquiring the protection such policies provide.

CHAPTER 6

Take Advantage of Your Benefits (or You're Being Kind of Dumb)

"Common sense is perhaps the most equally divided, but surely the most underemployed talent in the world."
—CHRISTIANE COLLANGE

You are now familiar with taxes, especially the *required* subtractions from your gross pay. Yet there are still more deductions listed on your pay stub. These represent the portion you pay for benefits. Unlike taxes, most deductions for benefits are *optional*.

In addition to wages, **benefits** are another form of compensation. Employees receive value from benefits. Employers pay real costs to provide them. Many benefits are smart to choose; others, well, not so much. This chapter highlights the winners and the losers.

Most benefits fall into one of these three categories:

1. insurance programs
2. spending accounts
3. retirement plans

Although the process of establishing your benefits varies from one employer to another, it probably involves "elections."

BENEFIT CHOICE ELECTIONS

During the **benefit election** time of year, there are neither campaigns nor politicians arguing for your vote. Any debate takes place between you and yourself as you attempt to make good decisions. Why human resources folks call benefit decisions "elections" instead of "decisions," "choices," or "selections"—which is what they are—is beyond me.

ANNUAL ENROLLMENT PERIOD

When you start your job, you make your initial benefit choices. After, you can usually make changes only once each year during the **annual enrollment period.** The choices you make at that time are locked in for the year and cannot be changed. However, you may be eligible to make changes sooner if you experience a **life event.**

You: I haven't had a date in a while. Last Friday, I met someone who asked me out. Is that a life event? It sure seems like one.

No. Examples of life events include:

➤ marriage or divorce
➤ birth or adoption of a child
➤ child no longer a dependent
➤ spouse's job changes (or gets one or stops working)
➤ death or disability of a spouse
➤ death or disability of employee

Though life events do happen, they happen infrequently.

You: Earlier, you mentioned benefits are a cost subtracted from my net pay. You also said benefits are a form of compensation. Now wait a second: How can something be compensation if it reduces my net pay? Is this some kind of joke?

No, it's not a joke. But it is an unpleasant surprise to learn that benefits cost you money. Most employers pay the overwhelming majority of a benefit program's cost. Typically you pay only a portion of the cost, not nearly the entire cost.

There are two primary reasons you might pay a portion of the benefit cost. First, your cost provides you with an incentive to select only the benefits you value. This ensures that your employer doesn't pay for providing unnecessary or unappreciated benefits. Second, the money you contribute makes it less expensive for the employer.

You: I still don't like it.

I understand, but it sure beats the alternative, which would require paying for insurance *entirely* on your own. Most people who have jobs without benefits would prefer jobs with benefits, even if it meant additional subtractions from their paychecks.

EMPLOYER-SPONSORED INSURANCE PROGRAMS

Not every employer offers benefits to every employee. Some employers offer no benefits to any employees. At other companies, full-timers receive benefits and certain part-timers or temporary workers do not. Sometimes eligibility for benefits is based on how long someone has been with the employer. There are many possible conditions to be eligible for benefits.

Here are some of the most common insurance benefits available to workers with comprehensive benefit programs.

HEALTH INSURANCE

If you are eligible for benefits, the most important program is usually a **group health (medical) insurance** plan. Having this benefit is critical for several reasons. First, it is expensive and difficult (occasionally impossible) to purchase health insurance as an individual.

You: My offer letter says health insurance is part of my benefits package. So why does my employer take so much money out of my paycheck for health insurance? Is this a bait and switch?

Not at all. There was a time—and not too long ago—when employers provided employee medical insurance at little or no cost to the employee. Today, with some notable and increasingly rare exceptions, employers require workers to pay part of the insurance cost. However, most employers still pay the bulk of the plan's cost. Furthermore, you receive an enormous savings by being part of a *group* health insurance plan.

You: Why do I need health insurance if I'm young and healthy? I haven't been to the doctor in three years. I don't even like doctors.

Choosing to decline health insurance is certainly an option. But it is usually a stupid one if you can possibly afford it. According to the Bureau of the Census, nearly 16 percent of all Americans didn't have health insurance in 2005. Nearly everyone in that group would like health insurance but can't afford it.

You should do everything you can to obtain health insurance. Without health insurance, you pay more for doctor's visits and prescriptions. The most innocent of activities can cause a financially devastating medical situation.

The romantic meal your significant other cooks leads to food poisoning. Your ski trip goes slightly awry. Either way, you're headed to the emergency room. Your resulting medical bills are thousands or perhaps tens of thousands of dollars. Just from one bad incident! These are bills you had not anticipated. Without health insurance, you suddenly find yourself with significant debt that takes a long time—perhaps years—to pay. With health insurance you are not financially devastated.[1]

You: Is there any situation in which it makes sense to decline health insurance coverage offered through my employer?

Yes. But typically only if all of the following are true:

1. You are married.[2]
2. Your spouse works.
3. Your spouse's employer offers a similar health insurance policy that can also cover you (or, if appropriate, your entire family).
4. This policy available to your spouse is less costly than purchasing two individual policies (one for you and one for your spouse).

Some employers slightly increase the pay of those who decline their company-sponsored health insurance coverage. Although you should not turn down health insurance solely for this reason, the pay increase is a nice side benefit if you would otherwise turn down the coverage to choose your spouse's policy.

---

[1] Although health insurance does relieve some of the financial pain from those incidents, your reluctance to eat anything with "a chunky butter sauce" or to do "just one more run down the mountain before the sun sets" is likely to stay with you for a while.

[2] Sometimes, domestic partners are offered the same benefit treatment as married couples. Check with your human resources department.

LIFE INSURANCE

Some level of life insurance might be provided at no cost to you as part of your benefits program. In addition, your employer might offer you the opportunity to purchase a higher amount of life insurance coverage, typically a multiple of your salary.

You: For instance?

Say that your salary is $45,000. A possible scenario is for your employer to provide $45,000 of life insurance at *no* cost to you. Often, you can also choose to increase that amount to a total of $90,000 or $135,000 of life insurance (2 times and 3 times your salary, respectively). If you do, the additional charge is usually just a few dollars per paycheck.

You: Should I get insurance through my employer or term insurance on my own?

Always accept the free coverage and thank your employer. Free is a price no one can beat. However, if you need additional insurance, it often makes sense to buy it privately—on your own.

You: Why? It's certainly much easier to just get the insurance through work.

That's true. But this path of least resistance might also be more expensive and less flexible. If you are young and healthy, and especially if you are a non-smoker, you owe it to yourself to get a quote for a private policy. You will likely find that a policy purchased outside of the group policy at work is less expensive.

In addition, life insurance you purchase privately is not dependent on your continued employment at your current job. When you go work for another company or take some time out of the workforce, you can keep your privately purchased life insurance. This advantage is known as **portability**. Life insurance purchased through your employer is typically not portable, since it is not available to you should you leave your job. In most cases, this is true regardless of the reason you leave: quit, layoff, or disability.

So, if you need life insurance, get a quote for term life insurance. If it is comparably priced, let alone cheaper, don't waste any of your money (even if only $5 or $10 a paycheck), on additional life insurance at work. Better to spend it on something you enjoy. Better still, save some of it.

DISABILITY INSURANCE

Disability insurance pays you a *portion* of your income if, due to an illness or injury, you are unable to work for an extended period of time. As with life insurance, some companies include a certain level of disability coverage at no cost to you. If you choose additional coverage, a cost is subtracted from your paycheck. Two types of disability insurance might be offered: short-term and long-term.

You: Why does the policy pay me only a portion of my income? Can I buy insurance that pays my entire salary if I am disabled?

Not usually. In most places, your monthly disability benefits are restricted to a percentage of your pre-disability pay. The government and insurers want you to have an incentive to return to work. If people make the same money whether working or not working, they lack financial motivation to rejoin the workforce.

SHORT-TERM DISABILITY INSURANCE

Like it sounds, **short-term disability insurance** covers disabilities that don't last very long. These policies usually begin payments after your sick time is exhausted. Although short-term disability payments typically do not last longer than six months, this insurance is a valuable benefit.

LONG-TERM DISABILITY INSURANCE

Not surprisingly, **long-term disability** insurance pays a benefit if you are disabled for an extended period of time. However, long-term disability insurance does not make payments until your waiting period expires. Although it can be longer, this **waiting period** is often three to six months. A common arrangement is to have disability insurances coordinated so the short-term disability pays benefits until long-term disability payments begin. In other words, your short-term policy pays benefits during the waiting period required by your long-term policy.

You: How long will long-term disability insurance pay benefits?

A long time.

You: That's real helpful.

Sorry. Duration varies by policy, but it usually lasts for many years, sometimes until you reach age 65 or longer. Of course, insurance companies stop paying if and when you are no longer disabled. Disability policies are based on the expectation of your returning to the workforce when physically possible.

You: Do I need disability insurance?

This answer surprises a lot of people. Long-term disability insurance is an important benefit at any age. Don't skip this one, even if you are young. Not convinced? Read these statistics:

> "Every year 12 percent of the adult U.S. population suffers a long-term disability. One out of every seven workers will suffer a five-year or longer period of disability before age 65, and if you're 35 now, your chances of experiencing a three-month or longer disability before you reach age 65 are 50 percent. If you're 45, the figure is 44 percent."[3]

Yet people spend far more time considering life insurance than disability insurance. When you are young, the odds of dying are far lower than the odds of your becoming disabled. Plus, if there are no survivors depending on your income, the financial burden caused by your death is minimal.

You: You said that already. Quit rubbing it in.

Glad you are paying attention.

A disability has entirely different financial implications. If you are disabled, an income is required to take care of you, whether or not you have dependents. Your personal needs might actually increase. *Absolutely take advantage of a long-term disability option.*

You: What about the other disability insurance options on this annual enrollment form? There are so many choices!

Let me simplify: there are only three *easy* questions to answer when evaluating corporate long-term disability insurance.

---

[3] Source: "Disability insurance can save your life", Ginger Applegarth, *http://moneycentral. msn.com/content/Insurance/Insureyourhealth/P35613.asp.*

> **Easy Question 1:** *Should I elect coverage for long-term disability insurance?*

Easy Answer 1: Hell, yes. Read the previous few paragraphs for the odds. One of the foremost rules of insurance is to *never risk a lot for a little.* Considering the protection long-term disability insurance provides and the real risk, you should not pass on this insurance.

> **Easy Question 2:** *There are replacement coverage level choices: 50 percent or 70 percent. Which should I select?*

Easy Answer 2: The increased cost for higher replacement coverage is usually nominal. Should you become disabled, the additional benefit is significant. Therefore, consider the higher level of protection.

> **Easy Question 3:** *I have the choice of paying the premiums* pre-tax *(before tax) or post-tax (after tax). What makes the most sense?*

Easy Answer 3: Select post-tax (after tax). Since not every employer provides this choice, some people don't have a question 3. Nonetheless, there are implications of each choice.

PRE-TAX PREMIUM PAYMENT

If you pay the disability payment pre-tax, your premium payment is subtracted from your *gross* income. This causes your taxable income to decrease, thereby saving you income tax. This means that a $10.00 disability premium could reduce your net paycheck by only $7.50.

You: I like that idea.

Indeed. However, your disability benefits are subject to income tax. This means that if you become disabled—and if you had always paid your premiums pre-tax—your entire benefit is received pre-tax. If your replacement coverage pays a $3,000 per month benefit, you receive $3,000 *less the amount of income taxes that must be paid.* Income taxes could easily reduce your benefit by several hundred dollars.

POST-TAX PREMIUM PAYMENT

When you pay your share of disability insurance premiums post-tax, the premium payment comes from your *net income.* This means your paycheck decreases by the amount of your premium payment: a $10 premium reduces your net pay by $10.

If you become disabled—and if you had always paid premiums after-tax—your entire benefit is received post-tax. This means that none of your disability benefit is subject to income taxes. If you receive a $3,000 per month benefit, you keep the entire amount. You pay no income taxes on the disability benefit.

You: So what do I do?

Pay premiums with after-tax dollars. By sacrificing the small tax savings of a before-tax premium payment, you receive a higher level of disability protection.

Imagine that you have long-term disability insurance with a replacement rate of 70 percent and that you pay premiums with your after-tax dollars. As you know, your current salary is subject to plenty of income taxes. Many years from now, you suffer a long-term disability.

You: Hey! What's up with that?

It's only an example.

You: Why can't you be the one who becomes disabled?

You can do what you want in your own book. As I was saying, although your disability benefit is only 70 percent of your working gross income, it is not subject to federal income taxes. You keep all of it. Because your salary while you worked was taxed—perhaps upwards of 20 percent—your net income might not change significantly despite your disability. It's a comforting feeling to have that kind of coverage. Choose to sleep better by paying disability premiums with post-tax dollars.

> **Workplace Disability Insurance Isn't Perfect**
>
> Disability coverage purchased through your employer typically ceases after you leave your job. In other words, it is seldom portable. Unfortunately, privately purchased disability insurance is usually more expensive and complicated than insurance available through your employer. However, if disability insurance is available through a club or organization to which you belong, consider it. Make sure you understand *how "disability" is defined* in any private policy. Ideally, you want "own occupation" coverage, which means you are considered disabled if you cannot perform your current position.

DENTAL, VISION, AND AD&D

You: AD&D? Does this cover a Ritalin prescription?

No. But you'll find the information in this section fairly simple to understand—if you can pay attention long enough.

DENTAL INSURANCE

As you'd expect, **dental insurance** covers some expenses related to oral health. Some dental policies are thorough and others less so. Typically, your only benefit choice is to either accept or decline coverage—there usually aren't multiple levels and plans to choose from.

You: Should I accept dental coverage?

Do you have teeth?

You: Yes.

Is your parent or another close relative a dentist?

You: Um—

Doesn't matter. You should probably accept dental coverage because the cost is usually very low and often covers most of the cost of your twice-annual checkups. And, although this is not the place for an oral hygiene sermon, it makes sense for you to go to the dentist regularly. So, pick up the insurance.

VISION INSURANCE

Sometimes vision is included in your medical insurance, sometimes it is offered separately. If offered separately, review the plan and anticipate your personal benefits by accepting coverage. Unlike dental, if you have excellent vision and eye health you might go a couple of years between eye doctor appointments. On the other hand, if you wear contact lenses or need new glasses every year, it probably pays for you to accept vision insurance.

ACCIDENTAL DEATH AND DISMEMBERMENT INSURANCE

Accidental death and dismemberment (AD&D) insurance provides a sizable benefit if you die in an accident or become dismembered. Typically, this benefit is a multiple of your salary (i.e., one or two times).

You: Wow, I wish I didn't have to ask this, but what does "dismembered" mean again?

I understand. If someone walks in as you're looking up "dismembered" in the dictionary and says "Hey, whatcha up to?" —well, that isn't going to be a real comfortable conversation for anybody. Dismembered means the loss of a limb or limbs.

Sometimes AD&D coverage is provided at no cost to you. If so, say thank you and move on. If you have the option to purchase a specific level of additional coverage, pass on it.

You: Why?

If others depend on your income, you need the protection life insurance coverage provides. Period. It doesn't matter if you die due to a bad bungee cord (an accident) or cancer (not an accident). Similarly, your need for disability insurance exists regardless of the type of disability—whether you lose your arm or your mind.

So take care of any life insurance and disability insurance needs as previously discussed, but pass on AD&D.

EMPLOYER-SPONSORED SPENDING ACCOUNTS

You: Cool! I had no idea I'd get one of these.

You don't. Maybe your sister, who works in sales, has a fat expense account she told you about. So you're pretty excited when you learn you have a spending account at your job.

Sorry. Although expense accounts and spending accounts sound similar they are quite different. Having an **expense account** means your sister can take clients to expensive lunches and have her company pay for it. You cannot do that with a spending account, but it is an attractive benefit in its own right.

You: Why? How does a spending account work?

Think about **spending accounts** (also called **reimbursement accounts**) as a series of straightforward steps.

1. You enroll.
2. You contribute your own money to your account. (You determine the amount. There may be a minimum and a maximum permitted annually.)
3. You incur an expense eligible for reimbursement.
4. You request reimbursement from your account.
5. You receive a reimbursement check.
6. Money remaining in your reimbursement account is typically forfeited at the end of the year.

You: Why should I do this? Seems like a bunch of work just to move money around. Besides, I have no idea how much money I'll spend on stuff eligible for reimbursement, so I could end up forfeiting money! I can't afford that. No thanks. I'll just pay these expenses as they come up.

You're right—forget it.

You: Really?

No.

You: Then tell me how a spending account could make any sense for me. Or anyone.

There's one key factor making reimbursement accounts worth considering: *The contributions put in the spending account are pre-tax but the reimbursements are post-tax.*

You: You said this was going to be straightforward. What are you talking about?

Let's take an example. Say you participate in a health care reimbursement account by putting $10 each paycheck into the account. Since you are paid every two weeks, you contribute $260 during one year from 26 paychecks.

Each $10 contribution reduces your gross pay. Assuming your tax withholdings are 25 percent of your gross pay, your tax withheld decreases by $2.50. Overall, your net pay decreases by $7.50.

Figure 6-1

Impact to Your Paycheck of Enrolling in a Reimbursement Account

	Before Enrollment	After Enrollment	Impact
Gross Pay	$ 1,000.00	$ 990.00	$ 10.00
Taxes	$ 250.00	$ 247.50	$ 2.50
Net Pay	$ 750.00	$ 742.50	$ 7.50

If you pay $260 (or more) of reimbursable expenses throughout the year and complete the reimbursement form, you will receive a check for $260.

Review what happens.

1. You divert $260 of pay before tax to your spending account.
2. You pay $260 in medical expenses from your after-tax income.
3. You receive $260 back from your spending account.

Note that numbers one and three cancel each other out. Number two happens regardless of whether you participate in the spending plan. Next comes number four:

4. Your tax decreases by $2.50 per paycheck or $65 for the year.

You are $65 richer by going through this process. No games, no gimmicks. You're basically taking money from one hand, giving it to another, and taking it back again. And by doing so, you permanently save tax. The more you contribute and the higher your income tax rate, the more you save.

Still not sold? Here's another way to look at it:

Wouldn't you take advantage of a coupon for 25 percent off even if you had to complete some forms? That's exactly what you accomplish if your top tax rate is 25 percent!

The primary drawback of a spending account is that you must typically use all your contributions to the plan in the year you make them. If you don't, you forfeit the amount of money by which your contributions exceed your eligible spending. Therefore, don't contribute more money to the plan than you reasonably expect to spend.

You: Does that mean I need to predict the future?

Sort of.

You: Sorry, but my time machine is at the shop.

Mine too. The risk of forfeiture causes many people to simply ignore the opportunity spending accounts provide. However, the best thing to do is to look over your records from the previous year or two and estimate your reimbursable expenses. Use an annual total as an indicator of the amount you might spend in the future. Think about expenses that can be reasonably predicted. At a minimum, put that amount in your account.

The different types of reimbursement accounts are described next.

HEALTH CARE SPENDING ACCOUNT

By participating in a health care reimbursement account, you divert a set amount of your paycheck to an account for future health care expense reimbursement. Then, when you incur an eligible medical expense, you complete a form and receive reimbursement from your account. The benefit of this process is tax savings. When determining what amount to put into a reimbursement account, think about co-pays, replacement contact lenses or glasses, out-of-pocket expenses for medications, and any other medical expenses.

TRANSPORTATION SPENDING ACCOUNT

This program is similar to a health care spending account, except reimbursements are provided only for expenses related to getting to work.

The primary reimbursable expenses are public transportation and parking at the office. Although the same advantages and drawbacks of a health care reimbursement account apply to a transportation account, it is far easier for most people to forecast their transportation expenses than their medical expenses.

You: What about parking I pay elsewhere, like at home?

Only the parking fees you pay at the office or related to commuting qualify.

You: Bummer.

I know.

DEPENDENT CARE SPENDING ACCOUNT

A dependent care account works like the other reimbursement accounts. Dependent care accounts typically allow reimbursement for the expenses of caring for your child (or children) while you are at work.

EMPLOYER-SPONSORED RETIREMENT PLANS

You: I'm a long way from retiring—can I just skip this and go to the next chapter?

Absolutely, positively not.

You: Why do I have to bother with retirement plans at my age?

Because you are the ideal age right now to be concerned about retirement. There will never be a better time.

You: But you don't even know how old I am.

That doesn't matter. Your primary source of income is probably wages from employment. When you fully retire, you stop working. Your salary stops. It stops immediately and entirely.

Yet your expenses continue. Expenses include your personal dreams that might include a second home, a boat, bingo, vacations, potato farming, and extensive golfing. There may also be less desirable but unavoidable expenses such as medical bills, college tuition for your children, and taxes.

Since your wages stop but your expenses do not, *you* need to develop a money source to pay for your retirement. This means investing time and money while you are still working to plan and save for your retirement.

Because of the miracle of compounding interest, *it is never as easy to fund your retirement as it is right now.*

You: So you are saying it is easier to plan for retirement when it is furthest away?

Yes!

You: That's weird.

The younger, the better. It might seem counter-intuitive or even illogical, but such is the result of the miracle of compounding interest we discuss in Chapter 1. With the understanding that retirement planning is important at any age, let's cover some basic retirement planning definitions:

➤ *Retirement Plan*—Retirement plans are accounts with specific tax advantages. The government makes these advantages possible as an incentive to get people to fund their retirement and not be a burden on society later. That's why there are penalties and other financial repercussions if the money is not left in the plan until retirement.

➤ *Pension Plan*—Administered by some employers, pension plans offer monetary benefits (i.e., retirement benefits) to retirees. Pensions are one example of a retirement plan. There are a few important types of pension plans.

➤ *Defined Benefit Pension Plan*—This is a retirement plan in which the retirement benefit is guaranteed to be a certain amount, based on salary and years of service. Since the amount received is guaranteed, the retirement *benefit* is *defined*. Defined benefit pension plans are also known as **traditional pensions** because, years ago, most pensions were defined benefit plans.

➤ *Defined Contribution Pension Plan*—This is a retirement plan with a certain amount of money invested. Since it is the amounts invested into the plan that are certain, the retirement *contributions* are *defined*. The retirement benefit is based on:

1. the amount (if any) of your contributions to the plan
2. the amount (if any) of your employer's contributions to the plan
3. the investment performance of the plan

Number 3 means you can theoretically do better with a defined contribution plan than with a defined benefit plan. Yet that is usually not the case—you are nearly always better off with a traditional plan. Therefore, you need a reality check.

You: I need a reality check?

REALITY CHECK

There is little chance you will have a defined benefit pension plan for your retirement unless you are:

➤ near retirement,

➤ work for the government, or

➤ a union employee.

You: Why not?

A company's cost to provide defined benefit plans is both extremely high and difficult to forecast. Therefore, most employers have determined they no longer want this costly and unpredictable expense. *As a result, numerous employers eliminate defined benefit pension plans every year.* The sooner you recognize the implications of this trend, the more likely you can thrive despite it.

You: So what you're really saying is, in addition to all the taxes and insurance premiums I pay, I also have to save for my own retirement. This isn't fair. And what about Social Security? I'm paying a ton of payroll taxes! Isn't part of those taxes for my retirement?

Gary: Hey, what you need is a tax-deferred annuity. Or a whole life insurance policy. I can guarantee that you'll pay no taxes on these investments and receive a phenomenal rate of return.

You: What is he talking about?

The purchase of a tax-deferred annuity or a whole life insurance policy is *not* the place to begin retirement planning. We'll discuss these options in greater detail in the next chapter.

Retirement planning has changed significantly. Today, it is more complicated and necessary than ever. In fact, many people who retired under the "old rules" live comfortably in their old age despite doing little or no retirement planning.

A brief historical perspective should help you understand why, without significant planning and action, today's working population will not be as financially secure in retirement as current retirees are right now.

THE OLD RULES

Formerly, retirement income came from three sources:
1. defined benefit pension
2. Social Security
3. personal savings

These three sources were often referred to as the three-legged stool of retirement. But things are much different today. First, as I mention earlier, relatively few people have a defined benefit pension any more.

Goodbye to the first leg of the stool.

And although you pay Social Security tax, the tax you pay does not go into an account for your future. Instead, your tax helps pay today's retirees. The government's plan is for your retirement benefit to be paid by those who are working when you retire. Your retirement benefit is to come from the tax paid, in part, by your children and grandchildren.

You: I don't even have children or grandchildren.

I know—scary, right?

You: So scary.

There are reasons to be skeptical of this arrangement. Countless articles discuss whether the government will be able to afford to pay today's workers their promised retirement benefit. If you're in the mood for some lower intestinal distress, go ahead and read a few of those articles online. Here's what I can tell you:

➤ In 1945, there were more than 40 workers paying taxes for each retiree collecting benefits.

➤ Today, there are slightly more than three workers per retiree.

➤ Experts estimate that by 2030 the number will decrease to two workers per retiree.

For most of the past half-century, the Social Security trust fund received more tax money than it paid out in benefits to retirees. That's the good news. The bad news is that the difference was *not* saved for eventual use by future retirees. Rather, it is being used for other governmental expenses. I won't provide an opinion on this arrangement because that would be inherently political, but it is only fair that you understand the seriousness of the situation.

You: How will this get fixed?

I do not know how it gets fixed. No one knows how it gets fixed.

You: Will it get fixed?

I do not know *if* it gets fixed. No one knows *if* it gets fixed.

You: So what are you supposed to do?

You must plan as though you will *not* receive a Social Security retirement benefit. If you receive any Social Security benefit, consider it "gravy" on top of your own savings.

If you *still* doubt the severity of the situation, why not listen to the Social Security Administration itself? Here's what it prints on the annual benefit statement it mails annually to taxpayers:

"Your estimated benefits are based on current law. Congress has made changes to the law in the past and can do so at any time. The law governing benefit amounts may change because, by 2041, the payroll taxes collected will be enough to pay only about 74 percent of scheduled benefits."

This is per the Social Security Administration! Personally, I think it's a fair warning. So I advise you to say...

You: Goodbye to the second leg of my stool?

Yup.

NO STOOL FOR YOU!

You don't need a degree in physics to figure out that a three-legged stool with only one leg remaining is not a place to rest comfortably. I prefer to compare your retirement to an entirely different piece of equipment—a **pogo stick.** That's what it is. And you need to do everything you can to enter retirement with a turbocharged pogo stick, not a little wimpy plastic one.

You: Okay, but I bought this book for empowerment. Now, quite frankly, I am nervous. What does all of this mean? What is it going to cost me? How much more is going to be taken out of my paycheck? Haven't you been keeping track? You've been going on for pages listing all these deductions from my paycheck. Am I going to owe money to my boss after working 40 hours? Should I just stay home?

Okay, relax. That's a lot of questions. I sense panic. There's no need to panic. I am simply demonstrating that the one responsible for your financial future is you. We'll cover the basic steps you can take to prepare for this new reality. But honestly, just by recognizing the "new rules," and even by feeling a bit nervous, you're already way ahead.

Your retirement plan contributions are an optional subtraction from your net pay. Because they are optional, many people don't make them. What a missed opportunity! Retirement plan contributions are quite different from other deductions. Take a look at this table:

Figure 6-2

Be the Best Payroll Deduction You Can Be

Paycheck Deduction	Who Gets the Money?	Examples
Taxes	Government	Helping the less fortunate and paying for advanced weapons systems, roads, and a whole lot of bureaucracy, including the friendly people at the Department of Motor Vehicles.
Insurance Premiums	1) Insurance company and 2) unlucky people who have claims	Those who become ill or disabled or who die. (Here's to your never receiving any insurance money.)
Retirement Plan Contributions	You do!	Toys for your grandchildren, Florida beach condo, vacations, doctors' bills in old age.

If you have a retirement plan at your job, you may have the opportunity to participate in *one* of the plans described below. The plan offered depends on the type of employer you work for.

➤ **401(k) plan:** Most "for-profit" companies can offer these plans to their employees.

➤ **403(b) plan:** Public schools, churches, and hospital organizations can offer these plans to their employees.

➤ **457 plan:** Frequently available to people working for certain state and local government entities—such as that friendly DMV associate.

You: What's the difference between these plans?

The differences are minor and unimportant. Remember, you can't choose *which* plan to participate in. To simplify, we will refer to all employer-sponsored retirement plans going forward as 401(k) plans, because they are the most common.

401(k) PLANS

You: Where do they get these ridiculous names? Are these number and letter combinations from failed disinfectant formulas? Cough syrups?

Earlier, I mentioned the several–thousand-page Internal Revenue Code. It's divided into numerous sections. Part *k* of the section numbered *401* describes the plan known as a 401(k) plan. That's where the name comes from.

You: For real?

Yes, not too creative, but remember tax professionals aren't known for their creative skills—and those who are have an excellent chance of being put in jail. In short, if the tax code authors had placed additional information about taxes in the IRC before they wrote about retirement plans, we could be asking each other how our 865(w) plans were doing.

You: Okay, so I get it that a 401(k) plan is a retirement plan. How does it work?

ELIGIBILITY

You must first be eligible to participate. The rules at some companies allow new employees to participate on their first day of work. Elsewhere, employees must wait a period of time, such as one year, before they can participate.

You: Okay, I've been told I'm eligible. Now what?

That's great, because at many companies no one comes around to tell you when you are eligible. You must remember when you are eligible.

This distinction is important, because eligibility alone does not usually cause participation. *Once eligible, you must usually take action to participate.*

You: What action?

Simply requesting an enrollment form from Human Resources and filling it out.

You: I got the form—that part was simple. It's the "filling it out" that is more complicated. What the heck is a contribution level?

The form can be intimidating. But only to people who don't understand how 401(k) plans work. Let's take a step back.

You: Fine by me.

When you contribute money to your 401(k) plan, you move money from your paycheck to your retirement account. *The money remains yours.*

You: Prove it.

The 401(k) account has your name on it. You receive statements detailing the money you put in and your current plan value. Most 401(k) plans allow you to check the value of your plan (your plan balance) online at any time.

Since the money you are contributing is still yours, your contribution is sometimes referred to as a **deferral.** You are simply deferring *your* income to *your* 401(k) plan for *your* eventual use in retirement.

Ultimately, a 401(k) contribution is like taking money from your right pocket—where your wallet is—and putting it in your left pocket. Actually, it's better: your contribution is not subject to the federal and state income taxes you would otherwise pay.[4]

You: Sorry to be a thorn here. I love metaphors, but I have to ask: Where exactly is my left pocket?

Your 401(k) plan is held by the plan's **custodian.**

You: Ron? The man in high school with all those keys?

No. The custodian is a company, not a guy with a mop. Your checking account has a custodian too: the bank. The 401(k) custodian provides periodic statements and brochures. You do not have to visit the custodian's office. Examples of 401(k) custodians are:

➤ Fidelity

➤ Ameriprise

➤ Vanguard

You: So the money is in my name but is also in a retirement account. How does that work?

Here's an example:

➤ Let's say you contribute $100 of each $1,000 paycheck to your 401(k) plan.

➤ Further, let's say your federal tax withholding rate is 25 percent.

You: Imagine I have said those things. Now what?

How much does your paycheck decrease due to your contribution?

You: $100—you just told me that.

Nope—your paycheck decreases by $75.

You: Why only $75?

Pretend you didn't contribute $100 to your 401(k) plan after all. Your taxable income would be $100 higher than if you had made the 401(k) contribution. But you aren't paid taxable income. Your paycheck is net income. Since your withholdings are 25 percent, you pay $25 of tax on the additional $100 of taxable income. Therefore, by not making a $100 contribution to your 401(k), your paycheck increases by only $75.

---

[4] The contribution is subject to FICA and Medicare taxes, however.

You: Gotcha. How much goes to my 401(k) plan as a result of the contribution?

I ask the questions.

You: I bought your book.

Fair point. Your 401(k) plan increases by $100—the amount of the contribution you make.

You: Not $75, like the amount my paycheck decreases?

No. One hundred dollars.

You: It sounds like I just made $25.

You did, by simply putting money in your left pocket.

You: Excellent.

Absolutely. You lowered your tax by $25. Instead of receiving (and probably spending) $75, you save $100. These are good things.

Figure 6-3

Effect of a 401(k) Contribution To:
Your Paycheck

	No Contribution	$100 Contribution
Gross pay	$ 1,000	$ 1,000
401(k) contribution	$ –	$ (100)
Taxable pay	$ 1,000	$ 900
Taxes (at 25%)	$ (250)	$ (225)
Net pay	$ 750	$ 675

Your Wealth

Net pay	$ 750	$ 675
401(k) contribution	$ –	$ 100
Total	$ 750	$ 775

Furthermore, your savings should grow significantly before you retire. In addition to the tax savings from your contributions, the *growth* of this money is also not taxed each year. You pay tax on it only when you withdraw the money. This concept—not paying tax until a later time—is known as **tax-deferred growth**.

CONTRIBUTION PERCENTAGES

You decide how much money to contribute to your 401(k) plan. Enrollment forms commonly ask you to indicate the percentage—not the dollar amount—you want to contribute. This figure is a percentage of your gross pay.

You: Huh?

It's admittedly a silly way to ask an easy question, but this is just how it is. Too many people get confused and stop—they don't enroll. Big mistake. This is really easy. Stay with me.

You: Okay.

Assume your annual salary is $36,000, paid twice a month. Your gross income each pay period is $1,500 ($36,000 divided by 24 paychecks per year).

You would like to save for retirement and feel comfortable reducing your take-home pay by $50 each paycheck.

You: Okay.

So you can afford to reduce your gross pay by $67.

You: Wait. I just agreed $50 was comfortable. Why are you taking $67?

If you are comfortable reducing *net* pay by $50, you can reduce *gross* pay by $67. Since you're in the 25 percent tax bracket, you pay $17 of tax on $67 of income received (not contributed to a 401(k) plan):

```
$   67 gross income
x   25 percent tax rate
────────────────────────
$   17 tax
```

The $17 of tax reduces your gross pay by $67:

> $67 gross income
> − $17 income tax
> $50 net pay

If you are in the 25 percent tax bracket and are willing to lower your net pay by $50, you contribute $67 of gross income.

You: I follow, but of course $67 is not a percentage, it's a dollar amount.

It certainly is. If the enrollment form asks for a dollar contribution (deferral) amount per paycheck, you write $67. If it asks for a percentage, divide $67 by $1,500 to get 4.5 percent.[5] If you indicate either of these figures on the enrollment form, you contribute more than $1,600 to your 401(k) plan annually ($67 x 24 paychecks), and you reduce your net pay by only about $1,200 ($50 x 24 paychecks).

You: But is 4.5 percent "good?" How much should I be saving for retirement?

I wish more people asked this question instead of the far more popular queries: "Do I really have to save now?" and "Does this make my butt look big?" Nonetheless, the answer to *your* question depends on your complete financial picture, which reflects whether you have credit card debts, an emergency fund, and so on. We cover financial priorities in the next chapter.

Here's what I can tell you now: Contributing 4.5 percent of your gross pay is *much* better than doing nothing. If you can afford more, contribute more. Aim to save at least 10 percent of your gross pay for retirement at the youngest possible age. Like Ben and Henry teach us in Chapter 1, the longer you delay saving, the more you will need to save to achieve the same financial objective. And that's hard to do. When in doubt, remember: few people get in trouble by saving too much too soon.

---

[5] Actually, it's 4.47 percent but I rounded. Employers who insist on a whole number won't allow you to contribute 4.5 percent. Instead, you'll have to select either 4 percent or 5 percent.

TURN TAXES INTO RETIREMENT SAVINGS

Wouldn't it be nice to increase your 401(k) contribution percentage without having to decrease your net income?

You: Sure, it sounds nice. It also sounds impossible.

Gary: Now who's making promises he can't keep?

In fact, it is possible. Anyone who consistently receives a federal income tax refund can likely execute this strategy. To eliminate the poor financial planning habit of consistent income tax refunds, in Chapter 4 we discuss how to reduce your tax withholdings and thereby increase each paycheck.

The raise you give yourself by adjusting your withholdings results in your paycheck containing additional funds you are not accustomed to receiving or needing for your living expenses. At the same time, you have been unable to contribute more to your 401(k) plan so far because you have lacked the cash to do so. With these facts, I sense an opportunity.

You: Okay, then. Keep going.

Would you be willing to adjust your withholdings but not take the new cash in your paycheck? Instead, could you save this additional money from reduced withholdings for your retirement? You can execute these two strategies simultaneously—a reduction in your tax withholdings and an increase in your 401(k) plan contribution level—in a manner such that your net pay is unaffected yet you significantly increase your retirement savings.

You: Is that legal?

Of course. If you consistently receive a federal income tax refund, consider implementing these dual strategies right away. Visit *www.totalcandor.com* for help with your personal numbers.

You: Sounds good.

Gary: That does sound good. But where's the commission?

Sorry, Gary. No commission.

EMPLOYER MATCH

You: I heard there's also a matching program. Is this some kind of corporate dating service? I'm already in a relationship.

Although people occasionally fall in love at work, a 401(k) plan is typically not the spark. An **employer match** is a contribution your employer makes to your 401(k) account. It is called a match because, in most cases, your employer makes a contribution only if you also make a contribution. When you take advantage of an employer matching program, you *and* your employer each make contributions to your retirement plan.

Any matching program is a good matching program, but some are *really* good. An employer may match your own $100 contribution with less than $100, exactly $100, or more than $100. Here are examples of employer matching programs and how they each work.

Figure 6-4

Sample Matching Programs and How They Work

Matching Program	Explanation
Dollar for dollar up to 3 percent	For every dollar you contribute, your employer contributes one dollar. After you contribute a total of 3 percent of your gross pay for the year, no additional employer contributions are made until the next year.
50 percent match up to 6 percent	For every dollar you contribute, your employer contributes 50 cents. After you contribute 6 percent of your gross pay to your account (and your employer has contributed 50 percent of that amount, or 3 percent of your gross income), no additional employer contributions are made until the next year.
No match	Regardless of your contribution level, your employer makes no matching contribution.
Dollar for dollar up to 5 percent	For every dollar you contribute, your employer contributes one dollar. After you contribute a total of 5 percent of your gross pay for the year, no additional employer contributions are made until the next year.

This table shows the *additional* percentage of gross income your employer contributes to your 401(k) plan based on your contribution level:

Figure 6-5

Employer Matching Contributions Under Various Matching Programs

Employee Contribution Level	Dollar for Dollar up to 3%	50% match up to 6%	No Match	Dollar for Dollar up to 5%
0.0%	0.0%	0.0%	0.0%	0.0%
1.0%	1.0%	0.5%	0.0%	1.0%
2.0%	2.0%	1.0%	0.0%	2.0%
3.0%	3.0%	1.5%	0.0%	3.0%
4.0%	3.0%	2.0%	0.0%	4.0%
5.0%	3.0%	2.5%	0.0%	5.0%
6.0%	3.0%	3.0%	0.0%	5.0%
7.0%	3.0%	3.0%	0.0%	5.0%
8.0%	3.0%	3.0%	0.0%	5.0%
9.0%	3.0%	3.0%	0.0%	5.0%
10.0%	3.0%	3.0%	0.0%	5.0%

You: This matching thing seems like my employer is paying for part of my retirement. Is that right?

You bet. Now you're thinking. An employer match is compensation. Your insurance benefits, vacation time, subsidized gym membership, and other perks (including that tasty office coffee) are all elements of your compensation. *A corporate match is a critical compensation component, but you get it only if you take advantage!*

FREE MONEY

Frequently, employer matches are called free money. Imagine you contribute 5 percent of your salary to your 401(k) plan. Look across the 5 percent row on Figure 6-5. Your employer—except in the "no match" program—contributes from 2.5 to 5 percent of your salary to your retirement account. If your salary is $36,000, these corporate matching programs provide you with between $900 and $1,800 of additional retirement savings each year. This is money your employer contributes, not you. It becomes your money and they're paying it.

> *You: Like free money.*

Precisely.

But if you don't participate in your 401(k) plan, you are on the top row of Figure 6-5—the one showing a zero percent contribution rate. Look across that row. Nothing but zeroes for the employer contribution. If you don't contribute, you don't get the match. Goodbye to free money.

It's hard to imagine anyone declining a raise, but that's what happens when you don't contribute at least the amount matched by your employer. Imagine the following conversation.

Employer: Congratulations, John, you're doing a great job. Times are tight and, as you know, we give raises only once a year—in October. But, although it's only April, we're going to give you an immediate bump in pay of 3 percent. Then we'll see what else we can do for you in October. But for now, we just want to let you know we're real happy with your performance and so we're giving you a taste of what you might get if you keep it up for the next six months.

John: No, thanks. I'm good. No raise needed.

Employer (to himself): John is an idiot.

John's decision above is no different financially than if he did not take advantage of an employer match. In both cases he voluntarily walks away from a 3 percent raise. Yet presented differently, we look at John's response above and immediately think "What a fool."

You: I believe he's an idiot. At least that's what his boss thinks.

True enough. In addition, nearly everyone in *John's department can probably receive a 3 percent raise just by participating in the 401(k) plan* yet they do not. So, financially speaking, they're all idiots.

You: We have a department like that—all idiots—at my company too.

Seems like every company does. But seriously, anyone not participating in the 401(k) plan up to the level of the employer match is turning down their employer's offer to pay them more. Don't be a fool *or* an idiot. Repeat after me: I will not turn down free money.

You: I will not turn down free money.

Excellent. How will you avoid doing so?

You: I will always contribute to my 401(k) plan an amount at least as much as my employer will match.

Great. What does that mean?

You: Since my employer matches the first 6 percent of my pay, I will contribute 6 percent or more.

Fantastic.

VESTING

You: I'm not sure my current job is the right one for me. What happens if I contribute to a 401(k) for the next few months and then quit? Do I lose this money?

Contributions you make to your retirement plan are always yours. This is true whether a company employs you for six years or six hours. It is your money regardless of the length of your employment or if you quit or are laid off.

Most employers have a **vesting schedule** for their *matching* contributions. **Vesting** means retaining your employer's matching contribution even after you cease working for the company. Vesting schedules apply only to employer contributions. Said another way, *you are always fully vested in your contributions.*

The vested money in your account is your **vested balance.** Money in your account that you do not get to keep if you quit today is your **unvested balance.**

Vesting schedules fit into one of the following categories.

➤ Graded: You gradually vest in your employer's contributions over several years.

➤ Cliff: You don't vest in any employer contributions during the early years of employment, but as of a certain date you vest all at once (like jumping off a cliff).

Here is an example of each type of vesting schedule.

Figure 6-6

Example of Graded Vesting Schedule

Length of Employment with *This* Employer	Amount Vested	Amount Unvested
up to 1 year	0%	100%
1 year	20%	80%
2 years	40%	60%
3 years	60%	40%
4 years	80%	20%
5 years or more	100%	0%

Example of Cliff Vesting Schedule

Length of Employment with *This* Employer	Amount Vested	Amount Unvested
up to 1 year	0%	100%
1 year	0%	100%
2 years	0%	100%
3 years	0%	100%
4 years	0%	100%
5 years or more	100%	0%

These are only examples. Your vesting schedule may differ. It's a good idea to understand *your* vesting schedule. If you don't, you might quit just before reaching a vesting milestone. What a shame! Don't give notice without knowing your vesting schedule. You could leave a few days before thousands of dollars become yours!

NO MATCH? NO EXCUSE!

You: I sent an email to HR and learned I have a 401(k) plan but no matching program. Why bother with a 401(k) plan if it has no match?

While an employer match makes not participating in your 401(k) absolutely crazy...

You: No, it makes it idiotic. You said so yourself.

Okay, crazy and idiotic. As I was saying, although a matching program sweetens the pot and provides extra incentive for an employee to participate, it still makes sense to participate in your 401(k) plan even if there is no match.

First, don't forget the tax-deferral benefits. Who doesn't like saving money on their taxes?

You: John. He is an idiot, after all.

Perhaps, but I know you and I will enjoy the tax savings. In addition, a 401(k) plan is a forced savings program. With a **forced savings program,** you automatically save without ongoing action on your part. Since you're less likely to spend what you don't see, a nice side-benefit of your 401(k) contributions can be reduced spending.

Because you don't get a three-legged stool and must create the most powerful pogo stick possible, you must save for retirement yourself. One of the best ways to save for retirement—and certainly the easiest—is through a retirement account such as a 401(k) plan.

Gary: Or a tax-deferred annuity.

No, Gary, not a tax-deferred annuity. I told you before, we'll get to that—in the next chapter.

You: I am getting the hang of this—ignore people fanatically obsessed with annuities. But I still don't see the rush to start retirement planning.

I'm only 24 (or 29, or 34, or however old I last told people I was). Can't I get to this later?

Such a common mistake. Re-read the "Miracle of Compounding Interest" in Chapter 1 if you are still struggling for motivation. Study the numbers. You should conclude you can't start soon enough. A delay in retirement saving is costly. As Henry learned, it's difficult to make up for a later start. Your retirement funding task becomes progressively harder the longer you delay starting.

You: Are there any downsides? Isn't this money locked up? I have bills now.

Yes, the money is locked up. **Normal retirement age** is 59½, so do not plan on accessing your retirement plan money until that age. Life is about choices; so is financial planning. Recall that contributing money to your 401(k) plan is like taking money from your right pocket and putting it into your left pocket. Here's some more information about your pockets.

You: That sounds slightly creepy.

Your left pocket is your retirement plan. Your right pocket contains your wallet and checking account, so it is where your paycheck comes in and your spending money goes out.

You: How much further can you possibly take this "pockets" metaphor?

Much further. Keep reading.

IMPORTANT FACTS ABOUT YOUR POCKETS

FACT 1: **When you move money between your pockets, the money in your left pocket increases by an amount greater than your right pocket decreases. This means you are wealthier simply by moving money between pockets!**

> When you contribute part of your salary to a 401(k) plan, you receive an immediate tax benefit, effectively raising your net worth by the amount of the tax savings. Furthermore, if you would have spent some of the money transferred from your wallet in your right pocket—a safe assumption for most people—you further increase your net worth by the amount you did not spend.

FACT 2: **Your right pocket is a sieve. Your left pocket never leaks.**

Money in your retirement plan is not spent. Further, it earns money and won't owe tax until you access it years from now. There are no leaks from your left pocket.

On the other hand,[6] you do spend most of the money in the wallet in your right pocket. That's your first leak. If you do manage to save some of the money in your right pocket, any amount it makes (such as bank interest income) is reduced by the increase in income tax it causes. That's your second leak.

FACT 3: **When you put money in your left pocket, your company might add more money to it for you.**

If your company has a match, that employer contribution goes only into your retirement plan. Of course, if you choose not to put any of your money in your left pocket and keep it all in your wallet in your right pocket, your company won't give you any additional money.

FACT 4: **Your left pocket has a lock on it. Your right pocket is open 24/7.**

When you contribute money to your 401(k) plan, consider it your retirement money. It's use? It's availability? Only for and only in retirement. Your retirement plan money is not for today's spending.

There are ways to access the money if you decide to do so, but that involves significant penalties. So while your left pocket is locked, you have the key. It's just an expensive key to use.

You: Why is it so expensive to use this key?

Several reasons. Here are the implications of taking money (known as a **distribution**) from your 401(k) plan before retirement:

1. You pay income taxes on virtually all the money distributed from the plan at a tax rate likely higher than your usual rate.

---

[6] Pun intended. My apologies.

2. By having to pay these taxes, you receive a check that's not remotely close to the amount distributed from your 401(k) plan. For example, if you take $10,000 from your 401(k) plan, you might receive less than $7,000.

3. In addition to regular income taxes, you also pay a 10 percent penalty tax for early withdrawal unless you meet extremely stringent exception criteria (which I'll tell you about in a minute). This penalty tax further reduces the amount you receive.

You: That's quite a disincentive.

Indeed, and yet there is still more to consider. Other negative long-term financial implications to keep in mind when considering taking an early distribution from your retirement plan are:

➤ The money you take from your plan is no longer able to grow in your retirement account. You spent it.

➤ You lose the future tax-deferral benefits on the growth of your existing 401(k) balance.

You: How hard is it to be an exception from that 10 percent penalty you mentioned?

The exceptions are few and not particularly subjective. This means neither your old guidance counselor nor your mother can help you here. The most common exceptions to the 10 percent penalty for an early 401(k) distribution are:

➤ death: hard for you to enjoy a distribution for this reason

➤ disability: yours must be total and permanent

➤ age 55 or older: cease employment where your 401(k) is (even if you then go work somewhere else)

➤ extreme medical expenses

➤ court order related to a divorce

➤ option to take substantially equal periodic payments: you must take a little bit of money out of your retirement plan every year until you are at least 59½. This doesn't exactly match what you had in mind, does it?

You: No, I was just thinking about money for a car.

Don't plan on meeting any exceptions. Remember, even if you meet an exception, it is only the 10 percent penalty tax that is removed. All the other negatives are still applicable, including the income taxes.

401(k) LOAN

You: Some guy on my floor just took out a 401(k) loan. What about those?

A **401(k) loan** is different from a distribution because a loan means you intend to pay the money back to your account. In essence, you borrow from yourself. Here's how it works, subject to additional restrictions and criteria possibly added by your employer.

➤ You request a loan from your plan.

➤ Typically, the loan amount cannot exceed the lesser of either 50 percent of your vested balance or $50,000.

➤ You must pay back the loan in 5 years or less (unless you are using the loan to buy a house, in which case the term of the loan can be much longer).

➤ You must pay interest.

You: Doesn't seem so bad—I'm paying the interest to myself, right? My interest payments are kind of like moving money from my right pocket to my left pocket, eh?

So smooth. A 401(k) loan isn't terrible, but it isn't desirable either. Most often, the loan is preferable to an outright pre-retirement distribution. You don't pay taxes and penalties and, yes, you pay interest to yourself. But there are negative repercussions to consider before borrowing from your 401(k) plan.

➤ During the time your money is on loan, it doesn't grow. The amount borrowed is temporarily gone, and since it doesn't exist it can't grow.

➤ If you do not pay back your loan, it becomes a distribution subject to taxes and penalties.

➤ Your loan repayments are made with after-tax money. In other words, you use money from your net pay to repay the loan. To make a loan payment of $100 if you are in the 25 percent tax bracket, you must earn $133 of gross income. You pay $33 in income tax and the rest can be applied to the loan. Then, when you receive money from your 401(k) plan during retirement, you pay tax on that $100 again! That's because 401(k) contributions are made with pre-tax dollars; loan repayments are made with post-tax dollars.

➤ If you terminate employment with the company you work for, the entire amount of the loan is due, usually within 60 days of your last day of work. This is typically true regardless of *whether you quit, are fired, or are the victim of a major layoff.* Any amount you are unable to pay becomes a distribution, likely subject to taxes and penalties.

Given the length of time people stay at their jobs, don't expect much time to pay back a loan. A 401(k) loan is a bit like playing with fire. Consider alternative sources of money and the necessity of the expense before tapping your 401(k) plan. *A 401(k) plan is a retirement plan and you should use it that way.*

You: Okay, but aren't you going to help me complete this 401(k) enrollment form? I already knew my name and Social Security number before reading this book, and you've only covered the contribution level. There are a lot more blanks on this thing.

Thank you for holding me accountable. Look at the sample 401(k) form at the end of this chapter. Other than your signature, only your investment choices remain. These choices indicate what happens to your money once that money is in your retirement plan. It is critical that you understand those investment options. That's why you will enjoy Chapter 8 on investments, from which you learn the information necessary to finish that form.

You: One last thing. For retirement planning, how much better is a 401(k) plan than Social Security?

In basketball, how much better is Jordan than Welter?

You: Who's Welter?

Exactly. Here's a summary of what you have learned so far about 401(k) plans and Social Security.

Figure 6-7

Social Security and a 401(k) Plan Do Not Have Much in Common

	Social Security	401(k) Plan
Employee contributions tax deductible?	No.	Yes.
Where does the money go?	Current retirees and other governmental expenses.	An account with your name on it.
Amount of your contribution?	Exactly 6.2.% of your gross pay; your employer also contributes 6.2%.	Virtually any amount you want (may vary by employer).
Free will of participation?	Involuntary tax.	Completely voluntary.
How are funds invested?	Not invested—there is no account.	Numerous choices.
Is the money taxed as it grows?	No money there to grow.	Tax-deferred.
Access to funds prior to retirement?	What retirement funds? Pay attention.	Although disincentives exist, you can always get to your money.
How is the money paid to you in retirement?	Monthly based on governmental formulas.	However you want.
Can you pass any of your money to your heirs?	Other than a one-time $255 death benefit, there is no money to pass on.	Yes—the entire balance remaining as of the day you die can be passed.
Annual warnings that you might not get what is currently promised to you?	Yes—on your Social Security benefits statement.	Of course not—this is your money.

Figure 6-7 makes it clear that Social Security and 401(k) plans aren't comparable. Is it any wonder participation in Social Security is required? Sadly, it is the only retirement program many people have. Not you, however. Take advantage of your benefits and the other retirement plans we discuss in the next chapter. For starters, get on the 401(k) plan as soon as possible.

Figure 6-8

Sample 401(k) Enrollment Form			
Personal or Participant Information			
Name			
Social Security Number			
Address			
Phone Number			

Salary Contribution Level			
I request to contribute _____ % or $ _____ from each pay period to the Fake Company 401(k) plan.			

Investment Elections or Selections			
Money Fund	%	Equity – Value Fund	%
Bond Fund	%	Equity – Growth Fund	%
Stable Value Fund	%	Equity – Income Fund	%
Balanced Fund	%	Equity – International Fund	%

Note: Percentages must add up to 100%.

Authorization/Signature	
I am choosing to participate in the Fake Company 401(k) plan and authorize Fake Company to make the above payroll deductions.	
Signature	Date

CHAPTER 7

Ira Roth is Not Your Congressman—
Do-It-Yourself Retirement Planning

"The great French Marshal Lyautey once asked his gardener to plant a tree.
The gardener objected that the tree was slow-growing and
would not reach maturity for 100 years. The marshal replied: 'In that case,
there is no time to lose, plant it this afternoon.'"
—JOHN F. KENNEDY

Although a 401(k) plan is a great retirement plan option, other impor-tant retirement planning opportunities exist. Additional accounts to become familiar with include:

➤ traditional (regular) IRA

➤ Roth IRA

➤ rollover IRA

➤ brokerage (taxable) accounts

Gary: Don't forget whole life insurance policies and tax-deferred annuities.

I didn't, Gary. We cover them where they belong—at the end.

You: Who is IRA and why does he insist on capitalizing all the letters in his name? Who needs this guy?

INDIVIDUAL RETIREMENT ACCOUNTS (IRAs)

IRA is the abbreviation for an individual retirement account. All three of those words are important:

➤ *Individual*—An IRA is not created through an employer. You must set up an account on your own with a custodian. (See Appendix B for examples.)

➤ *Retirement*—These accounts are most advantageous when used for retirement. Like a 401(k) plan, there are significant disincentives for using an IRA for non-retirement reasons. Don't put money into an IRA intending to use it for something other than retirement.

➤ *Account—An IRA is not an investment.* It's an account. Think about it like this: after you put $4,000 in an IRA, you're not done yet—you still haven't invested it. The money is in "cash." At that point, it's like trying to listen to an mp3 player on the way home from the store. Until you put music files on it, it isn't that useful. What you want to be able to say is: "I have an IRA that's invested mostly in stock mutual funds and I can meet you for dinner at eight."

TRADITIONAL IRAs

You: What's so special about a traditional IRA?

The advantages of a traditional IRA are similar to the advantages of a 401(k) plan. Specifically, tax benefits. Remember the two different tax benefits of a 401(k) plan?

You: I do, but I don't want to be a show-off.

Okay, I'll say them. They are:

1. a tax deduction on your contributions—*an immediate tax break*
2. no tax on the growth of the 401(k)—*tax-deferred growth*

With an IRA, you definitely receive tax-deferred growth. Whether you receive an immediate tax break depends on your income level and ability to participate in a retirement plan at work, such as a 401(k) plan.

You: Well, how do I know if I receive a tax deduction for a contribution to an IRA? Wow—I can't believe I just asked that question.

Here's a summary of the deductibility of a regular IRA contribution (for the two most common filing statuses).

Figure 7-1

Is Your Contribution to a Traditional IRA Deductible?
(Filing Status: Single)

Year: 2007

If you are covered by a retirement plan at work,	No	Yes
and your MAGI* is $52,000 or less:	**YES**	**YES**
and your MAGI is from $52,001 to $61,999:	**YES**	**PARTIALLY**
and your MAGI is $62,000 or more:	**YES**	**NO**

*Frequently, the definition of income in this chapter is the user-friendly term "Modified Adjusted Gross Income" (MAGI). Calculating your precise MAGI is not straightforward. However, you can estimate it by totaling your salary, interest, and investment income. It won't be exact, but it is a close approximation for most people.

You: Explain this to me.

Single people

A single individual ineligible to participate in a workplace retirement plan can deduct an IRA contribution regardless of income level. But someone eligible to participate in a 401(k) plan, *regardless of whether the person actually participates*, faces certain limitations. For example, if the individual's income (MAGI) is $62,000 or more in 2007, no part of the IRA contribution is deductible.

Married people

The rules are slightly more complicated for people who are married.

Figure 7-2

Is Your Contribution to a Traditional IRA Deductible?
(Filing Status: Married Filing Jointly)

Year: 2007

If you are covered by a retirement plan at work, and	No	No	Yes	Yes
if your spouse is covered by a retirement plan at work,	No	Yes	No	Yes
and your MAGI is $83,000 or less:	**YES**	**YES**	**YES**	**YES**
and your MAGI is from $83,001 to $102,999:	**YES**	**YES**	**PARTIALLY**	**PARTIALLY**
and your MAGI is from $103,000 to $156,000:	**YES**	**YES**	**NO**	**NO**
and your MAGI is from $156,001 and $165,999:	**YES**	**PARTIALLY**	**NO**	**NO**
and your MAGI is $166,000 or more:	**YES**	**NO**	**NO**	**NO**

Both spouses can deduct their IRA contributions regardless of their combined income if neither spouse is eligible to participate in a workplace retirement plan. Furthermore, both spouses can still deduct their contributions even if one or both spouses are eligible to participate in a retirement plan at work as long as the couple's combined income is $83,000 or less. However, if the couple's income exceeds $83,000 and either spouse (or both) is eligible to participate in a workplace retirement plan, the IRA contribution deduction will be limited.

You: What about the tax-deferred growth? Is that also limited by income level?

An important question. No. Regardless of your ability to deduct your IRA contribution, the investment *growth* within the IRA is tax-deferred. That's one reason to consider an IRA even if you aren't eligible to deduct your contributions.

Like a 401(k) plan, taxes are owed *only* on distributions. If you don't withdraw money until you retire, you don't pay tax on the growth of your IRA until that time. This is a good thing. Remember: the time value of money concept means it is far better to defer paying tax as long as possible.

You: How much can I put into one of these IRAs?

As of 2007, you can contribute up to $4,000[1] to a regular IRA, so long as you earn at least that much. If you do not earn $4,000 but are married and your spouse earns at least $8,000, then both of you can contribute $4,000 to your own IRAs.

ROTH IRAs

You: Who is Ira Roth? Is this known as an irregular or non-traditional IRA?

Because of the 1998 introduction of the Roth IRA, the IRA in the previous section is referred to as "regular" or "traditional." Roth and traditional IRAs are extremely similar, but there are a few critical differences to understand.

You: And they are?

Deductibility:

Although traditional IRA contributions *may* be tax deductible, contributions to Roth IRAs are *never* tax deductible.

---

[1] If you are age 50 or older (but not more than 70½) at any point during 2007, you can contribute an additional $1,000 to your IRA ($5,000 total).

Contribution Limits:

If you earn at least $4,000, you can *contribute* to a *regular* IRA. Only the *deductibility* of the contribution is limited at certain income levels. However, the ability to make Roth IRA *contributions* is limited to those with higher income levels as follows:

Figure 7-3

Can You Contribute to a Roth IRA?
Filing Status: Single

Your MAGI is $99,000 or less:	Yes
Your MAGI is from $99,001 to $113,999:	Yes, but not the full amount
Your MAGI is $114,000 or more:	No

Filing Status: Married Filing Jointly

Your MAGI is $156,000 or less:	Yes
Your MAGI is from $156,001 to $165,999:	Yes, but not the full amount
Your MAGI is $166,000 or more:	No

Year: 2007

To clarify, if you are a single individual earning up to $99,000 in 2007, you can contribute up to $4,000[2] to a Roth IRA. If you earn $114,000 or more, you are ineligible to contribute to a Roth IRA for that year. If your income is between those two figures, you can contribute an amount less than $4,000. Regardless of income level, Roth IRA contributions are never deductible.

You: Can I contribute $4,000 to both types of IRAs?

Individuals with at least $4,000 of earned income can contribute up to $4,000 *in total* to their IRAs. Provided their income does not exceed the limits above, they can contribute to a Roth IRA, to a regular IRA, or to a combination of both IRAs.

---

[2] Again, an additional $1,000 is permitted if 50 or over during 2007.

TAXES AT RETIREMENT

TRADITIONAL IRA

When you withdraw money from your *traditional* IRA, you pay income taxes. Taxes are calculated using your tax rate at the time you take the distribution. This tax rate is reflective of your retirement income tax situation. For many people, this rate is less than the rate paid during their working years.

Even without a decrease in tax rates during retirement, the significant financial advantage of paying tax later remains. This deferral enables your money to earn money that would otherwise have been paid as tax years earlier.

ROTH IRA

The Roth IRA has an even more advantageous long-term tax benefit. All retirement distributions from a Roth *are not taxed*.[3] So instead of *tax-deferred* growth, the investments inside a Roth IRA grow *tax-free!* Recall this conclusion from Chapter 1: those who start saving early can retire with significant account balances. Not paying tax on such large amounts leads to a huge financial savings.

You: When should I contribute to an IRA?

As soon as you can get the funds to do so. The sooner you make your contribution, the sooner:

➤ your money starts to earn money, and

➤ you stop paying tax on your money's growth.

You: How do I actually do this?

First, you must select a custodian for your IRA. This can be anyone from a local bank to a brokerage house to—

Gary: To me! I sell IRAs. Stick with me, my friend, and I could probably find a great annuity for you, too. We can even put the annuity inside the IRA.

---

[3] As long as you make an initial contribution at least five years before accessing money.

No one actually *sells* IRAs. They are simply available as an account type. An annuity is a poor choice for an IRA investment. We'll cover why in the Annuity section.

Gary: I'll be there.

I'm sure.

Choose a custodian who doesn't charge account fees. High fees add up and take too much of your money. One way to typically avoid fees is by arranging an **automatic investment program,** through which you automatically make electronic transfers of a fixed amount of money into your IRA at specific times. For most people, this is also an easier way to start an IRA than to come up with $4,000 to contribute at one time. Still another way to come up with money for your IRA contribution is to have part or all of your federal income tax refund (if you have one) direct-deposited into your IRA.

When you select a custodian for your account, you complete a simple form or two to establish the account. You also need to fund the account. You **fund the account** by depositing money into your IRA. When you make that deposit, your custodian asks for the tax year of that contribution.

You: Won't the custodian know what year it is? Or is this a good indication I've picked the wrong custodian?

Perhaps, but probably not. The contribution deadline for annual IRA contributions is when your income tax return is due. Since that isn't until April 15 of the following year, you are permitted to make your contribution up to that time.

For example, say you want to make a $4,000 IRA contribution from the money you earn for the year 2007. You can do so from January 1, 2007, until April 15, 2008. If you make a deposit to your IRA on March 5, 2008, you can specify the contribution year as either 2007 or 2008.

You: Which year should I choose?

If you have a choice, pick the earlier of the two years. This gives you more time later to make a contribution for the current year.

ROLLOVER IRAs

You: That makes sense. I also heard something about using IRAs as "rollovers." What's that about? That doesn't have anything to do with SUVs, does it?

Fortunately, no. So far, we have discussed IRAs funded by annual contributions. These are **contributory** IRAs. The primary time to consider a rollover IRA is when you terminate employment from a job in which you had participated in a retirement plan.

When you leave your job you have a few options for your retirement plan balance.

1. Do nothing; keep the money with your former employer.[4]
2. Do a rollover into your new employer's 401(k) plan.
3. Take a distribution from the plan.
4. Do a rollover into an IRA.

If you choose the first option and do nothing, only one change occurs to your account: neither you nor your former employer makes any further contributions to the plan.

If you select the second choice and roll over the money to your new employer, the plan at your new employer begins with the money from your old job's plan.

Taking a distribution from the plan is a regrettable decision. Since you pay massive taxes and penalties, you receive far less than your ending plan balance. Furthermore, this action leaves you with significantly less savings for your retirement.

If you choose the fourth option, to take money from your 401(k) and put it directly into an IRA, you create a rollover IRA. A **rollover IRA** is virtually identical to a contributory IRA—the principal difference being the source of the funding. Although you fund a contributory IRA with annual contributions, you fund a rollover IRA with a lump-sum deposit. This lump sum comes from either a previous employer's plan or another IRA.

---

[4] This may not be an option if your balance is so small that your employer requires you take the money via one of the remaining choices.

If done properly, you owe no tax when rolling over money to an IRA—the money is not taxed until you take a distribution from your IRA.

You: My 401(k) plan is still at my old job. So I guess I already chose option 1. Can I still roll it over into an IRA? And if so, why bother?

If you terminate employment and don't move your money, in most cases you effectively choose option 1. However, you can still choose another option later. There is no deadline. However, if your plan balance is too low, you might not have the "do nothing" option. In this case, you must choose another option quickly, or your former employer might choose the complete distribution option for you, which would qualify as a big mistake.

Assuming your 401(k) money is still at your former employer, a few advantages exist to rolling over your 401(k) plan into an IRA. One benefit is the virtually unlimited investment options. When your money is in the 401(k) plan, your only choices are the investment options available from your employer's 401(k) plan. This distinction is especially important if you are dissatisfied with these investment options.

Another plus of an IRA rollover is simplification. Since you might have several jobs during your career, you might participate in several 401(k) plans. If you leave your money in each of these accounts, you have money all over the place. It is easy to lose track of these accounts as the years and decades go by.

But if you move each 401(k) plan balance to the same rollover IRA every time you terminate employment, things remain simple. This approach means two accounts have all your 401(k) plan money: your current employer's 401(k) plan and one rollover IRA. Simplicity is a good thing.

You: How do I do a "rollover?"

A rollover is a good news/bad news situation. The bad news is you can really blow it: if you improperly handle a rollover, you pay a big price. As a result, many people do nothing because they fear screwing up. This is not the right answer.

Now, the good news: a rollover is easy. Furthermore, plenty of help is available. Just let people know what you intend to do and you should have no problems.

The key to a successful rollover is never cashing a check. Instead, your goal is a "trustee-to-trustee" (also known as "custodian-to-custodian") transfer. The check from your former 401(k) plan should be made out to your new IRA custodian *for the benefit of your IRA.* For example, let's say you formerly worked for Tilly Inc. and had a $10,000 401(k) account balance when you left Tilly. You decide to open a rollover IRA at the Salt Meadow brokerage house.

The precise action is critical: You want the custodian of the Tilly 401(k) plan to write a $10,000 check, payable *directly to Salt Meadow, for your benefit.* For example, if your name is Bill Frieder and you want to roll over your 401(k) account to Salt Meadow, the check should read:

"Pay to the Order of: Salt Meadow Inc., For the Benefit of Bill Frieder"

That is a rollover.

You can ask Salt Meadow to help you complete any paperwork Tilly or the 401(k) custodian requires.

You: Now why would they agree to help with my paperwork?

Like any financial institution, Salt Meadow wants you to have the highest possible balance in your account. Therefore, helping you successfully complete your rollover is in their best interests, too. Don't be shy about asking for help.

WHAT NOT TO DO

Do not ask Tilly to "just send a check." If a check is made out to you, the 401(k) custodian is required to withhold at least 20 percent of the balance for tax. So you'll get a check for $8,000, not $10,000. If you have a spare $2,000 sitting around, you can still deposit a total of $10,000 with Salt Meadow and complete your rollover.

But you don't have an extra two grand. As a result, you can deposit— or roll over—only $8,000. The other $2,000 is considered a distribution subject to taxes and penalties—despite the fact that you didn't receive the $2,000! This is bad news.

Make sure you indicate your rollover intent to your former 401(k) custodian. Make it clear you don't want any withholding, and have them confirm your intention. If you are clear, you will have no problems.

Should you ever wish to switch IRA brokerage houses, the "trustee-to-trustee" transfer is the best way to do so. For example, if you decide you no longer want to be with Salt Meadow and instead prefer the new-carpet smell of the just-opened office of Live Oak Advisors, you want Salt Meadow to transfer the funds directly to Live Oak.

You: Now what about this IRA conversion I keep hearing about? Sounds like some kind of financial cult. I'm willing to save more but I'm not so sure about participating in an unfamiliar religious ceremony.

ROTH CONVERSION IRAs

Our earlier Roth IRA discussion was limited to Roth **contributory** IRAs, those funded by annual contributions. There is, however, another type of Roth IRA called a Roth conversion IRA. A **Roth conversion IRA** is a *traditional* IRA converted to a Roth IRA.

You: What would cause someone to take the time to convert an IRA? Extreme boredom caused by overexposure to reality television?

Remember the different tax treatment of retirement distributions: Roth IRA distributions are *tax-free;* traditional IRA distributions are taxed. Wouldn't you prefer tax-free?

You: Of course! So why doesn't everyone convert their regular IRAs to Roth IRAs?

Because converting to a Roth has a cost.

You: There's always a catch!

Yes, but it is still an opportunity. Here's how it works. When you convert a regular IRA to a Roth IRA, you pay income taxes on the conversion amount.[5] However, you don't pay the 10 percent early distribution penalty. Still, these taxes can amount to a hefty sum. Conversion typically makes sense only if you have enough money *outside your IRA* to pay the taxes resulting from the conversion. You don't want to take money from your retirement account to pay taxes.

---

[5] No tax is due on non-deductible contributions made to a traditional IRA. For example, if your IRA balance at the time of conversion is $20,000 and you had previously made $4,000 of non-deductible contributions, only $16,000 is subject to income tax.

You: Can anyone do this conversion?

During 2007, as long as your adjusted gross income is $100,000 or less (not including the amount you convert), you can convert your regular IRA to a Roth conversion IRA. One exception is people whose filing status is Married Filing Separately who live with their spouse at some point during the year. Regardless of their income level, such people cannot convert their traditional IRA to a Roth IRA. Note that these rules are scheduled to change fairly dramatically over the next few years, so look for updates at *www.totalcandor.com.*

Until recently, you could not convert a 401(k) account directly to a Roth IRA. However, after you left your employer, you could roll over your 401(k) into a regular IRA and *then* convert the new regular IRA into a Roth IRA.

You: Pretty sneaky.

Indeed. Now it is simpler. Should you wish, you can convert your 401(k) into a Roth IRA when you leave your employer. Remember you have to pay the tax on conversion, however.

You: Are there any other types of retirement plans I should be aware of?

Gary: Oh yes—quite a few. Good commissions too! (Oops, that was for me. Forget that part). Ahem. But I do have some great opportunities for you.

Pay no attention to overzealous and under-trained salespeople. There are some lesser known, but still important, retirement planning accounts.

SELF-EMPLOYED RETIREMENT PLANS

Additional retirement plans are available to people with self-employment earnings. Usually, self-employed folks do not receive paychecks. Instead, their income comes from work as independent contractors or as business owners. Self-employed retirement plans include:

➤ SEP-IRA
➤ SIMPLE IRA
➤ Keogh

Targeted to the self-employed, these plans are not available to most individuals. Therefore, I won't cover the details of these plans here, except to say that these plans present compelling opportunities for self-employed individuals, especially since 401(k) plans are unlikely to be available to them. If you are self-employed, find a trusted advisor who can guide you in evaluating which, if any, of the plans listed on page 151 make sense for you and your company.

TAXABLE OR BROKERAGE ACCOUNTS

Anyone can open a taxable account any time. There are no income level restrictions or contribution limits. There are also no tax deductions and no tax deferrals; hence, the name taxable accounts. If one morning you wake up and go to the local branch of a brokerage house (such as Charles Schwab or Fidelity) and open a regular (non-retirement) account, you're opening a **taxable** or **brokerage** account.

Many firms have proprietary names for these accounts (e.g., Schwab One), but they are all treated the same for tax purposes. If you take full advantage of the retirement accounts discussed so far, you can put additional retirement savings in a taxable account. Taxable accounts are also useful for other significant savings goals, including a boat, second home, college education, or your garden-variety mid-life crisis.

TAX-DEFERRED ANNUITIES (TDAs)

Gary: Finally! I thought we'd never get here! Thanks for stopping by. I promise this won't take long. I really only have one question: would you describe yourself as someone who is (1) alive, (2) have money, and (3) wanting more?

You: Yes, I suppose so.

Gary: As I expected. You see? I know people. And it is exactly people like you, people who fit that very specific profile, who are the type of people who need annuities most of all. Let me show you some of your options. I have a great variable product which—

This needs to stop.

Gary: Oh, I am just getting started.

And now you are done.

You: Will he always be that obviously over-the-top? Completely disinterested in me?

Unfortunately not. He could be much smoother. For example…

Gary: Hello Mr. and Mrs. Melville. How are you today?

You: Just fine, thanks.

Gary: Can I get you some coffee or bottled water?

You: Sure, water sounds nice.

Gary: I understand you are here today looking for some advice and consultation. Furthermore, I understand—from our previous phone conversation—you are trying to get started investing. Is that right?

You: Yes, it is. I was told you could help us with that.

Gary: Indeed I can, indeed I can. Let me tell you why there is nothing out there better than this new tax-deferred annuity my company has just started to make available to select clients. I'm sure you've at least heard about mutual funds and 401(k)s and other financial instruments, but what you need is an annuity.

You: Why is that?

Gary: Glad you asked. You ask great questions. A tax-deferred annuity has a bunch of features that no other product has. It is tax-deferred—regardless of income. There are guaranteed minimum rates of return. Try finding that in the stock market: guarantees! Plus, if you are concerned about retirement planning, we can set up an IRA annuity—

Okay, that's all I can handle.

You: Wow—he was much smoother that time. I was starting to believe that an annuity might be a good idea—

Although he never explained what an annuity is.

You: No, I suppose he didn't.

That's one reason why I had to cut him off.

You: Thanks. So what is an annuity?

An annuity is a company's promise to provide a series of payments in exchange for an investment of money. In some instances, annuities make sense. However, if you have not yet maximized your 401(k) and IRA contributions, annuities are definitely not appropriate for retirement planning.

Most annuities carry significant restrictions and fees that prevent you from making simple changes. The principal advantage of an annuity, as the salesperson tells you, is tax-deferred growth.

You: But my IRA and 401(k) grow tax-deferred too.

Exactly. And with lower fees and fewer restrictions. As a result, it *really* doesn't make sense to own a TDA inside an IRA, yet it happens all the time. (As with my parents.)

Gary: You are really annoying.

WHOLE LIFE INSURANCE POLICIES

Many types of life insurance policies are available. A **whole life** insurance policy provides coverage throughout your entire lifetime. A whole life policy also accumulates funds, which are known as the policy's **cash value.** This cash value can be invested in many ways and will grow tax-deferred. The cash value feature of a whole life policy is a key point in selling these policies as retirement planning vehicles.

Gary: Amen, brother.

None of that changes the following: Buy life insurance only if you need life insurance. Don't buy a whole life insurance policy simply for its retirement planning benefits. If you do need life insurance, consider **term insurance,** a more cost-effective alternative I discuss in Chapter 5.

Like tax-deferred annuities, whole life insurance policies are often *sold* for retirement planning purposes—not *bought* for that purpose. There are better ways to save for retirement, particularly when you are young. Always maximize your 401(k) and IRA contributions before considering a tax-deferred annuity or a whole life insurance policy.

Gary: Shut up, will you?

Confusion acts as a benefit to the less reputable salesperson. As a general rule, never buy something you don't understand. Instead, go home and sleep on any investment decision you had not planned to make before you heard the sales pitch.

You: Why is Gary so hot on annuities and whole life insurance policies?

I'm not sure, but the high commissions associated with these products might have something to do with it. At times, as I said, these products make sense. They're just not the ideal choice in many of the situations in which they are purchased. In short, I see them as oversold.

PRIORITIES

You: Okay, so I should be careful about annuities and whole life insurance policies. But what do I do first among all the other options? Roth IRA? Regular IRA? 401(k)?

Interesting. Many people do not ask this question until they are close to retirement. Many don't ask it even then. Your posing this question now is a great step forward for you. You are not asking *if* you should take advantage of retirement planning but *how*. So I need to throw a question right back at you: Who are you, anyway?

You: What? I thought you were getting to know me pretty well by now.

I am certainly getting to know you. Still, I will learn more about you from this part of our conversation than any other.

At this point, *how* you should pursue retirement planning depends on whether (a) you are reading with the intent to implement a new financial plan or (b) you are day-dreaming about what it might be like to create a plan, but are actually focusing on if you can get a more expensive car while still paying the minimum on your credit card.

Be honest—which are you?

You: Must I answer? I think I might be a little of both.

That's not possible. I'll be quite clear: If you are part of the first group, congratulations. By planning now for your financial future, you are more likely to achieve financial success than those who don't plan. This is true regardless of the specific accounts and underlying investments you make—although the dreamers might drive nicer cars.

Dreaming alone just won't get it done. Focusing now on what you *want* to do now instead of what you *need* to do for your future is just an expensive form of procrastination.

But if you are ready to act now, you still face the dilemma of what to do first. Unfortunately, there is no "one size fits all" answer to this question. Your answer depends on a variety of factors, including:

➤ your current age and the age you expect to retire

➤ whether your employer has a matching program

➤ the type of matching program

➤ your current tax rate

➤ your expected future tax rates (while working and while in retirement)

➤ the rate of return of your investments

➤ the size of your other assets (e.g., non-retirement account investments, your house)

➤ your goals and objectives (e.g., paying for your children's education)

You: Now how am I supposed to know all of that?

No one has a crystal ball. Given that you don't know all the answers to the questions proposed above, you can see why it's not possible for me to tell you what you, dear reader #423963UV, should do. However, there are general guidelines. What follows are the guidelines in the order you should consider them.

1. *Never turn down free money.* If your company has a 401(k) matching program, you can give yourself a raise simply by participating in the program. If your employer matches 50 percent of your contribution and you defer $1,000 of salary to the plan, $1,500 is invested. *That's an instantaneous 50 percent return on your initial investment!* You can't expect to beat the immediate return of a matching program by doing anything else with your money.

   Of course, your investments should produce additional growth above and beyond the return provided by the employer match. As a result, participating in your 401(k) plan up to the level your employer matches is your number one priority.

2. *Pay off your high-interest credit card debt.* The interest rates charged by some credit card companies can exceed 20 percent. An investment expected to provide a similar return does not exist. Plus, the

return from paying off credit card debt is guaranteed: the reduction of the amount of interest you are charged each month. There is no risk with this strategy.

3. *Establish an* **emergency fund.** Ideally, save enough for three to six months of living expenses. Keep this money in cash, such as a savings account. If you have very strong job stability and job satisfaction, three months might be appropriate. If you could be let go in a minute and aren't feeling too marketable, you can't have too much saved. Aim for at least six months.

4. *Fund a Roth IRA.* The long-term tax benefits of a Roth IRA are phenomenal. You need only to create an account in person or online. An easy task to be sure, but one that holds too many people back. Just get it done and enjoy the results.

5. *Increase your 401(k) plan contribution rate above the amount matched.* This tactic loses in a toss-up for fourth place on this list of guidelines. One advantage of a 401(k) plan over a Roth is the ease of execution. As a forced savings program, once you begin to contribute to a 401(k) plan, you are likely to continue to do so for a long period of time.

WHAT'S THIS ACCOUNT GOT TO DO WITH AN IPOD?

You: Great. One more time—why don't you regard retirement accounts as investments? The HR guy says retirement plans are some of the best investments I can make. Do you disagree?

Funding a retirement account is a super strategy. But it's technically not an "investment." I emphasize the semantics because there are two steps in retirement planning.

1. Put money in the account.
2. Invest the money in the account.

Many people stop after step one! But you need to do both steps to be successful.

An account is *how* your money is *held*. IRAs, 401(k)s, bank accounts, and regular brokerage accounts are all accounts. You have investments *inside* each of the accounts, such as stocks, bonds, CDs, and mutual funds. But an account with $100 in it might not be invested yet. The money might be merely "parked" in cash.

Remember the mp3 metaphor. It's as though an account were an mp3 player and the investments were the songs:

You can buy one of the many available mp3 players and each can play almost any song.	You can establish one of the many available account types and each can hold virtually any investment.
Many different types of songs (rock, hip-hop, pop, country) can be downloaded to your mp3 player.	Many different types of investments (stocks, bonds, mutual funds) can be held in your account.
You can't listen to digital music without a player.	You can't have investments if you don't have an account.
Placing digital music files on an mp3 player is where the real customization comes in and the player becomes the most enjoyable and useful.	Investing makes the account set-up worth the effort. Now you're excited for the next chapter, the one on Investments, right?

You: Yes.

Gary: I got so screwed in this chapter.

What goes around comes around.

. . . .

Maximize Your (Investing) Performance

"It is better to have a hen tomorrow than an egg today."
—Thomas Fuller

D id you turn to this page right away? Have you skipped several sections to get to this chapter? Did you once think financial planning was *only* about investments? If so, you're not alone. But not discussing investments until Chapter 8 is an intentional decision.

A combination of excitement and ignorance causes many people to leave their investing *pre-requisites* unaddressed. For example, many folks fail to understand their paychecks, or participate in retirement plans, or establish needed emergency protection. Their investment decisions are based on hot tips, buzz, and false assumptions, not on the individual's entire financial situation. You, however, know better—unless you skipped reading the first seven chapters of this book.

WHY WALL STREET IS NOT ON "THE STRIP"

No financial topic receives more attention than investing. Investments have sex appeal. They are fun to talk about. They exhibit highs and lows. People share investment rumors and tall tales at parties and at the office.

You: You make it sound like a trip to Las Vegas.

And not without reason. Too many people treat investing like gambling by making emotional decisions, then, telling everyone:

➤ how great they did—the truth notwithstanding, or

➤ how the ride was so much fun, losing money was no big deal.

However, investing and gambling are eerily similar *only if* you invest without an understanding of what you're doing. With a basic investment education, your chances for long-term success become far greater than any game at Vegas.

You: What about—

Yes, even blackjack.

Gary: Michael, it would be much easier and quicker (and dare I say, more lucrative) if we just join forces and sell this reader an annuity.

That's probably true, but I would rather—Gary, I don't know why I even talk to you.

TAKE ADVANTAGE OF WHAT YOU ALREADY KNOW

You know more about investing than you think—no matter your stage of life, you make investment-type decisions every day:

➤ Going to class is an investment.

➤ Working is an investment.

➤ Attending your child's soccer game is an investment.

These are all examples of *investments of your time*. Your time, like your money, is limited. When you agree to invest your time in something, you expect a payback.

Figure 8-1

Potential Paybacks from Investments of Time

Investment	Possible Payback
Attend Class	Feel smarter and more confident
	Better grades
	Higher income potential
	Meet cute guy/gal in the row behind you
Work	Intellectual or physical challenge
	Salary
	Ability to golf, shop, or go on vacation
	Time in the car—alone
Attend Child's Soccer Game	Warm fuzzy feeling from your child's pure joy
	Closer long-term relationship
	Stronger marriage
	Leftover oranges after the game ends

You see a wide range of possible **paybacks.** They can be short-lived or last a lifetime. Some paybacks go to you and some go to others. Paybacks can be financial, emotional, physical—even nutritional.

FINANCIAL INVESTING

A financial **investment** also has anticipated future paybacks. Financial investments include savings accounts, bonds, stocks, and mutual funds. Your **portfolio** is the combination of all your current financial investments and is the key source of your passive income.

You: But where do I get money for all this investment stuff in the first place?

The only way to acquire money to invest is to save some first. (See Chapter 2.) Some people confuse saving with investing. Here's the distinction:

Saving represents the difference between what you earn and what you spend. If, during a given period, your net income is $3,000 and you spend $2,800, you save $200. *If the $200 stays in your checking account, you are saving it but you are not investing it.* Investing is what you do with the $200 you save.

You: Okay, enough lead in. Time for specifics. What should I invest in?

Gary: So glad you called today. I've had my eye on this stock all day. It's perfect: The company's been teetering on bankruptcy but I have some buddies who know this company real well and they tell me it's about to take off like a rocket.

Be wary of anyone who quickly answers the question of "What should I invest in?" An advisor needs much more information *about you* to provide good advice. So my answer is, "It all depends."

You: On?

Several things. But the best place to start is your "risk/reward" profile.

RISK AND REWARD

There are few investing certainties but here is one:

The greater the expected return, the greater the risk.

Risk is partially measured by the chance that the value of your investment becomes less than you invested. An investment's **volatility**—or the frequency and degree of its value's going up and down—is another characteristic of risk.

Expected return does not mean actual return. Rather, **expected return** is a statistical concept. It is the return you expect to earn—based on the investment made.

You: What I "expect to earn"? What if I "expect to earn" a million dollars?

It doesn't quite work that way. Think about flipping a coin ten times. Pretend that heads means your investment makes money and tails means your investment loses money. Statistically speaking, you expect to get five heads and five tails. But you know darn well it's possible to receive seven or eight heads. Also possible, though less likely: nine or ten tails. Expected return is not actual return, but only what you expect, based on probability.

THINKING LONG-TERM IS CRITICAL

If you flip the coin only once or twice, you might not get even one heads. The more times you flip the coin (say 100, 1,000, or 10,000 times), the higher your odds of getting very close to half heads and half tails. Similarly, *the longer you invest, the more likely actual return comes close to expected return.*

You: Why wouldn't I simply choose the investment with the highest expected rate of return?

Remember, to increase expected return you must increase risk.

You: But how do I know how much risk I should take?

Ultimately, this is a personal decision. The risk you should take is based primarily on the following factors:

- ➤ your risk tolerance
- ➤ your time horizon
- ➤ your investment experience
- ➤ your goals

RISK TOLERANCE

You: My risk tolerance is amazing. Last week, at the bar, in half an hour I had seven—

While your story might involve some level of risk, trust me—this is a whole different kind of risk tolerance.

The value of most investments changes daily. Your ability to handle these fluctuations is indicative of your **risk tolerance.** For example, if you feel unsettled about the possibility that an investment might lose money in a given year, you have a low risk tolerance. On the other hand, if the value of one of your investments decreases by 25 percent and you think,

"This is great. Now I can get more shares cheaper," you have a high risk tolerance.

TIME HORIZON

You: That was a good tolerance story you interrupted. Oh well—your loss. Now what is this time horizon thing?

Your **time horizon** is the length of time expected between your investment decision and your need for the money you invest. Your time horizon can be affected by a variety of factors, including:

➤ the account the money is in
➤ the goal of the account and, specifically, the investment
➤ your job security
➤ your age

Here's how each has an impact on your time horizon.

➤ Retirement *account* investment decisions have long-term time horizons (unless you are nearing or in retirement).
➤ If the specific *goal* of the investment is a house down payment within two years, you have a short-term time horizon to consider.
➤ The more *job security* you have, the less likely you'll need sudden access to your investments, implying a longer time horizon.
➤ The younger your *age,* the further away you are from retirement. Many more years of earning an income indicate a longer time horizon. The opposite is also true.

The longer your time horizon, the more risk you should be willing and able to accept. This relationship is critical, because accepting a higher level of risk means higher expected investment returns over time, a major contributor to growing your wealth.

INVESTMENT EXPERIENCE

Your **investment experience** is represented by the:

➤ length of time you have been investing
➤ amount of money you have invested
➤ types of previous investing

When you make money and lose money investing, you start to become an experienced investor. When you invest thousands of dollars over several years in different types of investments, you start to become an experienced investor. When you read books such as this one but never do anything other than put money in savings accounts and in the default cash option of your 401(k) plan, you remain a very inexperienced investor.

You: But why does the amount of my investment experience matter? Doesn't everybody start off as a rookie—with no experience?

Yes, we all start off inexperienced. But as you acquire experience, you learn about yourself. The results of this individual discovery play a major role in how you should continue to invest.

Just because you *think* you can stomach a 10 percent correction in the market (in which the value of your portfolio suddenly drops by 10 percent), it is another thing entirely when that correction happens—to you. What would be your reaction?

> ➤ Did you sell all your investments, telling yourself you'd get back in the market when things stabilized (a *risk-averse* reaction)?
> ➤ Did you do nothing (a *risk-neutral* reaction)?
> ➤ Did you take all your cash and put it in the market right then (a *risk-loving* reaction)?

The actions you take in a real-life investment situation demonstrate the value of investment experience. They are true indicators of your actual risk tolerance. Such is the value of investment experience.

INVESTMENT GOALS

Here are two ways to view your investment goals:

> ➤ rate of return: *how much* money you hope to earn
> ➤ *when* you will use the money

Each goal affects the risk you take. The higher the return you seek, the more aggressively you need to invest. This means accepting more risk. For example, if you seek an 8 percent return over the long term, you likely need to invest primarily in stocks, since that investment type gives you a better chance of achieving that rate of return than most alternatives. More on stocks a little later.

INTEREST RATES AND RATES OF RETURN

You: What's the difference between an interest rate and a rate of return?

Remember from Chapter I, the interest rate is the percentage of the deposit paid as interest during a year.

An investment's **total return** includes interest, dividends, and capital appreciation. The **rate of return** is the following percentage:

Rate of Return = Amount Earned (Dollars Return) ÷ Amount Invested

If, over a year, you earn $100 on an investment of $1,000, you earn a 10 percent rate of return, calculated as $100 ÷ $1,000 = 10 percent.

Basic algebra provides the formula for the amount earned:

Amount Earned (Dollars Return) = Amount Invested x Rate of Return

If you invest $1,000 and earn a 5 percent rate of return, you earn $50 in a year.

You: How about an example?

Good idea. Let's say that on January 2 of this year you purchased $1,000 worth of stock in Diag (a fictional company). Since Diag was trading at exactly $20 per share on January 2, you purchased 50 shares. Over the course of the next year, Diag paid you a dividend of $1.00 (two cents per share). Today is December 31, and this morning you sold Diag for $22 per share.

You: Sounds good. What was my total return from my ownership in Diag?

Your total return is $101. One dollar came from the dividends you received throughout the year. The other $100 came from capital appreciation. This $100 is the increase in the price of Diag stock from the beginning of the year ($20) to when you sold it on December 31 ($22) multiplied by the number of shares (50) you owned.

You: What is my rate of return?

Simply your total return divided by your original investment. This is $101 divided by $1,000 or 10.1 percent.

If you do not anticipate needing money from an investment for ten years or longer, you should accept a fair amount of risk. For example, when a 30-year-old invests for retirement, he has decades for his money to grow. Further, he's not planning on accessing that money in the meantime. This means he has a long-term time horizon. Therefore, he invests aggressively and rides out market fluctuations. This is how smart young 401(k) plan investors think.

TYPES OF INVESTMENTS

You: Okay—now will you tell me what to invest in?

Gary: Hey, I've been trying to but you won't put this piece of #!$*@ book down and come to my office, which, I might add, is nicely decorated with dark brown paneling and solidly healthy houseplants.

I cannot tell you what to invest in, specifically.

You: Jeez, Michael!

If you want to be told exactly what to do regardless of your personal situation, plenty of people will be happy to tell you (including Gary). In the late 1990s, such people hawked "can't miss" technology stocks. Day trading was all the rage. More recently, they're screaming you "can't lose" on condos and other real estate activities. And now oil companies are the "sure thing."

> *You: What's the interest rate now?*
>
> There is an interest rate for every occasion. You probably have different interest rates for your car loan, student loan, credit card, savings account, and mortgage. Someone else can have higher or lower rates than you on each financial product.
>
> A headline stating the comment "interest rates are rising" refers to a specific governmentally controlled interest rate as well as to an overall trend of interest rates. Some interest rates, such as fixed interest mortgages and teaser credit card rates, might not be immediately affected by changes in other interest rates.

By the time you finish reading *Beyond Paycheck to Paycheck,* there will be some other "hot" new investment. If you want to chase fads, buy a book on each new topic. But if you're hoping to read about a specific new investment opportunity in a book, it won't be the current fad; it will be the last one. When dozens of books come out touting the benefits of a specific investment, smart money knows the opportunity is long gone.

You: I want to be with the smart money. I'm ready to learn. What are my options?

There are several **investment vehicles** you can choose. Beginning investors should focus on the following:

Figure 8-2

Common Investment Vehicles for Beginning Investors

Savings accounts	Lower expected risk and reward
Certificates of deposits	
Bonds	
Stocks	Higher expected risk and reward

We also cover mutual funds and exchange traded funds, which can fall nearly anywhere along the risk/reward spectrum above.

SAVINGS ACCOUNTS

Other than stuffing your money in a mattress, stuffing it in a savings account is the simplest and safest of all investment possibilities. For that reason, savings accounts provide the lowest expected return. Remember, little risk equals little reward.

You can go to your neighborhood bank and open a savings account with a small deposit. You then earn and receive interest. Depending on (1) the amount you deposit, (2) the bank, and (3) overall interest rate trends, the interest rate you earn on a savings account can range from less than 1 percent to over 5 percent. Review Appendix B for examples of high interest savings accounts.

Any bank you consider should have **FDIC insurance** on your deposits up to $100,000. (Fortunately, nearly every bank does.) If your bank fails and your account is insured, the Federal Deposit Insurance Corporation (FDIC) replaces up to $100,000 of the money you lost. (The $100,000 limit may be higher if you have multiple accounts titled differently or if one of your accounts is an IRA.) While banks don't fail very often, it's still an important consideration. FDIC insurance is a key reason savings accounts are so safe.

Another reason savings accounts are so safe is that the account balance cannot go down. There's no chance an account with $100 on January 1 will have less than $100 on February 1, unless you take money out. Hence, you have no investment risk.

But let's say the interest rate paid to your savings account is 2 percent and the inflation rate is 3 percent. In other words, although the account grows by 2 percent, inflation grows faster. This environment causes the **purchasing power** of your investment to decrease. So while there is no investment risk with a savings account, there is a different risk to consider, and it's called inflation risk.

Inflation risk is the chance that the value of your investments fails to keep up with the general rise in prices (inflation). This risk is why you should invest most of your money more aggressively than in this very safe, conservative investment option—especially when you are trying to meet long-term investment goals.

You: So, when does a savings account make sense for me?

Along with the low rates of return that savings accounts offer, the lack of day-to-day fluctuations means that they are extremely safe. A savings account is appropriate when you need a high degree of safety for your money and are willing to sacrifice potentially higher returns to get it.

Therefore, savings accounts are a great way to invest emergency funds and cash you want available on short notice. Most of the rest of the money you have available should be invested more aggressively.

CERTIFICATES OF DEPOSIT (CDs)

Like savings accounts, certificates of deposits are conservative, safe investments. **CDs** offer a guaranteed rate of return over a fixed time period. As such, they let you see and choose from various lengths and interest rate combinations. Here are some possibilities, all with annual compounding:

- ➤ 4.75 percent   9-month
- ➤ 5.00 percent   12-month
- ➤ 5.25 percent   24-month
- ➤ 5.50 percent   5-year

If you invest $1,000 in a 5 percent, 12-month CD, your account will be worth $1,050 in 12 months. In exchange for that high level of security, you typically cannot access your money during the **term** (length) of the CD period without a penalty. Increasingly, exceptions from the penalty are available, but the general rule remains that you cannot access your funds for the term of the CD. The penalty is typically the **forfeiture** (surrender) of at least part of the interest earned.

You cannot lose money over the term of the certificate of deposit. Many CDs are covered by FDIC insurance.

You: What about CDs—when do they make sense for someone like me?

For CDs to make sense, they should offer interest rates higher than your savings account. Otherwise, why tie up your money?

You: Is this a trick question?

Nope. Just make sure you're paying attention at the bank, too. Longer-term CDs should provide higher interest rates than shorter-term CDs for the same reason.

CDs can be a good idea when you have a short-term goal with virtually no chance of needing the money any sooner. Let's say, for example, you want to buy a house in two years and already have some money saved for a down payment. You feel confident you do not want or need to purchase the house sooner. Your emergency fund is already established in a savings account. If the bank offers a two-year CD paying a decent amount more than a savings account, a CD could be a good choice for the money you are holding for your down payment.

Other than those folks nearing or in retirement, a very small percentage, at most, of portfolios should be invested in CDs.

BONDS

After CDs, the next least risky investment vehicle to consider is typically bonds. When you own a **bond**, you own the debt of another entity. If you ever received U.S. savings bonds as a gift, you were exposed to bonds.[1]

U.S. SAVINGS BONDS

You: I own some of those savings bonds. Whose debt is that?

Savings bonds represent the debt of the United States government. That makes it debt owed to me—and you, and nearly everyone else you know. Surely, you've heard that the U.S. has a national debt. But you might not have realized that a microscopic percentage of it is owed to you.

You: How much do U.S. savings bonds cost?

U.S. savings bonds[2] are **issued** to lenders—that's you—at half their face value. For example, if you purchase a $100 face-value bond, the purchase price is $50. Do not think of this as a half-price sale—you're not getting a better deal than everyone else because you got there at 6 AM the day after Thanksgiving. There are no "door-busters" at the U.S. Treasury—this is just how bonds work.

You: When do I receive interest payments from my U.S. savings bonds?

You do *not* collect any interest while you own savings bonds.

You: Sounds like a total rip-off.

It's not. You collect all the interest earned when you **redeem** (or cash in) the bond. Only at that point do you receive your original investment plus the interest you earned.

You: What is the interest rate on my U.S. savings bonds?

The interest rate on savings bonds depends on a variety of factors, as the rules have changed many times over the years. Bonds issued after

---

[1] Admit it: you were disappointed. You were hoping for a much cooler gift.
[2] This information is for a most common type of U.S. savings bond—Series EE.

April 30, 2005,[3] earn a *fixed* rate of interest for the entire length of time you own the bonds. This rate is determined at the time of purchase. For example, the rate for savings bonds purchased during early 2007 is 3.6 percent. Therefore, bonds purchased in April 2007 will continue to earn 3.6 percent regardless of the rates on future savings bonds.

You: When can I get my money from a U.S. savings bond?

For the most part, whenever you want—so long as it is 12 months or more since the bond was issued. However, there are implications if you cash in the bonds quickly after issue. The implications for redeeming bonds issued after April 30, 2005 are as follows:

Figure 8-3

Redemption Restrictions of Newly Issued Series EE Savings Bonds

Length of Time After Issuance	Can You Redeem?	Implications
Less than 12 Months	No	You must wait
12 to 59 Months	Yes	Forfeit the last 3 months of interest earned
60 or more months	Yes	No penalty—receive all interest earned

You: What else should I know about U.S. savings bonds?

U.S. savings bonds have tax advantages. First, although the interest is subject to federal income tax, it is not taxable by the state or local governments. If you live in New York City and earn interest on a U.S. savings bond, you pay federal income tax on that interest income, but not New York State or New York City income tax.

Another advantage of U.S. savings bonds is that you don't owe income taxes on the interest earned until the interest is paid to you. In this way, a U.S. savings bond operates like a tax-deferred account, since each year the

---

[3] Bonds issued before May 1, 2005 have altogether different rules. If you own such bonds, visit *www.totalcandor.com* for links to a summary of how older bonds work and a free calculator telling you how much your bonds are worth and their current interest rates.

bond increases in value—due to the interest earned but not paid—yet no taxes are due until redemption.

A third tax advantage of U.S. savings bonds is that the interest earned may be excluded from federal income tax under certain circumstances. If you pay for post-secondary educational expenses in the same year you redeem such bonds, you *may* be able to exclude the interest earned from your income tax return. The rules determining the amount of and eligibility for the exclusion are somewhat complicated. However, the more you pay in tuition and the lower your overall income level, the more likely you'll be able to use this exclusion.[4]

You: Any other types of bonds I should be clued into?

CORPORATE BONDS

A **corporate bond** is another type of bond. Companies such as General Electric and General Motors have an abundance of debt. If you purchase a corporate bond, you own corporate debt and are entitled to payment from the company.

You: When do I collect money by owning corporate bonds?

At different times. There are two separate sources of money you receive as a bond owner.

➤ interest
➤ principal

Typically, you receive interest income from corporate bonds twice a year (semiannually).

The **principal** (also known as the **face value** or **face amount** of the bond) is the amount that is stated on the bond itself. Most of the time, face values are nice round numbers, such as $1,000, $10,000 or $100,000. At the end of a bond's term, the bond reaches **maturity** and you receive the principal, regardless of the amount you paid to acquire the bond. The **term** of the bond is the length of time between when the bond is issued and when it **matures.** A bond's term can be as short as a few years to longer than 30 years.

---

[4] See IRS Publication 970 for more information—if you dare. Available at *www.irs.gov.*

You: Does the price of a bond change over time?

Bond prices do change. However, the price fluctuation of a bond matters only if you sell it before it matures. At maturity, you receive the full face amount.

The two things most likely to cause a bond's price to vary are:

➤ the risk of the bond (the likelihood the debt will be paid back), and

➤ overall interest rates.

DEFAULT RISK

Like people, not all companies are in top shape financially. Remember your credit score? It represents a measure of the risk to others of lending money to you. The likelihood of a company paying back its debts is also evaluated.

A person's inferior credit score and a company's poor debt rating have the same primary impact: both must pay higher interest rates on their debts. The risk a company does not pay back its debt is its **default risk.** Although a company's default risk doesn't change every day, it might change over time. If a certain company is considered more risky than previously, it is likely to pay higher interest rates on its new debts. Furthermore, the price of its existing bonds probably decreases.

INTEREST RATE RISK

Bond prices are often affected by changes in the market interest rate. The **market interest rate** is the interest rate for similar bonds *currently* sold. Market interest rates go up and down for a variety of reasons.

If the market interest rate decreases, the value of your bonds increases. Say a bond you own pays a 5 percent interest rate. If the market interest rate decreases to 4 percent, people want your bond.

You: Why do they want my bond?

Because newly available bonds pay only 4 percent, but your bond pays 5 percent. If you bought your bond when it was issued and sell it now, you will probably realize a profit. On the other hand, if the market interest rate increases, your bond becomes worth less, since people can purchase bonds paying higher interest rates than your bond pays. Of course, you don't have to sell your bond—you can keep collecting interest payments and hold it until maturity. At maturity, you receive the face amount of the bond, regardless of how market interest rates changed since your original purchase.

The moral of the story and a key lesson about bonds is:

Market interest rates and bond prices move in opposite directions.

If you buy bonds but do not plan on holding them to maturity, think twice, especially if the buzz says that market interest rates will rise.

Gary: [YAWN]

Excuse me?

Gary: You're boring us, Michael. The reader is ready to go and you're going over interest rates and bond prices. Hello?

Look, Gary—

You: Bonds do seem pretty boring.

I know. I tend to agree. But they are an important investment to understand. Besides, we're about to begin our stock discussion, which most people find significantly more interesting. Hang in there. There is just one more important bond type to learn.

MUNICIPAL BONDS

Another common type of bond is a **municipal bond**, for which the debtors are state and local governments, or similar agencies. *Municipal bond interest is tax-exempt on your federal income tax return.* Repayment is highly likely, because most governments have the power to tax if they need to raise funds to pay off their debts. The high likelihood of payback, combined with the benefit of tax-exempt interest, typically leads to municipal bonds paying the lowest interest rates of all bonds.

You: Okay, I made it through bonds. Most importantly, do bonds make sense for me?

Probably not to begin with. Individual bonds are *not* a great place for anybody to start investing, especially while they are far from retirement. Bonds have limited long-term growth potential compared to stocks—which we discuss next. Since routine changes in market interest rates can cause the value of a bond to fall, many bonds do not make sense for short-term goals, either. As you become more advanced financially and have a decent sum invested, bonds become an important part of your portfolio. But they are not where you should typically start.

STOCKS

Stock represents ownership of a corporation. Units of stock are called **shares.** When you own the stock of a company, you are a **shareholder.** Most investors can own shares only in publicly traded corporations—that is, corporations with stock available to the public. Not all companies are *publicly* traded. If a company is not public, it is *private*. Most small companies are private. But so are some very large companies—such as Hallmark. Because Hallmark is privately held, you can't buy Hallmark stock.

One example of a publicly traded company is McDonald's Corporation. If you own shares of McDonald's stock, you are a part owner of one of the most recognized companies in the world.

You: So if I buy shares in McDonald's, can I go into the one around the corner and be like, "Hey, I own this place"?

You could, but don't expect free fries. At the time of this writing, there are approximately 1.24 billion shares outstanding of McDonald's. **Shares outstanding** is the number of shares held by the public plus the amount of shares held by people who work at the company. So if you own 100 shares of McDonald's, you own about 0.000008 percent of the company. An investment to be sure, but not exactly clout at the local franchise.

You: So why does this matter? Should I buy Burger King instead? I love the King.

You can buy either one. Owning stock matters because every time someone orders a #1 combo for $4.99,[5] you share in an infinitesimal portion of the revenue. Nice, huh?

You: I'd prefer free fries.

Oh well. Let's talk about how to determine how much a company is worth.

---

[5] Sorry if you are reading this in bed and are now hungry.

MARKET CAPITALIZATION (MARKET CAP)

The value of a company is its **market capitalization.** At the time of this writing, the market capitalization of McDonald's is approximately $50 billion.

You: That's a lot of ketchup.

Indeed. Market capitalization, not share price, allows comparisons between two stocks. Many people confuse this point. They assume if stock A is trading at $10 and stock B is trading at $20, stock B is worth twice as much as A.

You: It's not?

Company A could be worth much less or much more than company B. You can't tell without calculating the market capitalization, which uses this formula:

stock price x shares outstanding = market capitalization

In the case of McDonald's, market capitalization is calculated as follows:

$40 stock price x 1.24 billion shares outstanding = $50 billion market cap

At the time of this writing, Hewlett Packard's (HP) stock price is also approximately $40 per share. But because HP has over 2.7 billion shares outstanding, the two companies are worth very different amounts.

Hewlett Packards's market cap:

$40 stock price x 2.7 billion shares outstanding = $108 billion market cap

So despite nearly identical stock prices, HP is actually worth more than double what McDonald's is worth!

You: Wow, interesting. But, more importantly, how do I make money by owning stocks?

Occasionally, I sense a pattern to your questions. There's nothing wrong with it either.

Gary: I can relate! If I could only get you in my office...

Two ways to make money from owning stocks are:

1. collecting money from the company (dividends)
2. selling stock for more than you paid (capital appreciation)

Not every company pays dividends. If you purchase a stock that does not pay a dividend, the only way to make money by owning that stock is through capital appreciation.

DIVIDENDS

Of the companies that pay **dividends** to shareholders, quarterly cash payments are common. At the time of this writing, McDonald's pays a dividend to its shareholders. In fact, McDonald's has paid a dividend since 1976. In 2006, the dividend amount was $1.00 per share. So, if you owned 100 shares of McDonald's stock in 2006, you received dividend payments totaling $100.

The **dividend yield** is the dividend paid per share each year divided by the current stock price. So, in the case of McDonald's at the time of this writing, it is calculated as:

McDonald's Dividend Yield = $1.00 ÷ $40 = 2.5 percent

CAPITAL APPRECIATION

Another way you can make (or lose) money through stock ownership is from share price changes. When you buy an investment and the value of the investment increases, you benefit from **capital appreciation.** Do that often enough and you can become rich. For that to happen, you need to *buy low and sell high.* Easier said than done, but that's certainly the goal.

The stock price for McDonald's and any other publicly traded stock changes nearly every second the stock market is open. (Stocks that trade on the New York Stock Exchange trade from 9:30 AM to 4:00 PM Eastern Time, but there is pre-market and post-market trading, meaning stocks trade nearly all the time.) If you sell your shares and the stock price is higher than when you bought them, you make money on your investment.

For example, if you bought 100 shares of McDonald's a few years ago at $37 and sell them for $40, you *make* $300, plus the dividend income received. If you bought McDonald's at $43 and sell them for $40, you would *lose* $300, offset by the dividend income received. The gain or loss in the value of an investment is a **capital gain** or a **capital loss**, respectively.

WHY DOES THE SHARE PRICE CHANGE?

In the case of stocks, the primary influencer of price is the balance between **supply and demand** for its shares. Without involving you in a crash course of introductory economics, let me say that **supply** is the amount of something available and **demand** is the desire and ability of people to acquire it. If demand increases for something and the supply remains the same, prices go up. If you ever participated in an auction or bid on a house that someone else also wanted, you saw the results of increasing demand. When the supply is fixed and demand increases, the price rises.

Back to the example of stocks, in which the supply (number) of shares is fixed for the short term. If people want to buy more of a particular stock than want to sell it, regardless of the reason, the stock increases in price. The reverse is also true: if people want to sell more of a particular stock than want to buy it, the stock decreases in price.

Many factors can cause a stock to become more desirable to buy instead of sell (or vice-versa). Some of those factors are company-specific and others are broader. Possible reasons that people change their opinions about wanting to own a specific stock include:

Company-Specific Measurements Influencing Stock Price
➤ revenue: a financial way of saying "sales"
➤ revenue growth: the rate at which sales increase
➤ earnings: profit (revenue minus expenses)
➤ earnings growth: the rate at which profits increase
➤ dividends
➤ dividend growth: the rate at which dividends increase
➤ performance of the competition

➤ price/earnings ratio (P/E ratio)

➤ emotion or psychology: ("I like this stock")

You: A P/E ratio? Man, I hated gym class.

I know...the rope burns—ouch! Don't worry, no physical education here. The **P/E ratio** is simply the price of the stock divided by the amount the company earns per share. If the stock has a higher P/E ratio compared to similar companies, it is considered more expensive than its "peers."

Issues outside the control of the company also affect stock prices. These are known as external factors. When interest rates are low, when the economy is performing well, and the world is at peace, stocks in general become more attractive (and their prices rise). Here are some examples of external factors influencing stock prices:

External Factors Influencing a Company's Stock Price

➤ interest rates

➤ domestic economy

➤ worldwide economy

➤ war

➤ tax policy

➤ emotions or psychology: ("The stock market scares me right now")

You: That sure seems like a lot to understand. Do I have to? No wonder people just go to Gary's office. This is hard.

Gary: Yes, come right in.

As you'll see in a moment, it doesn't have to be that hard. However, the fact that investing can easily be made to seem overwhelming clears the way for unscrupulous characters to take advantage of you.

Gary: Who exactly are you talking about?

Who do you think, Gary?

Gary: You're getting on my nerves. I am just trying to make a sale.

I know. That's my point. While you're trying to make a quick sale, I'm trying to educate and empower. Big difference.

Gary: Whatever. I'd be done already and on to the next ~~victim~~ client.

Admittedly, the easier way usually does take less time. But it's more expensive in the long run. Speaking of the long run, stocks have historically provided a far greater rate of return than any other commonly available investment vehicle. Despite the increased risk that accompanies the higher expected rate of return by stocks, there is no better place to invest your long-term savings than in stocks. Still, selecting an individual stock is complicated, and it's a big reason why I don't recommend that a beginning investor purchase individual stocks.

You: Okay, I've been paying attention. Earlier, you told me to put only a little bit of money in savings accounts and CDs. Bonds probably don't make sense for me right now. Now you say "I don't recommend that a beginning investor purchase individual stocks." Hello? What else is there? You're not going to sell me an annuity are you?

Gary: Are you, Michael? You little—

Of course not. I just feel the risk and complexity involved in choosing and managing individual stocks is greater than a new investor should take on. However, it is very important to have a basic understanding of what stocks are and how they work so you can make good decisions about what is likely to be your best option—mutual funds.

You: Okay. Mutual funds it is. Which ones?

Not so fast. Let's finish the last key points for understanding stocks.

STOCK CLASSIFICATIONS

Stocks are frequently categorized based on the following criteria:

➤ revenue or earnings growth rate

➤ market capitalization

➤ domestic (U.S.) vs. international

The spectrum of possibilities within each categorization follows.

GROWTH RATE

The stocks of companies with high growth rates are often called **growth** stocks. Growth stocks can be contrasted with the shares of companies generating slower growth rates. If experts believe a slower growth stock to be overly sold—that is trading too cheaply—it is referred to as a

value stock. Usually, a stock is considered a value stock, a growth stock, or neither. Generally, no stock is considered both a value and a growth stock—at least not by the same expert.

MARKET CAPITALIZATION

Definitions of market capitalization categories vary. However, companies are generally placed into one of the following three broad categories:

➤ small cap stocks

➤ mid cap stocks

➤ large cap stocks

Stocks with market caps smaller than that of small cap stocks might be referred to as "micro cap" or "nano cap" stocks. The risk involved in owning those shares is extremely high.

COUNTRY OF PRIMARY REVENUE GENERATION

Most large cap American-based companies, and an increasing percentage of mid cap and small cap American companies, have operations in other countries. Still, a disproportionate amount of the typical American-based company's revenue is generated in the United States. Similarly, the bulk of revenue for companies headquartered in other countries occurs outside the United States. Therefore, individual stocks are usually considered either domestic or foreign.

You: So now that you've gotten those distinctions out of your system, now can you tell me why mutual funds are where I should invest?

Sure, but not before I explain what mutual funds are.

You: Okay, that seems reasonable.

Gary: Stop explaining everything. Start selling! You don't get how this works, do you Michael?

Actually, I do.

MUTUAL FUNDS

Think about the old wallet you carry around. Empty it. Take out all the bills, the photographs, and the credit cards. How much is the wallet worth now?

You: Not much. I certainly wouldn't pay anything to get it back.

Right. Heck, it's time for a new one anyway. But before you toss the wallet, wait a minute. How much would you pay to get the wallet back if I told you there was actually one $20 bill still stuck inside?

You: I don't know. Maybe... probably twenty bucks.

Makes sense. That's what an old, beat-up wallet is worth—only what's inside it. The wallet itself has no value. Mutual funds work in a similar way.

You: So you're telling me to invest in old wallets?

Gary: I would never tell you to do such a thing. Come with me and I can set you up with an annuity that is invested in a secret gem of a nano-stock. It gets better: this annuity is part of a phenomenal whole life insurance policy with—get this—guaranteed cash value!

Wow, that was a mouthful—to ignore. Look, the wallet is a metaphor. A mutual fund itself, like any old wallet, has no value. A mutual fund has value only because of what it contains—that is, owns. Some mutual funds own stocks. Others own bonds. Many mutual funds own both stocks and bonds—different percentages of each.

Imagine you own shares in Fidelity Magellan, one of the largest and oldest mutual funds. As of this writing, Fidelity Magellan owns shares in many companies, including General Electric, Microsoft, and American International Group. If the value of what Fidelity Magellan owns (its investments) increases, then the value of your shares in the Fidelity Magellan mutual fund also increases. The reverse is also true.

At the end of each business day, the mutual fund calculates the total value of all the assets it owns. It then divides the total value by the number of mutual fund shares in existence to calculate the **net asset value** of the mutual fund. The net asset value is the price per share your shares in the mutual fund are worth at the end of that day.

Since this calculation is made only once per day, you cannot trade mutual funds during the day. You can *place* an order to buy or sell mutual fund shares during the day. However, the order is *executed*—the trade happens—at the end of the day (after the U.S. exchanges close at 4 PM Eastern Time).

You: There are like a zillion mutual funds, aren't there? How am I going to know which one to pick?

TYPES OF MUTUAL FUNDS

Mutual funds have become so popular that the number of mutual funds available is now greater than the number of stocks on the New York Stock Exchange. Fortunately, mutual funds are easily categorized based on the types of assets they own. Here are some examples of mutual fund categories.

- ➤ money market funds
- ➤ bond funds
- ➤ stock funds
- ➤ balanced funds

You: What's the difference between these funds?

A **money market fund** is a mutual fund investing in very safe assets. Its goal is to generate a rate of return in excess of what a savings account earns, with only a slight increase in risk. Money market funds are designed—but not guaranteed—to keep their share prices at exactly $1.00. Therefore, money is made not through share price increases but from periodic dividend payments[6] made to shareholders.

As you'd expect, **bond funds** (sometimes called **fixed income funds**) are mutual funds containing primarily bonds while **stock funds** (sometimes called **equity funds**) are mutual funds owning primarily stocks. A **balanced fund** is a mutual fund holding healthy amounts of both stocks and bonds.

There are numerous sub-classifications of stock mutual funds similar to the stock categories we discussed a few pages ago. Examples of **stock funds** you can invest in include:

- ➤ large cap growth
- ➤ small cap value

---

[6] These dividend payments are similar to interest payments, but because they are paid by a mutual fund they are called dividends.

➤ international small cap

➤ U.S. growth

You: Why are you so gung-ho on using mutual funds?

Two main reasons: ease of diversification and access to professional management.

DIVERSIFICATION

Remember the risk vs. reward lesson: the greater the risk, the higher the expected rate of return. But one way to reduce your risk while maintaining the expectation of high rewards is through **diversification.**

You: So is diversification an exception to the risk vs. reward lesson?

It's not an exception, it's a strategy. Diversification takes advantage of the risk/return trade-offs. When your investments are diversified, you own many types of investments, so that—statistically speaking—when some go up, others go down. As a result, your overall exposure to risk is reduced compared to having "all your eggs in one basket."

Here are some ways you can diversify your portfolio.

➤ Own many different stocks.

➤ Own various types of stock categories (i.e., international, domestic, large cap, small cap, growth, and value).

➤ Own stocks, bonds, and cash (like savings accounts).

DIVERSIFICATION USING MUTUAL FUNDS

There are a few easy ways to diversify using mutual funds. One is to purchase more than one mutual fund type. For example, you can purchase a domestic small cap value stock mutual fund *and* an international fund focusing on large cap growth opportunities. By doing so, you reduce your risk compared to purchasing only one fund type, since mutual funds as different as these do not historically move in lock step. This action lowers your risk without lowering your expected return, the benefit of the diversification strategy.

In addition, you benefit from diversification the moment you buy any mutual fund. This is because mutual funds own many stocks (or many bonds if a bond fund). Say you purchase 100 shares of McDonald's for

$4,000 ($40 per share). If McDonald's stock declines by 10 percent to $36.00, the value of your investment decreases by $400 (since the new stock price of $36.00 multiplied by your 100 shares is $3,600).

On the other hand, suppose you invest in a mutual fund that owns, along with dozens of other stocks, shares of McDonald's. Instead of investing directly in McDonald's, you purchase $4,000 worth of the Dodge and Cox Stock mutual fund. This fund owns more than 36 million shares of McDonald's as of this writing. Nevertheless, McDonald's represents only about 2.4 percent of the total value of the Dodge and Cox Stock Fund.

Assume the 10 percent one-day decline in McDonald's relates to company-specific news—such as the company's announcing poor earnings. Assume the rest of the market has an average day. In fact, to make it simple, the rest of Dodge and Cox Stock Fund neither loses nor gains value. Some individual stocks it owns go up, others go down, but at the end of the day, all the different changes net out to a big fat zero—other than the drop in the price of McDonald's shares.

What happened to your $4,000? Well, since only 2.4 percent of your investment decreased by 10 percent, you lost 0.24 percent of your $4,000, or less than $10. Quite different than the $400 loss! The diversification provided by the mutual fund reduced your exposure to company-specific events.

The opposite is also true. If McDonald's stock suddenly rises by 10 percent while the rest of the mutual fund nets no change, you are far better off if you invested your money directly in McDonald's. That's why your risk is so much higher with individual stocks compared to diversified mutual funds: much greater volatility.

PROFESSIONAL MANAGEMENT

In addition to diversification, another major benefit of mutual fund investing is access to **professional management.** As you already realized, selecting specific stocks and bonds is complicated. By investing in mutual funds, you don't need to decipher that complexity. Rather, you can defer to the investment decisions made by people who have decided, for a career, to focus on investment selection.

You might assume professionals can make better investment selections than you can. After all, it's their day job. But don't assume anything, because some mutual fund managers, like some cooks, politicians, and technical support representatives, stink. Most are good—well, maybe not most politicians—but you get the point.

You: How can I select a good mutual fund manager?

You can't select a mutual fund manager directly. You *can* select one indirectly by doing some basic research. Before choosing a mutual fund, find out who the manager is and how long he or she has managed the fund. You are looking for **outperformance**—meaning the fund has performed better (generated a greater return) than funds investing in *similar asset categories*. If the same manager has run the fund for several years of outperformance, consider this fund—as long as it otherwise meets your needs.

However, as printed all over every mutual fund's paperwork, *past performance does not necessarily predict future results*. Nothing is promised—a great manager can suddenly have a bad month, quarter, year or longer. Also, he or she can quit the fund or be transferred to a different fund. But at that point you can say you were unlucky—not careless—and change your investment.

You: Can little me really afford a professional manager? Sounds expensive. Can I call her?

You can absolutely afford a professional manager. And you can call her, too, although you're unlikely to be "put through." Instead, the odds are good you'll speak with a friendly customer service agent (who might even be in the United States).

To be clear, you are not getting a *personal* money manager, a professional who makes investment decisions on your behalf while considering your needs exclusively. Such attention is either unavailable or impractically expensive for a beginning investor with a modest amount to invest. The professional management provided by a carefully selected mutual fund is sufficient.

The mutual fund collects a fee for the professional management of your investment. Because the costs of such professional management are spread among so many investors, you don't pay a large lump sum.

The cost for professional management is expressed as a percentage of your investment. If the **expense ratio** is 1.2 percent, you pay $12 each year on a $1,000 investment. You are never billed or write a check for $12. Rather, the expense is deducted periodically from the net asset value of your shares. When evaluating funds, pay attention to the expense ratios in addition to performance. All things equal, a lower expense ratio is preferable, as higher expense ratios dramatically—and negatively—affect your investment balance over the long term.

In addition, you should consider a fund's **12b-1 fee.**

You: Its what?

The fund's 12b-1 fee. It's another expense frequently charged by mutual funds.

You: And it's not part of the expense ratio?

Nope, it's a separate fee.

You: Wow.

Indeed. Since the 12b-1 fee is not included in the expense ratio calculation, you need to review this charge. Again, with all else equal, a lower fee is better.

You: What about loads?

Gary: All right, who told you to ask that question? This is getting ridiculous—how am I going to make any money here? What about my retirement?

Loads are sales commissions you pay on certain mutual funds when you either invest or sell (redeem) shares. Sometimes, loads are due at both times. It is both preferable and realistic to purchase only **no-load funds.** These are funds without sales commissions (loads). Furthermore, a fund with a 12b-1 fee over 0.25 percent is usually categorized as a load fund.

Always ask about loads before making a mutual fund investment. To purchase a no-load fund, you might have to do more work or switch advisors.[7] However, if you were to calculate what you pay in loads per hour of assistance you receive from an advisor, you'd probably jump at the

---

[7] A section about advisor selection appears at the end of this chapter.

opportunity to either switch advisors or simply select the funds yourself. Besides, it's good work for you to do—basic research and filling out of simple forms. It makes you a better, more involved, investor.

You: How do I evaluate mutual fund performance so I know which ones to buy?

There are several ways to evaluate a mutual fund's performance. One is to compare the fund's long-term performance with other funds that invest similarly. At the same time, review the risk profile of the fund. Some funds achieve higher returns than others but do so by taking too much additional risk.

A number of rating services provide this kind of information. Morningstar is probably the best known. You can see the high-level results of these comparisons free at many of the financial web sites listed in Appendix B and at *www.totalcandor.com*.

Another way to measure mutual fund performance is to compare it to the **benchmark index** designated by the mutual fund. This index represents, in the opinion of the mutual fund's management, the average performance of the stocks or bonds most similar to the assets owned by the mutual fund. Ideally, select a mutual fund whose manager has consistently beaten her benchmark over at least five (ideally ten or more) years. A true star is one who beats her index in both good markets, where the index increases in value, and in poor markets, where the index decreases.

You: Speaking of averages, who is Dow Jones? Does he hang out with Ira Roth?

Dow Jones is a media company that owns, among other businesses, *The Wall Street Journal*. However, you are probably asking about the *Dow Jones Industrial Average (DJIA)*.

You: Yes—that's the one. What is that?

INDICES—THAT'S PLURAL FOR INDEX

The Dow Jones Industrial Average is an example of an index. You might have heard of some of these well-known indices:

➤ Dow Jones Industrial Average

➤ S&P 500

➤ NASDAQ Composite

➤ Wilshire 5000

Each index represents the performance of a different group of stocks. The stocks that make up an index change, but quite infrequently, and usually due to a major event, such as the bankruptcy or acquisition of a company in the index. What follows is a summary of these indices:

Dow Jones Industrial Average. This index, perhaps the most widely quoted financial statistic in the world, is the result of the movement of just 30 stocks! They are well-known stocks, including American Express, General Motors, Wal-Mart Stores, Altria Group, McDonald's, and Walt Disney. As of this writing, the latest change to the components of this index, other than a name change by one company, occurred in April 2004. The DJIA, unlike the other averages described below, is not a weighted average based on market capitalization. It is a complicated and less meaningful price-weighted average.

You: What the heck does that mean?

In a nutshell, it means the Dow Jones Industrial Average isn't as reliable a measure of overall stock market performance as the other indices we discuss.

But it is still the Dow Jones.

S&P (Standard and Poors) 500. This is a broader index and, as the name implies, includes the movements of 500 stocks. It is calculated as a market capitalization weighted average, which means that changes in the price of stocks valued highly count more in calculating the average than do changes by lower-priced stocks. For both reasons—more stocks as part of the index and a more meaningful calculation method—the S&P is a preferred measure of general market performance.

NASDAQ Composite. There are many locations where stocks are traded. The best known of these stock exchanges is probably the New York Stock Exchange (NYSE). The NYSE is on Wall Street in lower Manhattan—hence the cheesy question by one newsperson to another: "How did things go on Wall Street today?"

Another well-known exchange, especially during the height of enthusiasm around technology stocks in the late 1990s, is the NASDAQ (National

Association of Securities Dealers Automated Quotation system). It is also based in New York City, but not on Wall Street.

The NASDAQ Composite is made up of the more than 3,000 stocks trading on the NASDAQ. This index is often thought of as a useful barometer of the performance of technology stocks and other cutting-edge companies, which make up much of the exchange. It is a market capitalization weighted average.

Wilshire 5000. This index, despite its name, has over 6,700 stocks in it. It perhaps best represents the *total performance* of the American market, since it has virtually every domestic stock in it, regardless of the exchange it trades on. It is also a market capitalization weighted average.

You: I've also heard of index funds. Are they a good idea? What are mutual funds called that are not index funds?

Every mutual fund is either:

➤ an index fund, or
➤ an active fund.

The goal of an **index fund** is to mirror the performance of a specific index. For example, the Vanguard 500 Index fund attempts to match the performance of the S&P 500. Such an objective implies very little trading and decision-making by fund management. As a result, index funds are also referred to as **passively managed** funds.

Do not be concerned with identifying index fund management. The manager is not pursuing an active day-to-day investment strategy; she is merely **buying the market.** It is more important for you to focus on operating expenses. Since there is far less for the mutual fund company to do in the way of research and trading, operating expenses—including the charge for professional management—are typically very low. Try to find the lowest expense ratio. At the end of the year, there should be no difference in return by funds tracking the same index *except* differences caused by lower operating expenses.

Although all the funds come very close to meeting the return of the index they track, these operating expenses mean that index funds seldom achieve the same return as the index itself. With an index fund, you never do much better or much worse than the performance of the index the fund mirrors.

In contrast to passively managed funds, the other principal mutual fund management technique is **active management.** Actively managed funds seek to beat the performance of the market.[8] These funds can perform significantly better or worse than their benchmarks. More research is often required and performed by an actively managed fund. More frequent trading typically results. These activities—research and trading—usually lead to higher expenses for actively managed funds compared to index funds.

Over the long-term, index funds often beat comparable actively managed funds. The higher expense ratios of actively managed funds play an important role in their relative performance. In addition, since the returns of actively managed funds are often inferior to index funds investing in comparable stocks types, it is reasonable to question if the average professional manager is genuinely superior at picking stocks. After all, an alternative is to simply hold a portfolio that approximates the stock market, without focusing on specific stock selection.

You: A portfolio that approximates the stock market without focusing on specific stock selection? That sounds like an index fund.

Yes, and for good reason. That is the goal of an index fund.

You: I'm getting the hang of this.

Awesome.

You: Still, what do I do?

The debate between choosing active and index funds is not a new one. Furthermore, you can find intelligent people who advocate for either side. Personally, I think it's a good idea to start with index funds as you start investing. Since you are nearly assured to receive the investment performance of the market, it's a good way to begin. However, consider eventually investing in funds that represent each strategy. After all, doing so is another way to implement diversification into your investment portfolio—and diversification is rarely a bad strategy over the long-term.

---

[8] Few mutual funds have the stated objective of under-performing their benchmark index. Nevertheless, many do.

There is no better way to start investing than through mutual funds. You receive affordable professional management plus diversification for a fraction of the investment in time and money required to attempt to achieve similar results on your own.

You: Do you have any other recommendations for beginning investors?
Yes. Dollar cost—
Gary: You're teaching everything! What's the reader going to need me for?
Exactly.

DOLLAR COST AVERAGING (DCA)

Dollar cost averaging is a key investment strategy important for experienced *and* novice investors. While dollar cost averaging is easily understood, its favorable impact is often underestimated. When using the **dollar cost averaging** strategy, you purchase the same *dollar amount* of shares at regular intervals, regardless of the investment price. As a result, you buy fewer shares at high prices and more shares at low prices. What follows is an example of DCA in action.

Figure 8-4

An Example of Dollar Cost Averaging

Month	Investment Amount	Share Price	Shares Purchased	Shares Owned	Value of Investment	Total Invested	Gain (Loss)	Cumulative Return
Jan	$ 200	$10.00	20.00	20.00	$ 200.00	$ 200.00	$ 0.00	0.0%
Feb	$ 200	$ 9.00	22.22	42.22	$ 380.00	$ 400.00	$ (20.00)	−5.0%
Mar	$ 200	$ 8.50	23.53	65.75	$ 558.89	$ 600.00	$ (41.11)	−6.9%
Apr	$ 200	$ 8.00	25.00	90.75	$ 726.01	$ 800.00	$ (73.99)	−9.2%
May	$ 200	$ 9.50	21.05	111.80	$1,062.14	$1,000.00	$ 62.14	6.2%
Jun	$ 200	$10.50	19.05	130.85	$1,373.94	$1,200.00	$173.94	14.5%
Jul	$ 200	$11.00	18.18	149.03	$1,639.37	$1,400.00	$239.37	17.1%
Aug	$ 200	$11.50	17.39	166.43	$1,913.89	$1,600.00	$313.89	19.6%
Sep	$ 200	$ 9.75	20.51	186.94	$1,822.64	$1,800.00	$ 22.64	1.3%
Oct	$ 200	$10.00	20.00	206.94	$2,069.38	$2,000.00	$ 69.38	3.5%

In this example, you start buying shares in January at $10 per share. When you buy your last shares in October, the price is also $10. Logic suggests that you don't make money, since there is no stock price increase. However, by using DCA you purchase more shares at low prices (i.e., 25 shares in April at $8.00) and buy fewer shares when the price is high (i.e., only 17.39 shares in August at $11.50). As a result, you do not own exactly 200 shares, as you would if you had invested all $2,000 in January at $10.00 per share.

By the end of October, you have nearly 207 shares. Your investment of $2,000 is worth about $2,070, a 3.5 percent return over ten months. Not too shabby for a stock that didn't increase!

One additional note: *DCA is an automatic benefit of a 401(k) plan.* Your contribution amount is fixed, so you invest the same dollar amount each paycheck. Therefore, you automatically buy more shares at lower prices and less shares at higher prices—a direct result of dollar cost averaging.

You: I like "automatic benefits." What other big lessons are there on investing?

ASSET ALLOCATION

Another critical investment strategy is asset allocation. **Asset allocation** is the diversification of an investment portfolio across asset classes. These **asset classes** include stocks (consisting of various stock categories), bonds, and cash. **Asset allocation theory** states that you can *maximize your expected return for a given level of risk* by owning a specific percentage of your portfolio in each asset class.

One lesson from asset allocation you heard before: Don't put all your eggs in one basket. In other words, diversify.

Another message is to choose your asset classes carefully, based on your risk tolerance and time horizon. Unless you are already in or very close to retirement, you have a long-term time horizon for your retirement investments. Therefore, *your retirement plans should be invested nearly exclusively in stock mutual funds.* Remember, mutual funds are the easiest way for a beginning investor to get started, with easy access to diversification and professional management.

The precise determination of your target asset allocation requires a sophisticated mathematical model. However, you can visit *www.totalcandor.com* for guidance in determining an appropriate asset allocation.

REBALANCING

You: Sounds like a "Beat Your Sobriety Test" strategy. Hmmm—and you cut me off earlier when I was going to tell you my tolerance story.

Not quite. **Rebalancing** is the periodic review and adjustment of your asset allocation.

You: Why is that necessary? I thought you could just put DCA on autopilot and call it a day.

Over time, certain asset classes perform better than others. Let's say your ideal asset allocation is 80 percent stocks, 15 percent bonds, and 5 percent cash. One year later, you review your investments and discover you now own 88 percent stocks, 10 percent bonds, and 2 percent cash. This might happen if your stocks grow at a faster rate than your bonds and cash.

By rebalancing, you take action based on the new information. To once again achieve your target (ideal) asset allocation, you sell some stock funds and put the proceeds into bonds and cash. This keeps your risk/reward profile in check.

In addition, rebalancing is advantageous because it causes you to sell some investments high. Only the better-performing asset classes grow to disproportionate levels and cause you to sell them. These investments are your "winners." The same way DCA causes you to "buy low," rebalancing causes you to "sell high." And anytime you buy low and sell high, you make money!

You: I like the sound of that.

RANDOM INVESTMENT TERMS

You: What about all those random investment terms people use? I probably ought to know them by now—but, honestly, I don't.

No problem. Here are some commonly used investment terms and their definitions:

A **bull market** is an increasing market (or a market expected to increase) for a particular asset class (e.g., a bull market for housing, a bull market for small cap stocks). When no investment class is referred to, the speaker is usually speaking about stocks in general. As you'd expect, most people love bull markets. It's no coincidence that a 7,000-pound statue of a bull stands near Wall Street.

However, there is no bear statue in lower Manhattan. A **bear market** is a declining market. A bull market and a bear market are opposites. People optimistic about a market are **bulls** and market pessimists are referred to as **bears.**[9]

You: For real?

Indeed.

You: All right then.

The term **bubble** has recently become part of the everyday investing language. Bubbles commonly referred to are the technology bubble of the late 1990s and speculation over a possible housing bubble in 2007.

A **bubble market** is a market in which assets are considerably overpriced, often due to psychological factors. Only afterward can a market be identified as a bubble market. When a bubble market **pops,** there is a significant **market correction:** a downward adjustment of prices. A market correction is different from a bear market in that a correction is more severe and quicker. A very sudden and very deep market correction is a **crash.**

You: Why would I invest if the market is going to crash?

You wouldn't. But you don't know about a crash until after it happens. By then it's too late.

Many experts agree that stocks should continue to return approximately 8 percent per year *over the long-term,* in line with their historical performance. Some years stocks do far better than 8 percent, and some years they do far worse. I don't know which years fit in each category. Neither does anyone else.

Gary: I do. I have access, baby. I just got off the phone with—

What's your net worth, Gary?

---

[9] You are not required to be either to root for Chicago sports teams.

Gary: Got to go.

One of the worst investment strategies is to try to **time the market** (engage in **market timing**). People who embrace this technique frequently buy and sell stocks based on their opinion of where the market or an individual investment is headed.

You: But how do they know?

They don't. If they did, they would be phenomenally rich. Although they talk a lot, very few market timers make money that way over the long term. Far more people are badly hurt through market timing than helped—but it is harder to find them; they don't brag. Another market timing strategy to avoid is short selling.

You: Hey—no short jokes!

Selling short is a bet that a stock will decrease in value. Logistically, when you sell short, you sell shares you don't own and buy them back later. If the price when you buy them back is lower than when you sold them, you make money. If not, you lose money.

Short selling is a market timing strategy. It also goes against the historical trend of stocks rising over time. Therefore, it is a strategy to avoid.

You: So you're saying I should do what, exactly?

Start by determining a reasonable asset allocation at *www.totalcandor.com*. Then, dollar cost average your way into index mutual funds. The easiest way to start investing is with your workplace retirement account. Since you probably have a long-term time horizon for retirement investing, you'll invest primarily in stock mutual funds. Your 401(k) plan automatically follows a dollar cost averaging strategy. Enroll at once—at least 10 percent—and you are well on your way!

You: This investments chapter is nearly over. You really aren't going to tell me what to specifically invest in, are you?

Gary: I can help you with that: Pork bellies! Gold! Oil! Soybeans!

Pork bellies, gold, oil, and soybeans are all examples of **commodities.** They have higher expected risk and reward than stocks. Commodities have no place in the portfolio of a beginning investor. (Even for sophisticated, wealthy investors, commodities should be a small percentage of their portfolios.) Again, stock mutual funds are where to start investing.

REAL ESTATE

You: What about real estate?

Land and anything on it *can* be an investment, too. **Real estate** includes homes, apartment buildings, and undeveloped land. Today, many people consider their home their most valuable and most important investment. For many people, their home is also their *only* investment. If you buy a house and don't save another dime, you aren't saving and you aren't investing.

You: But I'll just sell my house later and live off that money.

And where will you live when you sell your house?

You: In a cheaper place.

It won't be as cheap as you think. You get accustomed to a nice place after all those years. Plus, the homes around you are going up in price the same way yours is. People often dramatically overestimate how much money they are willing to pull out of their home to live on when they retire.

Buying a home is an important financial milestone. But don't consider it your sole retirement plan.

You: Ok, so I should buy a home at some point. When?

There are many factors to consider when making a rent vs. buy decision. Review the various viewpoints and financial calculators before taking the plunge. (See Appendix B for a list of useful financial web sites.) You might never make a bigger, nearly irreversible financial commitment in your life than the purchase of your home. Often, it makes sense to buy a home only when you reach the point in your career and personal life where you are confident you will not need or want to move for at least five years.

You: What about flipping condos?

Remember what I said about financial fads appearing in books?

You: Yes. Too late.

Exactly—and so we're done with that topic.

Still, real estate is an investment to consider. Don't be intimidated by real estate—it's just another asset class like stocks and bonds. Furthermore, you can invest in real estate without becoming Ralph, the guy who fixes the leak or calls the electrician, as you might be if you own an apartment building.

One way to gain exposure to this asset class without the responsibility of active real estate ownership is through the purchase of real–estate-focused mutual funds. You also incur less risk investing in real estate this way. A real–estate-focused mutual fund provides the benefit of diversification—you own a little bit of many properties. Still, don't make real estate a large part of your overall portfolio. It's just one part of your portfolio's overall asset allocation.

EXCHANGE-TRADED FUNDS (ETFs)

You: What's an ETF? I think I read somewhere ETFs can be better than mutual funds but now I don't even remember what they are. Ha! Maybe ETF is the abbreviation for "Easy to Forget"?

For an investor, ETFs operate similarly to index funds and provide the same benefits. Like index funds, there are ETFs for virtually every index. The advantages some ETFs have over index funds are even lower expenses and the ability to trade during the day (rather than only at the end of the day).

Each ETF buy or sell order typically triggers a brokerage commission. This is the principle disadvantage of ETFs, since you can otherwise select no-load index funds and completely avoid commissions.

You: So Yes or No on ETFs?

If you invest small amounts in a recurring manner (i.e., dollar cost average), ETFs usually don't make sense because you pay numerous commissions. However, if you plan to make a large investment and hold it for a long time, consider ETFs. The lower ongoing expenses available with many ETFs could more than make up for the infrequent commissions you pay. Still, make sure to verify that the expense ratio of the ETF you are considering is lower than the expense ratio of a comparable index fund.

INVEST IN FINANCIAL PLANNING SOFTWARE

You: How do you keep track of all this?

Numerous financial planning software programs are available. Two of the most popular are Intuit's Quicken and Microsoft's Money. Regardless of the program you choose, financial planning software helps in both the establishment and monitoring of your personal financial plan.

For around 50 bucks, the job of managing your financial affairs is made much easier and less time-consuming. It's money well-spent and, depending on your tax situation, may be tax deductible. The software takes some time upfront to set-up, but saves you significant time fairly quickly. Plus, by using financial software, you're far more likely to notice if something goes awry—furnishing you with another opportunity to help yourself financially.

WORKING WITH FINANCIAL PROFESSIONALS

You: What if I want help from a professional but I am afraid I'll get Gary? I fear I won't know it's him until it is too late. How can I get someone reputable?

Gary: C'mon! I'm not that bad.

I beg to differ.

No one else cares about your financial well-being as much as you do. It's simply human nature, regardless of who tells you otherwise. This does not mean you can't use professionals. Professional advice is seldom a bad idea, especially if you're choosing between solid advice and procrastination. However, never delegate *responsibility* to another individual, only *expertise*. Always be careful whom you trust.

Although many excellent financial professionals are available, there are also those who take advantage of others' ignorance for self-profit.

Gary: That's an oversimplification!

Big word, Gary. In reality, these are not the planners you want to work with. Others might do their best but are not great planners. Their advice might lack awareness of alternative, more appropriate opportunities available to you because such options are beyond the scope of their expertise.

If and when you decide to seek the help of a financial professional, interview several candidates and ask each the following question:

How are you paid?

The response you want to hear is "Fee-only." You don't want the planner to say "Commissions" or "You don't have to pay me anything; I get paid by other companies based on the products you buy." (The last two responses mean the same thing.) Commissions are unattractive from your standpoint because you want *your* best interest to be the only thing influencing the planner's advice, not the amount of commission the planner earns by recommending one course of action over another.

Choose a financial planner with good references from people whose financial situations are similar to your own. Such references are among the best ways to find any good professional.

Lastly, consider working with advisors who have obtained the CERTIFIED FINANCIAL PLANNER™ (CFP®) designation, indicating he or she has met certain experiential and educational requirements. Furthermore, these planners commit to working by a code of ethics and have passed a comprehensive financial planning examination.

FINAL THOUGHTS ON INVESTING

Don't let Gary—or anyone else—tell you they have the *right* investment for you if they haven't bothered to get to know you and to determine, among other things, your risk tolerance. Also remember, "If it's too good to be true it usually is."

Here's the reality: Choosing the *right* investment is not the most critical part of investing.

You: Hold up. I think you just said "Choosing the right investment is not the most critical part of investing." Can you say that?

I can say it and I did say it. It might not be how most people talk, but it is total candor.

You: Ok, then what's more important than choosing the right investment?

Getting in the game. You must invest. *Being a great investor is not as important as being an investor.*

A *Money* magazine article about a Putnam Investments survey[10] shows important findings about a man they call "Average Joe." Joe is 42 years old. He contributed 2 percent of his paycheck (and received a 50 percent employer match) for the last 15 years. When he started, he made $40,000 per year, and every year he received raises of 3 percent.

Clearly, his wealth is affected by the performance of the funds he selects. But how much is his current 401(k) balance affected?

➤ Scenario 1: If Joe picked bottom quartile (meaning relatively poor) funds: $39,700

➤ Scenario 2: If he picked top quartile (all the right) funds: $41,900

Note the small difference. After 15 years, just a little more than two grand. What if Joe had selected a more appropriate investment strategy? In other words, what if Joe were more aggressive—if he had selected more stock mutual funds? (He should have been investing for retirement aggressively all along, since he still has more than 20 years to go before he retires.)

➤ Scenario 3: If Joe had a more aggressive asset allocation: $48,200

Compare the results of selecting an appropriately aggressive allocation (Scenario 3) to choosing the "right," but overly conservative, funds (Scenario 2):

$48,200 vs. $41,900

While Joe's plan balance is more than 15 percent higher by investing appropriately, $48,200 isn't getting it done. Not after 15 years of investing.

Joe is still just Average Joe—he's stressing out, worrying about how to invest.

---

[10] Press Release 9/28/05: "Putnam Study Reveals Simple Secret for Successful 401(k) Investing" at: *https://content.putnam.com/shared/pdf/press_401k_investing.pdf* and "How Even Average Joe Can Retire Rich," Updegrave, Walter, Money magazine, January 2006, p. 50.

You: I'm stressing out too. $48,200 sure seems like a lot of money to me.

It is, but Joe should have plenty more since he's already been saving and investing for 15 years. I don't know Joe, but I bet $48,200 isn't going to permit him to live out his retirement dreams.

More importantly, Joe is stressed about the wrong things. He shouldn't be stressed about *how* he invests. He should be stressed about *how much* he invests.

What if Joe had invested more money? Let's say he picked the same poor investments but invested 6 percent of his pay instead of 2 percent. With a $40,000 annual income, he would save a little over $4 more per day than before (for a starting daily savings total still less than $7 per day, pre-tax).

➤ Scenario 4: If Joe saved 6 percent of his pay: $119,200

That's a big difference.

See how choosing the *right* investment is not the most critical element? Don't drown in information overload trying to pick the "right" funds. Proper asset allocation, dollar cost averaging, rebalancing, and careful selection of fund management remain important. Do those activities, but don't stress over them.

Feel proud and sleep well after you enroll in your 401(k) plan and select the investments in it. If the funds you select don't perform the best of those offered, that's okay. In fact, it's unlikely you will ever pick the very best fund out there.

Where should you focus your energy?

You: On getting in the game in a major way.

Indeed. Few people get in trouble by saving and investing too much.

CHAPTER 9

. . . .

Death Happens: Estate Planning

"True, you can't take it with you, but then,
that's not the place where it comes in handy."
—BRENDAN FRANCIS

E state planning is death planning.
   You: Fun stuff!

Perhaps because death is such an uplifting topic, estate planning is often one of the most neglected parts of financial planning. Although conversations about estate planning can make you uncomfortable, avoiding estate planning entirely might be extremely painful for your heirs.

As you know, life's two certainties are death and taxes. These days, however, there is little certainty about *death taxes*. The current death tax (estate tax) laws cause constant changes. Congress incessantly talks about changes to these dynamic laws, but usually does nothing. Yet you can and should plan your estate in this uncertain environment.

   You: How is that possible?

Only an individual with a net worth over $1 million has any real possibility of having heirs who must pay the estate tax. These millionaires should consider one or more of the plentiful legal and occasionally sophisticated estate tax strategies available to minimize the estate tax paid on their death.

. . . .

But millionaires are not reading this book. You are.

You: How do you know I don't have a million dollars? Besides, I might have more than that one day if I take advantage of the miracle of compounding interest, right?

Indeed, you might acquire significant assets by implementing the financial lessons presented throughout this book. And I hope you do. But ultimately, *Beyond Paycheck to Paycheck* teaches *basic* personal financial planning. Most millionaires already understand the basics. Heck, paying attention to the basics is a great way to become a millionaire in the first place. This book was written for you—not for those *already* extremely affluent. If they are reading this book, they may be screening it as a possible guide for their loved ones.

You: Okay, back to me. I am currently $995,000 (plus or minus) short of reaching millionaire status and paying estate tax. Why should I care about estate planning?

Tax is just one part of estate planning. Other **estate planning** concerns include deciding who receives your money and who takes care of your kids. You also need to communicate your wishes about the type of medical treatment you want to receive if your health deteriorates to the point where you are no longer able to make such decisions for yourself.

You: Do I really need to take care of these things at my age? When you told me to focus on disability insurance, you already told me how low my chances of dying are.

If you're too young now, what is the right age to address these concerns? Sadly, people less than 30 years old do go into comas. Admittedly, the odds favor estate planning *not* mattering to you for many years. But open your newspaper and look at the obituaries. Most people listed there were in their sixties, seventies, or older when they passed away. But almost every day one or two people on that list are much younger. Their cause of death could be anything—from a rare form of cancer to being hit by a drunk driver to most any other unpleasant event. It happens. Every day.

You: How do I do this—how do I put together an estate plan?

You have two real choices. The first, and most practical, is to hire a competent attorney. The second is to do it yourself using software.

Consider legal software only if your affairs are very simple—such as someone who has no spouse, children or significant assets, but is an over-achiever in search of an estate plan. Legal software is sold online and at stores selling business software.

WORKING WITH LAWYERS

Many attorneys establish basic estate plans for their clients for a fixed fee. Get a quote before starting to work with a lawyer. Many of them provide an introductory meeting with no financial obligation on your part. In addition to your learning a thing or two, this meeting gives you a chance to see if you like the attorney. If you are married, bring your spouse to any estate planning meeting. Ideally, obtain lawyer recommendations from people who have similar levels of asset and estate complexity to your own.

ESTATE PLANNING DOCUMENTS

There are several **estate planning documents** most people need to ensure that their affairs are handled according to their wishes. Obviously, each document needs to be created while you are alive. However, each document plays a different role based on whether you are alive or dead.

Figure 9-1

Common Estate Planning Documents

Important Role During Your Lifetime	Important Role Upon Your Death
Durable power of attorney	Will
Durable power of attorney for health care	
Living will	
Revocable living trust	

The following documents do not transfer *assets* at death, but shift *responsibility* if you are medically unable to make decisions for yourself while you are alive.

DURABLE POWER OF ATTORNEY

A **power of attorney** is a document authorizing another person, an **agent,** to act on your behalf. A power of attorney is often granted temporarily for a specific purpose.

With a *durable* **power of attorney** your designated agent can continue to act on your behalf after you are no longer **competent** (medically able to handle your affairs). For example, if a brain tumor renders you incompetent, your designated agent can sell your house and use the money for your medical expenses. Without a durable power of attorney in place, it is extremely difficult for someone to take appropriate financial actions on your behalf.

The scope of your designated agent's abilities is typically limited to financial and business decisions, not medical decisions. Still, this document allows for the agent to make gifts, make changes to insurance policies, and sell property, so choose your agent carefully.

DURABLE POWER OF ATTORNEY FOR HEALTH CARE

A **durable power of attorney for health care** might be known in your state as a **medical power of attorney** or a **designation of health care surrogate.** This document allows the agent you designate to make medical decisions concerning your care if you cannot do so yourself. Such decisions might include whether to resuscitate and whether to use life support. Think about this document in the context of serious—but not expected to be life-ending—medical decisions such as those made while you are in a short-term coma or in surgery.

Creating a durable power of attorney for health care implies having conversations with your loved ones that are not fun. As a result, many people avoid these discussions. As you will see, the consequences of avoidance can be severe.

LIVING WILL

You: Wait—isn't that an old Will Smith song?

No, "Living Will" isn't the track after "Gettin' Jiggy Wit It."

A **living will** states your wishes for medical treatment should you become terminally ill.

You: That sounds kind of similar to how you describe a durable power of attorney for health care. What's the difference?

Great question. Basically, the living will explicitly states your wishes during specific life-ending medical circumstances. The durable power of attorney for health care gives someone else—the agent—the ability to carry out your decisions for you.

You: So it's one or the other?

Nope—it's both.

You: Huh?

No one can create a living will covering every possible medical condition and treatment option. The living will covers only the most common, dreaded scenarios. Typically, this means that in addition to being physically or mentally incapacitated, you are, in the opinion of at least two doctors, in:

➤ a terminal condition,

➤ an end-state condition, or

➤ a persistent vegetative state.

If such a situation should come to pass, your desired treatment—including no treatment—will have already been spelled out in your living will. There is no guesswork. As a final document, you can say pull the plug. Yet, things are likely to go smoother if you also have a durable power of attorney for health care in place and your designated agent instructs the doctors to carryout the wishes specified in your living will.

In addition, there is, of course, the chance of something happening to you unaddressed by your living will. You don't want anyone wondering—or still worse, arguing over—what you would want done in a critical situation. With a durable power of attorney for health care, you name one individual as your agent to make such decisions for you. Ideally, you discussed these types of situations with your agent (at least once anyway), while you were still in good health. Those conversations prepare your agent to make an informed decision based on what he or she thinks you would want.

In addition to designating an agent who you've spoken with about your wishes, it is also advantageous to choose someone who agrees philosophically with your choices in these end-of-life matters. Furthermore, it is preferable to choose someone who lives locally, so they can be in the hospital quickly and available to make difficult decisions. Ultimately, becoming someone's health care agent is not an honor; it's a responsibility.

Any wonder why most people *don't* have these documents? This stuff is really hard to talk about. The good news is you don't need to revisit these topics each month or each year. Just put the documents in place and forget about them for a while.

You: What happens if I don't take care of this? What's the default option?

It's to hope it never matters. You don't want your loved ones to go through the experience of being powerless to carry out your wishes in a life or death situation.

"What happens?" you ask. It all depends. Remember Terri Schiavo? Everyone agreed she was medically incompetent to make her own decision about further treatment. Unfortunately, that's where the agreement ended. The arguing between her parents and her husband over what action Terri would have wanted was terrible.

Eventually the fighting led all the way to a Congressional subpoena! Although the Schiavo case was in the national news for a few months in late 2004 and early 2005, her husband had originally petitioned for the removal of her artificial life support about *seven years* earlier, at which time she had already been in a coma for several years. It is much better to avoid extraordinary legal wrangling by detailing your true wishes *and* by designating someone to communicate your wishes for you—whatever those might be.

You: So you're saying I should get those documents soon?

Yes, at least the three documents discussed so far. In fact, most financial professionals advise addressing your entire estate plan right away. However, I grant you a *temporary* reprieve from the documents we are about to discuss *if all of the following are true*:

➤ You have never been married and are not now engaged.

➤ You have never had any children and are not now expecting any.

➤ You don't own any real estate.

➤ You are under 30 and in excellent health.

➤ You do not own a business or anything other than standard brokerage and retirement accounts.

➤ You are comfortable with the way your state government would handle your affairs if you pass away—most likely giving your assets to your next of kin, as defined by the state.

If every condition above applies to you, then you may be able to delay putting together a will and considering a revocable trust. But only until the time when any one item on the above list is no longer true.

It can't hurt to address your estate plan early. Anyone already married, with a child, or not matching any item on that list above should make a full estate plan a high priority.

WILL

A **will** specifies who receives your assets and who is responsible for (provides **guardianship** to) your minor children upon your death. If you die without a will, you die **intestate.** In this case, the state you live in decides how your affairs are handled. Sometimes their actions match your wishes. Many times they do not.

A will is an important document, but it is not perfect. The primary disadvantage of assets transferred through a will is the resulting probate process. **Probate** is a court proceeding. Probate is typically not desirable because:

➤ It costs you money[1] (think more lawyers and potential state fees).

➤ It is public (nosy people can find out what was passed on and to whom).

➤ It can take a while (so your heirs might not receive their inheritance for a longer period of time).[2]

---

[1] On second thought, you're dead. It costs your heirs money.

[2] The negative impact of probate varies by state. Your lawyer can tell you how much pain probate causes in your state.

Still, you need a will to specify guardianship and to transfer certain assets. However, a revocable living trust should be considered for a more efficient and effective transfer of your assets.

You: A what?

REVOCABLE LIVING TRUST

You: That didn't help.

Look at it like this: of those three words, which do you already know?

You: "Living." I also know what it means to "trust" someone, but I don't think you're using the word "trust" that way.

Okay, then let's start with "living." The word "living" refers to a trust created while you are alive. A **trust** is an entity you create capable of owning assets **titled** in its name.

A Thing About Titles

If you are single, most of your assets are probably titled in your name, alone. When you are married, many of your assets are titled **joint tenancy with right of survivorship (JTWROS)**. Unmarried couples who wish to have their assets pass to one another upon death should also consider titling their assets JTWROS. The JTWROS title simply means that when you die, the asset goes to your **joint tenant** (typically your spouse) without regard to a will.

For example, imagine a bank account titled Colleen and Phil Smith, JTWROS. If Colleen passes away, the money in that account passes to Phil. It does not matter if Colleen's will states all her money goes to their daughter, Grace. The money in this JTWROS account goes to Phil because the asset's title takes precedence over what the will says. Furthermore, since the asset doesn't pass through the will, the probate process is not necessary for this account.

> ### Example: Unnecessary Havoc
>
> **Y**our will says everything goes to your spouse. However, you also have an old bank account opened during your bachelor days with your roommate Skippy. It was for shared living expenses. He moved out years ago and you have no idea what happened to him. (Skippy was kind of weird, now that you think about it—who introduces himself as "Skippy" at age 28?)
>
> **Gary: Did somebody just call me?**
>
> No.
>
> **Gary: Oh, I thought I heard someone say "Skippy."**
>
> Forget it.
>
> Anyway, Skippy gave you his checks and his ATM card when he left town. You figured there was no need to do anything else and began using this bank account as your own.
>
> When you pass away, $1,500 remains in the account. Your wife expects to receive the money, but she won't. Since the account is still titled JTWROS between you and your old roommate, this asset bypasses your will and the money goes straight to good old Skippy, wherever he is.
>
> *You: Wow. I guess titling is important.*
>
> Yes, so consider consulting with an attorney if your living situation is not straightforward in the eyes of current law. Those in relationships unrecognized by their states, as well as those with children from outside of their current marriages are people likely to benefit from competent legal guidance.

So instead of titling your assets in your name alone or JTWROS, your assets can be titled in the name of a trust. A trust has a trustee, a trustor, and a beneficiary.

> ➤ The **trustee** manages the assets inside the trust. That's probably you.
>
> ➤ A **trustor** puts assets into the trust. So, my friend, that's also you. (In addition to being a junior level associate at your day job, you're

now the trustor and trustee of your very own trust. See if *that* gets you a date Saturday night.)

➤ The **beneficiary** gets the loot. You, as trustor, determine the beneficiaries when you create the trust. You typically select two different beneficiaries: one for while you are alive and the other for when you have passed away. Most often, you designate yourself as the **primary beneficiary** while you are alive, allowing you to enjoy the income from your trust as well as to pay the taxes. The **contingent beneficiary** is often your spouse or another loved one.

➤ Of course, your *first choice* contingent beneficiary might die before you do. Therefore, you should also select a *second* contingent beneficiary. Your second contingent beneficiary selection is only relevant if your first contingent beneficiary is no longer alive when the primary beneficiary (likely you) dies. Your children, or a trust for your children, are often the second contingent beneficiary.

You: What's the "revocable" part mean?

Because the trust is revocable, you can make changes to it for as long as you live. You can even eliminate the trust entirely! If you change your mind about how you would like your assets distributed, you can make changes to the trust. Only when you die does the trust become **irrevocable** and no longer changeable. At that time, you're not around anyway, so you won't have a problem giving up control then, will you?

You: Enough about me.

After you establish a trust, preferably with a lawyer's assistance, you then transfer assets to the trust. The current custodian of most of the assets you consider transferring to a trust is a bank or brokerage house—or several. There is usually no reason to switch custodians when you change the title of your accounts to your trust. You continue to enjoy the use of the money and pay taxes on the income.

For example, your trust might be called "the Michael Rubin Revocable Living Trust Dated April 26, 2005, FBO Michael Rubin."[3] You would retitle

---

[3] FBO = For the benefit of. Also, use your name, not mine, though I appreciate the gesture.

your bank accounts, brokerage accounts, and investment properties and by doing so, they become part of your trust. Remember, while you are alive, there is no difference in how the accounts function. The only change you should notice is that statements received are addressed to you *as trustee for your trust* rather than to plain vanilla you.

You: So why bother? How does a trust help me? Why not just stick with a will?

Because, eventually, you will die.

You: Excuse me?

Sorry to be so blunt, but this is estate planning. When you die, the assets in your trust are transferred according to the terms of your trust. *Probate is not required for assets already in the trust.* This helps to reduce costs and preserve privacy. If estate tax is a concern, trusts, under certain circumstances, might help there, too.

You: So are you telling me I need to set up a trust?

No, I am not. The appropriateness of setting up a revocable living trust depends primarily on your current and expected financial and family situations. For example, a revocable living trust is often a wise choice for people who own real estate outside of their home state, for those with significant assets, and for those with children from a previous relationship. On the other hand, a revocable living trust is not typically necessary for someone just starting out in life with no spouse, children, or significant assets. A competent attorney can provide guidance as to the necessity of a revocable living trust.

You: If I set up a trust, do I still need a will?

There are three good reasons you need a will even if you establish a trust. First, some items cannot easily be put into your trust. Personal property, such as your DVD collection, clothes, and furniture, is often transferred via a will. If you want to surprise your brother with the timelessly sentimental gift of an old ratty tee shirt, you'd probably address that in a will.

You might also forget to put certain items in your trust. When written properly, the will covers your possessions not elsewhere addressed.

The person who receives your assets does not have to be the guardian of your children. For example, you might have one person you completely trust with financial matters but who ~~watches too much porn~~ wouldn't create a good home for your children. Another person might be a great surrogate parent but ~~loves the ponies~~ isn't exactly responsible with money. Solution: a) will the money to a trust to be managed by the first person with the requirement that the money is to be used for the benefit and well-being of your children, and b) will guardianship of your children to the second person.

The final reason you need a will is to specify guardianship of your minor children. Assets transfer via a trust, not children. For these three reasons—to handle items you can't transfer to your trust, to handle items you forget to transfer to your trust, and to establish guardianship of your children—you need a will.

ESTATE PLANNING SUMMARY

Unfortunately, anyone can get in a fatal or near-fatal accident at any age. Tomorrow is promised to no one. Yet you can make decisions today that enable a future tragedy to be a little easier for your loved ones to deal with.

Assuming you have accumulated modest assets, you are now aware of most of your key estate planning considerations. If you have a sizeable net worth, it is imperative you contact an attorney well versed in estate planning. You don't want your buddy two years out of law school to do this for you, even if she makes a ton of money doing corporate litigation. Estate planning is a specialty, so see someone who spends most of her day doing estate planning. Although the laws are constantly changing, a good attorney can draft documents to account for many of the anticipated legal changes.

For everyone else—those whose assets are not yet significant—consider preparing the appropriate documents highlighted in this chapter. While a few computer-based solutions do exist, they are not substitutes for attorneys, so they cost much less. Still, if you have a very basic plan, software should suffice until you can afford an attorney. At a minimum, software-aided documents beat having no documents at all. Should any estate planning document you create ever be needed, your heirs will appreciate your efforts and concern.

CHAPTER 10

Take This Book and Use It!

"You can't escape the responsibility of tomorrow by evading it today."
—ABRAHAM LINCOLN

HOW DO YOU GET THERE FROM HERE?

Your understanding of financial planning alone does not lead to financial success. Only by understanding what to do, *then actually doing it*, can you become successful. This chapter reemphasizes the *doing it* part of this reality. Along with the FIRST THINGS FIRST checklist in Appendix A, reread this chapter periodically to evaluate where you are versus where you want to be.

But what about ...?

Anything not previously covered is either:

➤ too specific for an introduction to personal financial planning, and might be covered in a subsequent Total Candor book or event, or

➤ not very good for you.

TOTAL CANDOR'S TOP INTRODUCTORY FINANCIAL PLANNING STRATEGIES:

You: So this is where I start?

Absolutely

You: When do I start?

THIS MONTH

1.   An employer match is not a corporate-sponsored dating service. (More information in Chapter 6)

It is free money, however. If your employer offers a match, taking advantage of it is a no-brainer first financial planning step. By not contributing to a 401(k) plan that offers a match, you are turning down free money. That's not the way to create wealth. Enroll in your 401(k) plan—at least to the level your employer matches—so you don't turn down free money for your retirement.

2.   Get rid of expensive debt first. (Chapter 3)

The appropriate way to measure the cost of a debt is the interest rate charged—*not* its balance. The higher the interest rate, the more costly the debt. Pay down your most expensive debt first. If you make only the minimum payment on your credit card, you primarily pay interest each month, barely reducing the amount you owe.

3.   Protect your loved ones while you still can. (Chapter 5)

You might have a spouse, children, or other loved ones whose well-being depends on your income. If you unexpectedly pass away without life insurance coverage, those people would probably be financially devastated. Although numerous life insurance products exist, the best bet for most people is a *term* life insurance policy. Term life policies enable you to afford the most coverage at the cheapest cost. *Whole* life insurance policies collect significantly higher monthly payments for the same coverage amount. Therefore, they are rarely the best use of funds for people just beginning to plan their finances, although they are often sold aggressively—by Gary.

4.   Don't risk a lot for a little. (Chapter 5)

Consider this strategy whenever you evaluate an insurance purchase. For example, renter's insurance is remarkably inexpensive, yet protects you financially from some fairly horrific events. For just a few hundred bucks a year, you can protect your possessions from most unforeseen circumstances. If you do not purchase renter's insurance, you risk a lot (virtually everything you own) for a little (a relatively small premium). Similarly, make sure that you have the appropriate coverage levels if you are a homeowner.

You: That seems like enough for one month.

I agree. It is doable, but that's enough for this month.

You: So then what?

Soon you will have accomplished those four things and the month will be over. Keep the momentum going by taking on the following tasks over …

THE NEXT SIX MONTHS

5. **An emergency fund comes in really handy if you have an emergency. (Chapter 7)**

Although most emergencies are unexpected, you can reasonably expect to encounter an urgent situation at some point. A financial emergency might be a sudden loss of income, a significant medical expense, or a large unplanned home repair. If you have an emergency fund, these scenarios won't dramatically disrupt your overall financial plan. It makes sense to have between three and six months of living expenses saved in an emergency fund. For many people in their first few months of their careers, that is not realistic. But an emergency fund is an obtainable goal shortly thereafter, especially if you focus on adding to it each month. Since you never know when you will need to tap your emergency fund, it should be invested very safely, such as in a high interest rate savings account.

6. **Pay what's due. (Chapter 3)**

If it's your debt, pay it off. You actually begin to lose many of the less dramatic options for getting out of debt when you begin to miss payments. Your goal should always be to pay more than the minimum on your high interest rate credit card accounts. Even more important, however, is to never miss a single payment. If you do, things can dramatically turn for the worse quickly, as additional fees and interest can be charged, making it increasingly difficult for you to get out of debt.

7. BIG SAVINGS on your medical, transportation, and child care expenses! (Chapter 6)

If your employer offers spending accounts, take advantage. Through these plans you save the equivalent of your top tax rate multiplied by all your spending eligible for reimbursement. Consider the risk of forfeiture of unused funds when determining the amount to put in your accounts. The extra paperwork and recordkeeping are worth the effort. The tax savings can be used to build your emergency fund.

8. There's a diamond in the Roth. (Chapter 7)

For all the advantages of the *tax-deferred* growth available from a traditional IRA and a 401(k) plan, you gotta love *tax-free* growth even more. Such is the upside of a Roth IRA. Available to a single worker with an income of up to $113,999 and to a married worker with combined income of up to $165,999, a Roth IRA contribution provides an unmatched long-term opportunity to accumulate significant wealth—tax-free.

9. If there's no will, there's no way ... (Chapter 9)

... your heirs are going to be happy about your not having one. A will, especially when you have either a family or significant assets (let alone both), is essential. If you lack a will, the government determines everything from who takes care of your minor children to how to distribute your assets. The odds of the government's decisions gelling precisely with your wishes aren't too great. Don't miss your chance to leave your family in good shape. Get a will. While you're at it, create a durable power of attorney, a durable power of attorney for health care, and a living will, documents authorizing others you designate to make decisions on your behalf should you become, from a medical perspective, incompetent or unable to manage your affairs.

10. Establish appropriate spending and saving habits. (Chapter 2)

Begin implementing the ten simple saving strategies I discuss in Chapter 2. Furthermore, make it an explicit goal to start repaying more debt or saving more money each month. Doing either one generates more cash for you going forward. You can then use these extra funds for additional saving or to further reduce your debt.

11. Track your progress. (Chapter 8)

Financial planning software should be one of your first investments. By enabling you to see where you are financially, this software serves as a wonderful motivator. You find it far easier to stick to your convictions as you easily track your debt decreasing and your net worth increasing. And if that's not what you're seeing, the software provides the wake-up call you need now, not years from now.

12. Know your odds. (Chapter 5)

Although people worry more about death than disability, for young people without dependents, disability is a far greater financial threat. First, at younger ages you are more likely to become disabled than to die. Second, the financial implications of your untimely passing are minimal if no one else depends on your income. If you become disabled, however, where's the money coming from to take care of you? Don't overlook long-term disability insurance, especially if you have a plan available to you at work or through a group.

You: Okay, this is good. There's plenty to do, but I see the corresponding checklist in Appendix A and I'm motivated to cross some of these things off. I bet I could cross off a couple of tasks already.

Excellent. I sense your increased confidence! That feeling will continue to grow as you further create and implement your financial plan during the next several months. From there, you can then take the steps necessary to go to the next level by beginning to work on the strategies listed in this last section ...

THIS YEAR AND EVERY YEAR

13. Pay the entire thing the entire time. (Chapter 3)

Pay the new outstanding balance of each credit card each month. That might seem impossible now, but it won't be if you take care of each of these previous strategies. As you begin to track your spending, you'll spend less. As you begin to understand the true cost of your credit card debt, you'll be motivated to come up with the cash to pay off more of your debt sooner. Eventually, you might use fewer cards, meaning less bills to keep track of and less bills to pay. Have confidence you can do this, and you will.

And your life will change forever.

14.   Have a good time, but stay in balance, with mutual funds. (Chapter 8)

Mutual funds can own stocks, bonds, and even cash, all of which create value for the shareholder. Since mutual funds own many different investments, mutual fund shareholders benefit from diversification, which lowers the overall risk. In addition, you benefit from the expertise of the professional investment managers who make the investment decisions for the mutual fund. Although you can turn over responsibility for specific stock and bond selection to mutual fund management, you should rebalance your portfolio annually, as gains in one asset class might cause your overall asset allocation to become out of line from your original target.

15.   Save early, save often. (Chapters 1, 2 and 7)

There is no surer way to move from *income generation* to *wealth creation* than by saving. Nothing amplifies the positive impact of this strategy more than saving while you are young. Regardless of the amount you have already saved and your current age, you can never make a bigger impact on your future financial situation than you can right now. Remember you are funding your retirement with a pogo stick. Raising your 401(k) contribution higher, even above the level matched, can only help.

16.   A tax refund is not a savings program. (Chapter 4)

Many people make an interest-free loan to the government each year by receiving a big income tax refund. Many people rationalize their sizable refunds by calling them savings. Then they use this "savings" for large purchases such as new televisions and vacations. A tax refund is not a savings program. It's just poor financial planning. Review the withholding calculator section in Chapter 4 and adjust your withholdings. By doing so, you can give yourself a raise—now.

Use the extra money from the raise you just gave yourself to increase your 401(k) contribution level. *You can decrease your withholding and increase your 401(k) contribution simultaneously, enabling you to save much more for retirement while leaving your net pay unaffected.* The only thing this strategy "costs" you is that large tax refund you shouldn't want in the first place. Visit *www.totalcandor.com* for assistance executing this strategy.

17.   You can take your 401(k) plan with you. (Chapter 7)

And you should. When you leave your job, consider either rolling over your 401(k) plan into your new employer's 401(k) plan or rolling it over into an IRA. Doing so helps simplify your life because it gives you one less account to keep track of. Simpler is better because simpler gets done. Invest an hour of time to roll over your 401(k) the right way when you leave your employer, instead of spending days trying to figure it out a few years later.

18.   Trust yourself. (Chapter 9)

Many people assume trusts are only for the extremely wealthy. And while there is certainly a place for trusts among the affluent, a revocable living trust often makes sense for people living a middle-class lifestyle. This is especially true when they own investment assets, such as those held in brokerage accounts. A trust provides for a cleaner passing of your estate—large or small—to your designated beneficiaries. Unlike transfers done by a will, assets in a trust can avoid the costs and delays related to probate.

19.   Spending more than you make always decreases your net worth. (Chapter 2)

If you spend more than you make, you either reduce the balance of an existing asset or create additional debt. Either one lowers your net worth. If you are currently in credit card debt, it is because you spent more than you made. The only way to get out of debt is to do the opposite: spend less than you make and apply the extra money to paying off the debt.

20.   Respect the identity theft epidemic. (Chapter 3)

If someone steals your identity, it will probably take a long time to have your financial affairs straightened out. In the interim, the task of repairing your credit might seem like a full-time job. Minimize your chances of becoming a victim by monitoring your credit reports, by being intelligent about your online activities, and by shredding just about everything that comes in the mail besides birthday cards.

# # #

You are now empowered with the ownership of your financial future. But for it to matter, you must get started. Refer to Appendix A for Total

Candor's FIRST THINGS FIRST checklist. If you haven't already done so, implement the financial planning strategies under the caption "This Month" right away. Then, begin to put a few of the "Next Six Months" strategies into practice. As you see your net worth increase, you will become more comfortable and confident in your own abilities.

Undoubtedly, you will make some mistakes along the way. Everyone does. The key is to make your mistakes small ones and to make them sooner rather than later. Larger mistakes made when you are older and closer to retirement are harder mistakes from which to recover. Your best opportunity is the one you have today. Really.

KEEP LEARNING!

If you learned from and were motivated by *Beyond Paycheck to Paycheck*, imagine how you'd feel after attending a financial planning educational event featuring the author! Be on the lookout for Total Candor workshops in your area and additional books that are part of the Total Candor series. Register for access to additional personal financial planning information at *www.totalcandor.com*.

Total **Candor**.sm

Appendix A

FIRST THINGS FIRST Checklist

THIS MONTH

Strategy	See Chapter	Do it. Check it. Enjoy it.
Contribute to your 401(k) plan, at least up to the amount the company matches.	6	☐
Start paying down your high-interest credit card debt.	3	☐
Obtain term life insurance if you have dependents.	5	☐
Obtain renter's insurance if you rent.	5	☐

NEXT SIX MONTHS

Strategy	See Chapter	Do it. Check it. Enjoy it.
Establish an emergency fund of at least three months of living expenses.	7	☐
Never miss a loan payment.	3	☐
Take advantage of your reimbursement accounts.	6	☐
Establish a Roth IRA.	7	☐
Put a will, durable power of attorney, durable power of attorney for health care, and a living will in place.	9	☐

continued on next page

continued from previous page

Strategy	See Chapter	Do it. Check it. Enjoy it.
Increase your savings by beginning to implement the Simple Savings Strategies.	2	☐
Track and improve your financial life using financial planning software.	8	☐
Obtain long-term disability insurance.	5	☐

THIS YEAR AND EVERY YEAR

Strategy	See Chapter	Do it. Check it. Enjoy it.
Don't carry a balance on your credit cards.	3	☐
Rebalance your investments annually.	8	☐
Save aggressively (primarily in retirement accounts) for your long-term goals.	1, 2, and 7	☐
Adjust your withholding to ensure you don't receive large income tax refunds.	4	☐
Roll over your 401(k)s each time you leave a job.	7	☐
Consider a revocable trust.	9	☐
Spend less than you make.	2	☐
Monitor your credit reports and shred credit card solicitations to reduce the chance you become an identity theft victim.	3	☐

Total Candor™

Appendix B

Useful Resources

Ready to move *Beyond Paycheck to Paycheck?*
Here are some useful resources.
Check for updates at *www.totalcandor.com*.

Resource	Web Site
Brokerage Houses (Custodians)	
Ameriprise	www.ameriprise.com
E*Trade Financial	www.etrade.com
Fidelity	www.fidelity.com
Charles Schwab	www.schwab.com
T. Rowe Price	www.troweprice.com
TDAmeritrade	www.tdameritrade.com
Vanguard	www.vanguard.com
Software	
Personal Finance	
Money	www.microsoft.com/money
Quicken	www.quicken.com
Estate Planning	
Perfect Attorney Platinum	www.cosmi.com
Willmaker	www.nolo.com/willmaker

Resource	Web Site
Tax Preparation	
CompleteTax	www.completetax.com
TaxACT	www.taxact.com
TaxCut	www.taxcut.com
Turbo Tax	www.turbotax.com

High Interest Bank Accounts (for Your Emergency Fund)

Emigrant Direct	www.emigrantdirect.com
ING Direct	www.ingdirect.com
HSBC	www.hsbcusa.com
Many, many more. Just visit:	www.bankrate.com

Useful Financial Web Sites

Total Candor	www.totalcandor.com
Bankrate.com (compare interest rates)	www.bankrate.com
Internal Revenue Service	www.irs.gov
Social Security Administration	www.ssa.gov

Magazines

Kiplinger's Personal Finance Magazine	www.kiplinger.com/personalfinance/magazine
Money	www.money.cnn.com
Smart Money	www.smartmoney.com

Credit Bureaus

Free Credit Reports Annually (no strings attached)	www.annualcreditreport.com
Experian	www.experian.com
TransUnion	www.transunion.com
Equifax	www.equifax.com

Amazingly Comprehensive Glossary of (Mostly) Important Terms

accidental death & dismemberment (AD&D) insurance A total crock. Financial protection if you die from an accident or lose a limb. You don't need this *insurance*. Review Chapter 5.

active income *Money* you acquire by working.

actively managed fund A *mutual fund* seeking to beat the performance of the *market*. Contrast with *passively managed fund* and *index fund*.

actual value An *insurance policy* clause stating you receive payment for what lost or damaged items were worth at the time they were destroyed. Contrast with *replacement cost*.

after-tax dollars See *post-tax dollars*.

agent A person authorized to act on another's behalf, typically through a *power of attorney*.

allowances Unnecessarily confusing term whose definition is as mystifying as it is unimportant. What is important is how allowances work. The more allowances you claim on your W-4, the less taxes withheld from your paycheck. Visit the *IRS* web site (*www.irs.gov*) and calculate the right amount of allowances for you, especially if you consistently receive a sizable *income tax refund*.

annual enrollment period A designated time when employees can make changes to their *benefit elections* without experiencing a *life event*. There is usually only one such time period a year.

annual percentage rate (**APR**) The *interest rate* without the impact of the *rate of compounding*. Also known as the *stated rate* or *nominal rate*. It is more meaningful to focus on *annual percentage yield* (*APY*).

annual percentage yield (**APY**) The *interest rate* including the impact of compounding. When comparing different investment options or loans, it is better to focus on APY than on *APR*, because APY represents the financial truth more accurately.

annuity (**1**) A company's promise to provide a series of payments in exchange for an investment of money. (**2**) A financial product typically paying a high commission to the salesperson. Annuities are not appropriate for most investors, especially in retirement accounts. Annuities, however, do have a place in financial planning. That place is not for people under 50 years of age unless they have an extremely high income, are completely free of *bad-debt*, and have taken advantage of every other tax-deferral method available, including maximum participation in their *401(k)* and *IRAs*. See *whole life insurance* and *Gary*.

arson I told you I'm not defining this. I can't believe you checked. See Chapter 5 for an explanation.

assessed value Worth of a property for *property tax* purposes. Sometimes the assessed value is significantly different (usually less) than the value the property could sell for.

asset Something you own, such as *investments,* a home, a car, baseball cards, or shoes. If your most valuable assets are made of cardboard or smell funny, you need more assets.

asset allocation The *diversification* of your *investment portfolio* across multiple types of *stocks* (including various stock categories), *bonds,* and *cash.*

asset allocation theory The concept you can maximize your *expected return for a given level of risk* by owning a specific percentage of your *portfolio* in each *asset class.*

asset class A type of *investment*. Examples include *stocks, bonds, cash,* and *real estate.*

automatic investment program (AIP) An arrangement with a brokerage house or *mutual fund* company to transfer a set amount of money into your account to be invested according to your instruction. You can do this in an *IRA* or a *regular account.* Often, low balance account fees are waived when you set up an AIP.

average tax rate A percentage calculated by dividing tax owed by total income.

bad debt *Loans* resulting from purchases with no chance of future financial payback. Examples include credit card debt, retail store debt, and a home equity loan where the money is used for a first class trip to the Super Bowl—even if your team wins. Contrast with *good debt.*

balanced fund *Mutual fund* holding both *stocks* and *bonds.*

bear An individual who believes we are in or about to enter a *bear market.*

bear market A *market* that's declining or expected to decline for a specific *asset class* (i.e., a bear market for stocks with no revenue, a bear market for stocks specializing in the delivery of pet food sold online). Contrast with *bull market.*

before-tax dollars See *pre-tax dollars.*

benchmark index An appropriate comparative measurement of a *mutual fund's* performance. According to fund management, this *index* represents the *return* of the *stocks* or *bonds* most similar to the fund's investing style.

beneficiary The person you designate to receive certain money and/or assets as a result of your death. Examples of places where you select a beneficiary are your life insurance policy, 401(k) plan, and will.

benefit elections Your workplace choices related to *insurance, spending accounts,* and *retirement plans.* Typically, you choose whether to participate in a given program and the extent. For example, you choose whether to accept health insurance, then select a specific health insurance plan, and finally determine whether to insure your spouse. You can usually make benefit elections only when you are hired, during the *annual enrollment period,* or as a result of a *life event.*

benefits Employer-provided compensation in addition to your wages. Examples include *insurance* programs, *spending accounts,* and *retirement plans.*

bond The *debt* of another entity, typically paying *interest* and *principal* according to a schedule.

bond funds *Mutual funds* owning primarily *bonds.* Also known as *fixed income funds.*

borrow To accept money from someone or some organization with the expectation of paying it back in the future. This action creates a *loan.*

brokerage account An investing account with fewer tax advantages and restrictions than a *retirement account.* Also known as a *taxable account.*

bubble market A condition in which *assets* are considerably over-priced, usually due to psychological factors. Bubble markets are only easily recognized after the bubble has popped.

bull (1) An individual who believes we are in or are entering a *bull market.* (2) Most of what comes out of *Gary's* mouth.

bull market An increasing *market* or a market expected to increase for a specific *asset class* (i.e., a bull market for companies specializing in flood repair, a bull market for all railroad stocks except those carrying passengers). Contrast with *bear market.*

buying the market See *index fund.*

capital appreciation The gain resulting from the value of an *investment* increasing.

capital gain An *investment* sale in which you receive more than you invested.

capital loss An *investment* sale in which you receive less than you invested.

cash Easily accessible *money*—in your wallet, in checking or savings accounts, or underneath your car's floor mats. You often receive no or a minimal *return* from cash.

certificates of deposits (CDs) An *investment* providing a guaranteed *rate of return* over a fixed time period in exchange for an agreement by the investor not to access the *investment* during the time period. CDs are widely available at banks and are often protected by *FDIC insurance.*

cheap How you might feel and what other people might initially think when you first implement the new savings strategies detailed in Chapter 2. But you're actually being *fiscally responsible.* It is amazing how much more money you can spend later if you don't spend it all now.

claim (verb) Contacting the *insurance company* to report a *covered event.* (**noun**) See *covered event.*

collateral What you must forfeit if you do not pay your debt. When your debt has collateral, it is *secured debt.*

collision The part of your automobile *insurance policy* providing coverage if you get into an accident. For example, just as you take a sip from a "just a little too hot to be totally perfect double latte," your car collides with another driven by someone struggling to figure out how to use his cell phone's conference call feature which is "like seven levels down from the main menu," and who is in turn hit by a third car in which the driver is furiously sending a text message about "how heavy traffic is" and "wondering if there is an accident ahead."

commodity A highly risky investment vehicle with potential for superior performance not belonging in the *portfolio* of beginning investors. Examples include oil, soybeans, and corn.

competent Considered capable, from a medical perspective only, of handling one's affairs. Ironically, people in great health who make really bad decisions are technically competent. Contrast with *incompetent.*

compounding See *rate of compounding.*

comprehensive Part of your automobile insurance policy providing coverage for most non–accident-related damage. Examples include vandalism, a tree falling on your car, and theft.

contingent beneficiary A person you designate to receive benefits resulting from your death if your *primary beneficiary* dies before you do.

contribution percentage Amount of your gross pay you choose to defer to an *employer-sponsored retirement plan,* such as a *401(k).*

contributory IRA An *IRA* funded by annual payments to your *IRA.* Contrast with a *rollover IRA.*

corporate bond The *debt* of a corporation, typically paying *interest* and *principal* according to a schedule.

cost of debt *Interest rate* charged on amounts *borrowed*.

coverage Protection provided by an *insurance policy*.

coverage limit The maximum the *insurance company* pays for a *claim*. When you purchase your policy, you typically select your coverage limits, subject to required minimums and permitted maximums.

covered event Occurrence an *insurance policy* provides *coverage* for. You must make a *claim* to receive a benefit from your coverage.

crash A sudden and severe *market correction*.

credit bureau A company, such as Experian, Equifax, or TransUnion, which collects information used to determine the risk of lending money to you. These companies prepare your *credit report* and your *credit score*.

credit cards Dangerous source of *unsecured debt*. Using credit cards requires remarkable self-discipline. There are few other ways to easily spend money you don't have while obligating you to pay it back for many years at very high interest rates. Few other legal ways, that is. Contrast with *debit cards*.

credit report Information compiled by a *credit bureau*, primarily concerning your previous borrowing activity. This information is used to determine your *credit score*.

credit score Measurement of risk used by potential lenders. Your credit score is based on sophisticated mathematical calculations affected by the amount you borrow, the age of your accounts, your payment history, and the amount you are allowed to borrow. Your credit score influences the amount you can borrow in the future and at what cost (interest rate).

custodian The organization administering an account. For example, your *401(k)* custodian could be Fidelity or Vanguard.

debit cards A convenient tool allowing you to pay for things with, in effect, an instant electronic check. The money you spend with a debit card comes directly out of your bank account. You can't borrow with most debit cards. If you tell yourself you use *credit cards* for the "convenience" but can't pay the entire balance, consider using debit cards. You won't spend what you don't have.

debt Amount owed to another as a result of *borrowing,* such as a credit card, student loan, car loan, mortgage, or bad Vegas experience. A debt is a *liability* that decreases your *net worth.* Also known as a *loan.*

deductible (1) Amount you pay if you make a *claim* that results in a payment by your *insurance company.* You select the amount of your deductible when you purchase a policy. (2) An expense eligible to be subtracted to calculate *taxable income.*

deduction Expense eligible to be subtracted to calculate *taxable income.* Examples include moving expenses, *IRA* contributions, and charitable contributions.

default risk The chance of a company not paying back its debt due to bankruptcy or other financial problems.

deferral percentage See *contribution percentage.*

defined benefit pension plan A *retirement plan* in which the retirement benefit received is guaranteed and is typically based on your salary and years of service. Since the amount you receive is guaranteed, your retirement *benefit* is *defined.* Also known as a *traditional pension* because most pensions worked this way at one time. Contrast with *defined contribution pension plan.*

defined contribution pension plan A retirement plan in which the only thing guaranteed is the amount you and/or your employer put into the plan. Since contributions are certain, the retirement *contribution* is *defined.* Ultimately, your retirement benefit is based on the amount you contribute to the plan, the amount your employer contributes to the plan, and the performance of the investments in the plan. Contrast with *defined benefit pension plan.*

delayed gratification The potential for something later in exchange for giving up something today; a requirement to save and invest. Waiting for the microwave to beep instead of taking it out when it "might be warm enough" doesn't cut it.

dental insurance Covers a portion of expenses related to a visit to the dentist. Hope that one was helpful.

designation of health care surrogate See *durable power of attorney for health care.*

disability insurance Pays a portion of your income if you are unable to work for a certain period of time due to an illness or injury.

discretionary expenses Money spent on "wants," such as DVDs, concert tickets, and dining out. Most "fun" expenses are discretionary. Contrast with *non-discretionary expenses.*

distribution Withdrawal from a *retirement account.* Usually, you need to wait until you are 59½ before you can take a distribution from your retirement account without paying a penalty.

diversification A *risk* reduction strategy in which you own many different types of investments. By diversifying, when some *investments* go up, others are likely to go down.

dividend yield The *dividend* paid per *share* each year divided by the current *stock price.*

dividends Payments made periodically (often quarterly) to *shareholders* of certain companies' *stock.* Part of a *stock's total return.*

dollar cost averaging (**DCA**) Strategy of periodically investing the same *dollar amount*, regardless of *investment* price. This causes you to buy fewer shares at higher prices and more shares when prices are lower. A *401(k) plan* automatically takes advantage of DCA.

down payment An initial payment made in connection with a sizable purchase such as *a mortgage* or a car.

durable power of attorney A *power of attorney* that is still effective even if you are deemed no longer *competent.*

durable power of attorney for health care Document authorizing an *agent* to make medical decisions for you if it is determined you are unable to do so for yourself. Also known as a *medical power of attorney* and *designation of health care surrogate.*

early distribution *Retirement account* withdrawal prior to age 59½ that does not meet the rare exception criteria.

effective rate See a*nnual percentage yield (APY).*

emergency fund *Cash* savings of about three to six months of living expenses for unexpected expenses or sudden loss of *income.*

employer match The amount of money your employer puts in your *retirement account* as an incentive for you to participate in the plan. Not every employer has an employer match. See *free money* and *idiot.*

employer-sponsored retirement plan A huge opportunity, this benefit allows you to contribute a percentage of your income into a *retirement account*. This account grows *tax-deferred* until you access the money, ideally in retirement. A *401(k)* plan is the employer-sponsored retirement plan most likely available to you.

equities *Stocks*. Often used to describe a key category of *mutual funds* (i.e., equity funds).

equity See *home equity*.

equity funds See *stock funds*.

estate The *net worth* you leave behind when you pass away.

estate planning Proactive decisions and documentation about how you want your affairs handled during life-threatening medical conditions and after your death.

estate planning documents The best way to ensure that your wishes are followed, both after death and during incompetence. Common estate planning documents include a *will*, a *trust*, a *living will*, a *durable power of attorney*, and a *durable power of attorney for health care*.

estate tax Tax owed upon your death based on the amount of your *net worth*. As of 2007, an individual can have up to a $2,000,000 *estate* without owing any estate tax. Absent any future law change the $2,000,000 cap amount becomes unlimited in the year 2010 before being reduced to $1,000,000 in 2011. (Personally, I would not want to be very old, very rich, and just a little sick in December of 2010.)

exchange-traded fund (ETF) An *investment* with both *stock* and *mutual fund* characteristics. You can buy and sell an ETF throughout the day like a stock. However, an ETF works similarly to an *index fund*. ETFs can be a good choice for a *lump sum* you wish to invest in a *passively managed* way.

exemption *Tax* benefit generally claimed by the person providing more than half the financial support of an individual. In 2007, each exemption is potentially worth a $3,400 reduction in *taxable income*.

expected return Statistically speaking, the *reward* you should realize given the amount and types of *investments* in your *portfolio*. By properly implementing *asset allocation*, any increase in *risk* should increase *expected* *return*. But remember one thing about statistics: with one foot in a fire and another in an ice bucket, you're perfectly comfortable—on average.

expense account Ability to take clients out to expensive lunches and be reimbursed by your employer. If you find it anywhere, you're likely to find it in sales. Not given to the new guy in accounting.

expense ratio Fees paid to a *mutual fund,* expressed as a percentage of your investment. Rather than billing you, mutual funds take their fees by reducing the *return* you earn. Pay attention to the expense ratio when evaluating mutual funds. If you own a mutual fund with an expense ratio of 1.2 percent, you will pay about $12 on your $1,000 investment each year. Also see *12b-1 fee.*

face amount See *principal.*

face value See *principal.*

FDIC insurance Protection by the governmental agency, the Federal Deposit Insurance Corporation, if your bank fails or goes out of business. Specifically, the FDIC replaces the money you lose as a result—most often up to $100,000.

federal income tax Typically, the largest *income tax.* Paid to the federal government.

FICA Federal Insurance Contributions Act. See *Social Security tax.*

filing status Classification you choose for your *income tax return* that affects your *tax rates* and possible *deductions.* Common choices include *Single, Head of Household, Married Filing Jointly,* and *Married Filing Separately.* See page 61.

fiscally responsible The recognition that you alone control your financial future and are willing to take appropriate actions. Contrast with *cheap.*

fixed income fund See *bond fund.*

flat tax A tax in which the rates don't change regardless of income level. Sales tax is an example of a flat tax.

forced savings program A system for automatically saving money without ongoing conscious effort. Enrolling in your *401(k)* plan is an excellent example of using this strategy.

forfeiture A financial penalty, often the surrender of some or all of the *interest* earned, due to an early withdrawal, usually from a *CD* or *annuity*.

401(k) loan Money borrowed from your *401(k) plan* with the intent of repayment. Preferable to an *early distribution* but still unattractive.

401(k) plan *Employer-sponsored retirement plan* frequently available to people working at for-profit companies. One of the easiest methods to save, early participation makes a huge difference in achieving long-term financial success.

403(b) plan An *employer-sponsored retirement plan* similar to a *401(k)* except typically available for people who work for public schools, churches, or hospitals.

457 plan An *employer-sponsored retirement plan* similar to a *401(k)* except usually available to people working for certain state and local government entities—including elected representatives who might be corrupt and/or from New Jersey.

free money An *employer matching* contribution to your retirement plan for which you don't have to do anything—other than save—to receive. Turning down an employer match is like denying a raise. See *idiot*.

Gary He personifies all that is wrong in financial services. There's a great chance you'll never meet Gary. I hope you don't. But he's in this book so you can recognize him in case you do run into him—or her. Gary's chief concern is his own financial well-being, not yours. Reduce the impact Gary can have on your financial life by sleeping on major financial recommendations he makes and by asking for and actually checking his references. I hope the Gary's of this world will disappear as people wise up, but in the meantime do what you can to stay away from him.

good debt *Loan* for *investment* purposes likely to lead to future gain greater than the debt borrowed. Most student loans and home mortgages are examples of good debt. Contrast with *bad debt*.

gross income Total amount of *money* you earn without taking into account any payroll subtractions such as *withholding* taxes.

group health insurance Medical coverage through your employer, union, or professional association, typically far less expensive and more comprehensive than what is available for you to purchase on your own.

growth stock *Shares* of a company with an anticipated high growth rate in earnings.

guardian Person designated to take care of your minor children should you die.

head of household *Filing status* option generally available for someone not married or living with a spouse *and* who is supporting at least one additional person besides himself/herself.

home equity The value of your home minus the sum of your remaining *mortgage* balance and any *home equity loan*. For example, if you own a home worth $220,000 and have a mortgage of $150,000 and a home equity loan of $10,000, your home equity is $60,000.

home equity loan Amount borrowed from your *home equity*. Whereas a mortgage is used to acquire a home, a home equity loan is usually created later. The money from such a loan can be used to do something logical, such as home improvements or, alternatively, pay for a fourth luxury car in a two-person household.

homeowner's insurance Covers the home, your possessions, and *liability* from an event at the home. This insurance, advisable for all homeowners, is typically required if you have *a mortgage*.

identity theft Stealing personal information to commit fraudulent financial transactions.

idiot Someone who doesn't take advantage of the *free money* an *employer match* provides. Don't be one of these.

income subject to tax The total money you receive from any source, with a few specific exceptions. The most common exceptions are gifts and inheritances. Yes, even lotto winnings are income subject to tax.

income tax Your money spent by the government for the common good. At least that's how I imagine the government views it. You might have your own opinion. The amount owed is based on your *taxable income*. For employees, most income taxes are paid via *withholding*.

income tax refund Typically, the result of poor planning, since it amounts to an *interest-free loan* from you to the government. Don't be so generous to the government. Adjust your *withholding* and review Chapter 4.

income tax return Annual chore of calculating your income tax for the previous year by determining your income, *deductions*, and *exemptions*. If the amount of tax you paid throughout the previous year exceeds your total *income tax*, you receive a refund. If your total tax bill is less than the amount you already paid, then you will owe even more.

incompetent Considered no longer able, from a medical perspective, to handle one's own affairs.

index The average performance of a group of selected *stocks* over time. Examples include the Dow Jones Industrial Average and the NASDAQ Composite.

index fund A *mutual fund* with the goal of mirroring the performance of a specific index. For example, the Vanguard 500 Index fund attempts to copy the performance of the S&P 500. An index fund does little trading. Also known as a *passively managed* fund. Those index funds mirroring large indices (such as the Wilshire 5000) engage in a *buy the market* strategy. Also see *exchange traded fund*.

individual retirement account (IRA) A privately arranged *retirement plan* providing tax benefits as an incentive for long-term retirement savings. Key benefits include *tax-deferred growth* and a possible income tax *deduction* for each *IRA contribution*. Since IRAs are not offered through an employer, you need to work with a *custodian* yourself—which is easy. Along with *401(k)s*, IRAs are another fantastic way to save for your retirement. Also known as a *traditional IRA* or a *regular IRA*. Contrast with *Roth IRA*.

individual retirement account contributions The amount you put into your IRA. There is a maximum contribution amount allowed per person per year. In 2007, the maximum amount anyone under 50 can put in an IRA is $4,000, assuming he or she has earned at least that amount.

inflation The overall trend of prices to rise over time. Historically, inflation in the U.S. has averaged between 3 percent and 4 percent annually.

inflation risk The chance your *investment's* value doesn't keep up with the general rise in prices.

insurance Financial protection against possible but unlikely events.

insurance company An organization that collects *premiums* and distributes funds to the *insured* when there are *claims*.

insurance policy Written document of the who, what, when, where, how, and why of the *insurance* you purchase.

insured Something covered because you paid *premiums* to insure it. For example, most of the possessions in your apartment are insured after you purchase *renter's insurance.*

interest Payment for the use of *money.* Interest is collected from banks on *savings accounts* and *CDs.* Interest is paid to banks on *debts,* such as *mortgages* and *credit cards.*

interest-free loan *Money* you give to someone for a period of time without charging interest. Sometimes parents do this for their children— no problem, that's just Mom and Dad helping out. Millions of people give interest-free loans to the government every year by receiving a sizable income tax refund. If that sounds like you, fix it. Review Chapter 4 and adjust your *withholdings.* Also see *allowances* and *W-4.*

interest rate Amount of income you receive during one year divided by the amount of your *investment.* Also, the payment due to cover the cost of borrowing for one year divided by the amount borrowed. In both cases, the interest rate is expressed as a percentage.

Internal Revenue Code (**IRC**) The laws which define federal taxation in the United States. The two enormous volumes containing these laws are among the longest and least readable texts in the history of the world.

Internal Revenue Service (**IRS**) The governmental agency in charge of administering and enforcing federal tax laws. Don't look for anything funny here.

intestate One who dies without a *will.* The state decides how the affairs are handled for those who die intestate. If you aren't a careful driver, you can become an interstate intestate.

introductory rate A low credit card or mortgage rate valid only for a specific period of time before it increases, sometimes dramatically. Also known as a *teaser rate.*

investment Short-term sacrifice for *potential* long-term gain. Non-financial examples include spending more time studying or practicing the trombone. Financial investments include *stocks, bonds,* and *mutual funds.*

investment experience The depth of one's background in the financial markets, affected by the length of time invested, amount of money invested, and types of previous investing.

investment goals The specific hopes one has from investments, including rate of growth over a certain period of time.

investment vehicles Your options for growing your *savings*, such as *stocks, bonds, mutual funds,* and *real estate.*

IRA See *individual retirement account.*

irrevocable No longer able to be changed. A *revocable living trust* becomes irrevocable at the death of the *trustor.*

issue date When bonds are originally sold.

itemized deductions Specific subtractions in the calculation of *taxable income,* including charitable contributions, certain medical expenses, *state income tax,* and *property tax.* Except in rare cases, only those whose total itemized deductions exceed their *standard deduction* benefit from itemizing their deductions.

joint tenancy with right of survivorship (JTWROS) A *title* whereby when one owner of the *asset* dies, the asset immediately passes to the *joint tenant* (often the spouse) without regard to what the will says.

joint tenant One who smokes marijuana in a rented apartment. Not really. If two people are joint tenants in an *asset* and one dies, the other receives the asset without regard to what the *will* says. Married couples are often joint tenants in their home. See *title* and *joint tenancy with right of survivorship (JTWROS).*

left pocket A Total Candor analogy for the location of your retirement savings. Since retirement savings are still your money, saving for retirement is like taking money from your *right pocket* and putting it in your left pocket—no real pain.

liability (**1**) The part of your automobile *insurance policy* providing *coverage*—and often a lawyer to represent you—if you are sued as a result of an accident. This includes injuring or killing somebody or destroying or damaging someone's property. A liability insurance feature is usually part of your automobile insurance policy as well as your *renter's insurance* or *homeowner's insurance* policy. (**2**) See *debt.*

life event An occurrence allowing for changes in your *benefit elections* outside of the *annual enrollment period*. Examples of life events within most companies include marriage and divorce, birth or adoption of a child, and a spouse's job change.

life insurance A policy paying a *net death benefit* to your designated *beneficiary* if you die. If there are people depending on your income, you are a good candidate for life insurance. If so, start by getting quotes for *term insurance*.

living will An *estate planning document* spelling out your final wishes for specific medical treatment if you subsequently become terminally ill and unable to address such matters yourself.

load A sales commission payable to a salesperson at the time of *mutual fund* investment, the time of sale (redemption), and sometimes both. It is preferable and realistic to restrict yourself to the purchase of only *no-load funds*.

loan See *debt*.

local income tax Tax owed to a local jurisdiction, typically a city or county, based on your income or residency in that location. Examples range from New York City, "the Big Apple," to Jackson, Michigan, host of the Jackson County Rose Festival.

long-term care insurance Pays a portion of the cost of nursing home care. Typically not appropriate for those under 50 to consider for themselves. But talk to Mom, Dad, Grandma, and Grandpa.

long-term disability insurance Subsequent to the expiration of a *waiting period*, pays a portion of your income if you are unable to work for an extended period of time due to an illness or injury. Often such policies pay for many years, sometimes until age 65 or later.

lump sum An infrequent or one-time significant amount of money. Often resulting from a *rollover* from a *401(k)* or perhaps an inheritance, a lump sum should be treated very carefully because you don't get too many of them and they can be a huge part of your financial future.

marginal tax rate See *tax bracket*.

market (1) A place (formerly physical, increasingly virtual) in which people and organizations can buy and sell *investments*. There are different markets for different categories of investments. (2) A place to buy meats, vegetables, and to ponder the genuine need for whole tomatoes, chopped tomatoes, diced tomatoes, tomato paste, and ketchup.

market capitalization The total value of a company. Calculated by the simple formula: market capitalization = *stock price* x *shares outstanding.*

market correction (1) A sharp and relatively quick downward adjustment of investment values. (2) When you come back from the grocery store and your spouse says "No, I can't 'just use ketchup' in a recipe that calls for tomato paste. Now we need to go back."

market interest rate Prevailing interest rate for a specific *investment* or financial product. Market interest rates go up and down for a variety of reasons.

market timing Strategy in which an individual buys and sell *stocks* frequently based on guesses of where the *market* or even a specific *investment* is headed. Since guessing requires an amazing degree of intellect and/or luck, it is not a long-term winning investment strategy.

married filing jointly Most common *filing status* for married couples. By choosing this filing status, a married couple can file one *tax return.*

married filing separately *Filing status* option for a married couple requiring each spouse to file a tax return. This usually, but not always, results in greater combined tax owed.

maturity (1) The date a *bond's principal* payment is available. (2) The point in life when you realize the most arrogant people are also the most insecure.

medical power of attorney See *durable power of attorney for health care.*

Medicare A program funding a portion of the health care expenses of qualified older Americans and those with certain disabilities.

Medicare tax Part of the *payroll tax.* The Medicare *tax rate* is 2.9 percent, half paid by you, half by your employer.

miracle of compounding interest The phenomenon of your money making money. The more you save and the longer you invest, the more dramatic the benefits. Unfortunately, this miracle also works in reverse if you borrow excessively: the *interest* payments you owe grow through compounding as well, making it increasingly difficult to pay back your *debt*. This is the miracle of compounding interest in its evil form.

money Currency in the form of dollars and cents that enables people to easily exchange products and services with one another.

money market fund A *mutual fund* investing primarily in very safe *assets*. A money market fund aims to generate a *rate of return* higher than *savings accounts* with only a slight increase in *risk*. Money market funds attempt to keep their share prices at exactly $1.00. Income comes from periodic *dividend* payments to *shareholders*.

mortgage A home purchase *loan*. Note, the home is *collateral* for the loan.

municipal bond The debt of a state government, local government, or similar agency. Municipal bond interest is, for the most part, exempt from *federal income tax*.

mutual fund An *investment vehicle* owning many other investments, including *stocks* and *bonds*. Mutual funds are a great way to invest the majority of your *savings*. Mutual funds enable *shareholders* to affordably benefit from *diversification* and *professional management*. Also see *index fund*.

net asset value Price of a *mutual fund share* calculated by dividing the total value of its *assets* by the number of *shares outstanding*.

net death benefit The amount your heirs will receive from your life *insurance policy* after you die. In the case of a *term insurance* policy, this is the same as the amount of life insurance you purchased. In the case of a *whole life insurance* policy, it could be more or less than the amount you originally purchased.

net income Money you receive from your paycheck, after taxes are *withheld*. Often referred to as *take-home pay*.

net worth What you own less what you owe, represented by the formula: net worth = *assets* – *liabilities*. Also known as *wealth*.

no-load fund A *mutual fund* you can purchase without paying a sales commission *(load)*. You know you have a no-load fund if, after writing a check for $1,000, your first statement shows a beginning investment balance of $1,000. If you see only $950, you paid a 5 percent load. Don't do that—ask the question in advance.

nominal interest rate See a*nnual percentage rate (APR)*.

non-discretionary expenses Money spent on "needs," such as housing, groceries, and transportation to your job. Contrast with *discretionary expenses*.

normal retirement age Other than by rare exception, the age at which you can take a *distribution* from your *retirement account* without penalty. According to current regulations, this age is 59½.

outperformance Higher *returns* received by an *investment* compared to similar investments or an *index* of similar investments. Contrast with *underperformance*.

passive income Money you receive without working for it at the time you receive it; for example, income from *investments*. Contrast with *active income*.

passively managed fund See *index fund*. Contrast with *actively managed fund*.

payroll tax Comprises two different taxes: *FICA*, (also known as the *Social Security tax*), and *Medicare tax*. Payroll taxes are assessed only on wages and net earnings from self-employment, not on investment or other types of income.

pension plan Retirement program administered by an employer. Two common types of pension plans are *defined benefit* and *defined contribution*.

pogo stick Your only source of retirement funding is you. Instead of the traditional three-legged *stool* of retirement planning, plan as though your personal *savings* is your only retirement funding source. A three-legged stool with only one leg remaining is much too dangerous to sit on. You have a pogo stick. Turbo-charge it.

portability The ability to take something with you. For example, *term life insurance* purchased privately is portable because you can choose to keep it regardless of the number of companies you work for after you purchase the insurance.

portfolio All your current financial *investments*.

post-tax dollars *Money* already taxed. See *after-tax dollars*.

power of attorney Document authorizing an *agent* to act on your behalf. Often granted temporarily for a specific purpose.

premium *Money* paid to an *insurance company* to protect you from financial losses due to *covered events*. The bill you receive from your insurance company is to collect premiums.

pre-tax dollars *Money* not yet taxed. These dollars are worth less to you if they come through your paycheck because you will pay tax on them. When possible, use pre-tax dollars for any spending that would otherwise require *after-tax* dollars. For example, if you have the option, participate in your health care *spending account* program at work. Also known as *before-tax dollars*.

price/earnings (P/E) ratio The price of a *share* of *stock* divided by the company's earnings per share. If the stock has a higher P/E ratio compared to similar companies, it is often considered more expensive than its peers.

primary beneficiary Person you designate to receive any benefits due to you as a result of your death. Contrast with *contingent beneficiary*.

principal (1) Amount borrowed (in the case of a loan). (2) The value of a bond at *maturity*. Also known as the *face value* or *face amount* of the bond.

probate Court proceedings for certain *assets* passing at death.

procrastination Doing nothing about your financial situation. Since you are no longer ignorant, you realize that procrastination is not a strategy. Get going. Also see *waiting for …*

professional management Those making the specific investment decisions for a *mutual fund*. Affordable access to these professional managers is a key benefit to *mutual fund* investing.

progressive tax A tax system in which the higher your *taxable income*, the more, *as a percentage*, you pay in tax. Contrast with *flat tax* and *regressive tax*.

property tax Tax based on the *assessed value* of certain types of *property*. A house is a commonly taxed property.

purchasing power The value of *money*, in terms of its ability to purchase goods and services. Due to *inflation*, the purchasing power of a dollar generally decreases every year.

rate of compounding The frequency with which *interest* is posted to an account. Common rates of compounding include daily, monthly, and yearly. See also *APR* and *APY*.

rate of return The total value an *investment* provides in the form of *capital appreciation, interest,* and *dividends* expressed as a percentage. Calculated by dividing the *return* provided by the amount originally invested. Compare to *return* and *total return*.

real estate Land and anything attached to it, including homes and apartment buildings. Real estate is one of many possible *investment vehicles*.

reality check What you need if your only plan is to rely on the government or your employer for a comfortable retirement. Recognize what the *stool* was, what a *pogo stick* is, and start accepting *fiscal responsibility* for what you need to do in this new financial world you live in.

rebalancing The periodic review and adjustment of your *portfolio's asset allocation*.

redeem To cash in (e.g., a *bond*).

refund anticipation loan Available to someone expecting an *income tax refund,* money provided to you immediately rather than waiting through the *IRS's* processing time. Avoid refund anticipation loans due to their high fees and absurdly high *interest rates*. When filing, provide your direct deposit information to speed your money's return back to you.

regressive tax A tax system in which the *tax rate* decreases as income increases.

regular IRA See *individual retirement account (IRA)*. Contrast with *Roth IRA*.

reimbursement account See *spending account*.

renter's insurance Protection of your possessions and personal *liability* resulting from an event occurring in an apartment or a house you rent.

replacement cost coverage A loss under an *insurance policy* with this feature results in payment based on the cost to *replace* the items destroyed. Contrast with *actual value coverage*.

retirement account See *retirement plan*.

retirement plan Account with specific tax advantages to encourage retirement saving. Also known as a *retirement account*.

return See *total return*.

revocable Changeable. See *revocable living trust*.

revocable living trust A reversible arrangement whereby a person transfers assets to a *trust* primarily to ease the transfer of assets upon death, in part to avoid *probate*.

reward The upside of *risk*, the *return* of an *investment*.

rider A supplement to an *insurance policy* providing additional *coverage* (usually for additional items or *covered events*) for an additional *premium*.

right pocket A Total Candor analogy for the location of your wallet, where your money is available to spend at a moment's notice. Your first step is to keep filling your right pocket by generating income. The second step is to move as much of it as possible to your *left pocket* (your retirement savings). See *left pocket*.

risk The possibility things don't work out the way we'd like or expect them to. One example of financial risk is the chance an *investment* becomes worth less than the amount invested.

risk tolerance The ability to handle fluctuations in investment value without panicking. Your risk tolerance is not a skill; it is a personality trait. Still, education can help, since people can become more comfortable in risky situations when they know they are not taking unreasonable or ignorant risks.

rollover IRA An *IRA* funded via a *lump-sum* deposit from another *retirement account*, typically a *401(k) plan*. Contrast with a *contributory IRA*.

Roth conversion IRA A *Roth IRA* created by paying tax on an existing tax-deferred retirement account such as a *regular IRA* or *401(k)*. This completely optional process is available to most individuals whose income level is below $100,000 as of 2007.

Roth IRA An *IRA* in which *contributions* are never *tax-deductible* and growth and distributions can be *tax-free*.

Roth, William Former U.S. senator from the state of Delaware for whom the *Roth IRA* is named. For those of you who like trivia. No, this won't be on the test.

sales tax Tax assessed to the final purchaser of a product based on the retail price of the purchase.

savings Difference between your income and your spending. There are plenty of suggestions and strategies in Chapter 2 to create savings but there are no shortcuts. Savings is represented by the simple formula: your savings = your income – your spending.

savings account The most basic and conservative of all investments. The *risk* is minimal so the *expected return* is low.

savings bond Part of the *debt* of the United States government. Interest earned from a savings bond is *not* taxable on your state income tax return. It is usually taxable on your federal income tax return when the savings bond is *redeemed*.

secured debt Loan with *collateral*, such as the home in the case of a *mortgage*. Note that it is the lender who has the "security."

self-employed Those whose primary source of *active income* is from their own business compared with an employee who receives a paycheck.

self-employed retirement plans Retirement plans available to those with self-employment income. While a detailed discussion of these is beyond the scope of this book, if applicable to you consider visiting a local brokerage house or a financial web site listed in Appendix B to learn more. Examples of self-employed retirement plans include Keogh Plans, SEP-IRAs, and SIMPLE 401(k)s.

selling short A bet that a *stock* decreases in value. Logistically, when you sell short, you sell stock you don't own and buy it back later. If the price when you buy is lower than when you sell, you make money. Since selling short is a *market timing* strategy that goes against the historical trend of stocks rising over time, it is something you should refrain from doing.

shareholder One who owns *shares* of a company.

shares Units of *stock* ownership.

shares outstanding The total number of shares held by the public plus the amount of shares held by people who work at the company.

short-term disability insurance Pays a portion of your income if you are unable to work due to an illness or injury for a certain period of time, typically not exceeding six months.

single (1) In tax, a *filing status* for an unmarried person, typically when not financially supporting anyone else. (2) In baseball, a base hit. (3) In dating, not attached or a liar.

Social Security A benefits program providing payments chiefly to current retirees, the disabled, and the widowed.

Social Security tax Part of the *payroll tax*. The tax rate for *Social Security* is 12.4 percent. You pay 6.2 percent and your employer pays an additional 6.2 percent.

spending account A benefit plan in which you can pay for certain expenses with *pre-tax dollars*. Examples of spending accounts include health care, transportation, and dependent care. Also known as a *reimbursement account*.

standard deduction A subtraction nearly everyone can take to calculate their *taxable income*. The amount of the deduction varies based on *filing status*. For example, someone filing as *single* in 2007 has a standard deduction of $5,350, and a couple who chooses to file as *married filing jointly* receives a standard deduction of $10,700. Use the standard deduction unless your *itemized deductions* exceed your standard deduction.

state income tax Tax owed to a state based on residency or income earned there. As of this writing, all but nine states tax wages. If you live and work in different states with *income taxes*, you usually must file *tax returns* in each.

stated interest rate See a*nnual percentage rate (APR)*.

stock Ownership of a corporation. Units of stock are called *shares*. Historically, stocks have been the best long-term *investment*. For short-term investing, stocks are often too risky.

stock category Classification of *stocks* simplifying *mutual fund* selection and *diversification*. Often based on *market capitalization, growth* vs. *value* profile, and primary country of revenue generation. Examples include small cap stocks, international stocks, and value stocks.

stock fund A *mutual fund* holding primarily stocks. Also known as an *equity fund*.

stock price Value of one *share* of stock in a corporation based on the *supply and demand* for the *stock* at a specific moment in time.

stool (1) An outdated analogy for funding your retirement: a three-legged stool represented a *defined benefit pension, Social Security,* and *savings*. (2) Feces, like from a bull, which is exactly what the first definition of stool is for today's workers. Better to see *pogo stick*.

supply and demand An economics concept about which entire courses, even the bulk of certain collegiate majors and dissertations, are devoted to teaching. I am not going to come close to dignifying it here. However, I can tell you that supply and demand, discussed briefly in Chapter 8, significantly affects *stock prices*.

take-home pay *Money* you receive from your paycheck after *taxes* are *withheld* and your portion of *benefits* costs are subtracted.

tax *Money* paid to the government for the services it provides, both locally and nationally. Your opinion on taxes has no legal bearing on the amount you pay.

tax bracket Income *tax rate* paid that corresponds to a specific level of income. Current bracket examples include 10 percent, 15 percent, and 25 percent. Since your top tax bracket is also the highest tax rate you pay, it is also known as your *top tax rate* or your *marginal tax rate*.

tax-deductible An item qualifying as a *deduction* from your *income taxes*.

tax-deferred growth Concept of not having to pay taxes on your investment's growth until its *distribution*. Available in *retirement accounts* such as *401(k)s* and *IRAs*.

tax-exempt Income not subject to *income tax*. For example, *interest* earned from *municipal bonds* is tax-exempt for purposes of *federal income tax*.

tax-free Income that is never taxed, such as qualified retirement distributions from a *Roth IRA*.

tax rate A percentage representing the tax owed divided by the value of the item taxed. All else being equal, the higher the tax rate, the higher your tax.

tax schedule A list of all the different *income tax rates* by level of *taxable income*. See page 67 for examples.

taxable account See *brokerage account*. Also known as a regular account.

taxable income Your *income subject to tax* minus *deductions* and *exemptions*.

teaser rate See *introductory rate*.

term Length of time. Examples include an auto *insurance policy* with a six-month term and a two-year term *CD*.

term insurance Less expensive and less complicated version of *life insurance* compared to *whole life insurance*. Consider term insurance at once if there are people depending on your *income*.

time horizon The amount of time expected between when an *investment* is made and when the money is expected to be needed. The time horizon can be affected by a variety of factors, including the account the money is in, the goal of the account, job security, and the investor's age.

time value of money The concept that a dollar today is worth more than a dollar in the future due to *inflation* and the *miracle of compounding interest*.

title (1) Legal document signifying ownership, like to a car or a house. (2) The way in which an *asset* is owned. Examples include in *trust* or *joint tenancy with right of survivorship (JTWROS)*.

top tax rate See *tax bracket*.

Total Candor (1) Complete truth, nothing held back, honest assessment of the facts, answering even unasked questions. (2) A business founded in 2005 with a mission of overcoming financial ignorance through in-person events, books, and other media. Please visit *www.totalcandor.com* for more information.

total return The total value an *investment* provides in the form of *capital appreciation, interest,* and *dividends*. See *return*. Compare to *rate of return*.

traditional IRA Also known as *regular IRA*. See *individual retirement account (IRA)*. Contrast with *Roth IRA*.

traditional pension See *defined-benefit pension*.

trust A financial arrangement whereby the *trustor's* money is held by a *trustee* for the *beneficiary*.

trustee The organization or person administering a *trust*.

trustor The person putting assets into a *trust*.

12b-1 fee Expense collected by a *mutual fund* primarily for the purpose of promoting the funds to new investors. Doesn't do much (if anything) for you as an existing investor. All else equal, look for funds with lower 12b-1 fees. Also see *expense ratio*.

umbrella insurance Protects you only if the coverage level of another one of your *insurance policies* is exceeded.

underperformance Lower *returns* received by an *investment* compared to similar investments or to an *index* of similar investments. Contrast with *outperformance*.

unsecured debt Loan for which the lender has no *collateral*. *Credit card debt* is unsecured. Since this is the riskiest type of debt for the lender, higher *interest rates* are charged.

unvested The current value contributed to your *retirement account* by your employer subject to *forfeiture* upon termination of your employment. Make sure you review your *vesting schedule* before quitting a job.

value stocks Companies with slower growth rates that—in the eyes of some—are overly sold (trading too cheaply) but have promise for a rise in their *stock price*.

vested balance The value of your *retirement account*—including any *employer match*—that remains yours if you leave your employer immediately.

vesting schedule A timetable specifying when *employer-matching* contributions to your *retirement account* remain yours (rather than be subject to *forfeiture*) should you terminate employment.

vision insurance Covers a portion of expenses or offers a discount related to a visit to the eye doctor, often including eyeglasses and contact lenses. Vision insurance is sometimes available as part of a health insurance plan and sometimes as a distinct benefit.

volatility The frequency and degree an *investment* might go up or down. Volatility is a type of *risk*.

W-2 The tax form that wage earners receive, typically in late January, showing their earnings from wages for the previous year.

W-4 A bewildering and unnecessarily complicated tax form you complete when you start a new job or need to adjust your *withholding*. You select the number of your *allowances* by completing this form. Review Chapter 4 for suggestions. You can change and resubmit this form whenever you like.

W-6 No such thing—yet.

waiting for ... Along with *procrastination* and not having enough *money*, a frequent explanation for why people aren't saving. Regardless of where you are right now, today is the best day to start saving. You can make a bigger difference now than you will ever be able to in the future.

waiting period Time when you are disabled but not paid benefits by your *long-term disability insurance*.

wealth What you own less what you owe. Your *assets* minus your *liabilities*. Also known as *net worth*.

whole life insurance A financial product paying a high commission for the salesperson. I am not a fan of whole life insurance at any age. Moreover, it is clearly not a priority if you have not taken care of the basics, including paying down *credit card debt*, establishing an *emergency fund*, *investing* in *mutual funds*, and *saving* for retirement. If, based on your review of Chapter 5, you need *life insurance*, purchase *term insurance*.

will An *estate-planning document* indicating who receives your *assets* and who becomes the *guardian* of your minor children after you have "left the building."

withholding *Tax* paid directly from your paycheck. This is the stuff that really pisses you off.

write-off See *deduction*.

Acknowledgments

After several paragraphs listing each and every one of their professional connections, many authors end their acknowledgments by quickly thanking their family. Paradoxically, they also claim family as the most important part of their lives. I think that's nonsense.

Total Candor: Without a great home life, you're a miserable SOB. No one wants to be around such a person. Ultimately, everything starts at home. And so do my acknowledgments:

This book would not have happened without the unwavering dedication, support, and loyalty of my beautiful wife, Laura.

My young daughter, Hannah, likely won't remember the time I spent writing this book. Yet she seems to have already learned a fair bit about saving—her food. Frequently returning to search the corners of her high chair moments after the "all gone" announcement, she never wastes a single piece of rice cake, cereal, or anything else possibly edible. Is my sense of pride truly inappropriate?

Mom, your faith in my abilities gave me the confidence to start Total Candor. Well, that plus Dad's near-fanaticism I work for myself someday. And to my grandparents, all anyone can hope for in life is to have three generations of legacy in awe of us when we reach your ripe young age. Of course, at the rate this generation has kids, we might have to live to be 120 years old to even see our great-grandchildren.

~~I would be remiss if I didn't~~ Who talks like that? Thanks to all my friends and family who repeatedly ask me many of the same financial planning questions *you* do. It was this sense of déjà vu that led me to start Total Candor, LLC and write *Beyond Paycheck to Paycheck* to provide this desperately needed education. Among others, Steven Rubin, Daniel Rubin, Jennifer Rubin, Doug Rand, Jonathan Rand, Lisa Rand, and Bradley Tillotson all supported me with ideas and feedback as I wrote, re-wrote, and re-wrote once more.

I've been blessed with knowing and working with people who have tremendously shaped my career including Sandy Jose, Joel Anderson, and those of us who love Geoffrey. (He's not just a giraffe, you know).

It takes a genuine team of people to convert a word processor document into a real book, including expert readers, targeted readers, editors, proofreaders, web site designers, book designers, printers, and indexers. I can't possibly thank everyone, but I will specifically express my sincere gratitude for efforts "above and beyond" to the team at 1106 Design.

And to Gary. Yes, even a personal finance book can benefit from a real character.

You: And what about me?

Without you, there would be no Total Candor in the world. So, tell a friend. We'll both thank you.

Index

Share the Wealth (with Free Shipping* too!)

We can all benefit from a financial education. Do you have friends or family members ready to move *Beyond Paycheck to Paycheck*? If not, should they be? Consider this education as a gift. Why not let this book change your financial future *and* that of the people you care about most? Don't be surprised if you're thanked many times over the years. (It should at least have a more lasting impact than a bottle of wine.)

Internet: *www.totalcandor.com/sharethewealth*
Email: sharethewealth@totalcandor.com
Phone: (603) 373-0373
Fax: (603) 457-5617   Fax this form (or a copy).
Mail: Total Candor LLC
P.O. Box 4283
Portsmouth, NH 03802-4283

❐ Please send _____ copies of *Beyond Paycheck to Paycheck,* at $24.95 each, to the following address:

Shipping Address

Name: _____

Street address: _____

City: _____ State: _____ Zip: _____

Billing Address

❐ Same as shipping.

Name: _____

Street address: _____

City: _____ State: _____ Zip: _____

Email address: _____

Would you like to receive emails from Total Candor?_____

*Shipping: When using this form, there is no shipping charge to continental United States addresses for orders received by 12/31/07. Contact us for shipping rates to other addresses.

Payment Type:

❐ Check Enclosed   ❐ Visa   ❐ Mastercard   ❐ American Express

Credit Card #:_____

Name on Card:_____ Expiration date: _____

Signature: _____

Remember to join us at *www.totalcandor.com* for additional educational resources and to learn about events in your area.

REMEMBER SIMPLE SAVING STRATEGY NUMBER FOUR:
ENJOY FREE STUFF!

By reading *Beyond Paycheck to Paycheck,* you've taken a critical step down the road from income to wealth. If you'd like to continue our conversation, your next step is an easy one. Benefit from your **free membership*** to *www.totalcandor.com.*

Take advantage of this offer by joining via the registration page at:

www.totalcandor.com/ihategary

Total **Candor**™

Join today and enjoy the following features:
- Information and periodic member-first discounts on our live *events*
- Useful financial planning *calculators,* including those referenced throughout the book
- Revealing and timely financial planning *articles* and *information*
- *Links* to other useful web sites
- Occasional financial planning *humor*
- Other Total Candor *media*
- Additional facts about *Gary*
- And *more ...*

We add content frequently, so join us, bookmark us, and visit us often.

Thanks,

Michael Rubin
Founder
Total Candor LLC

*This offer may be discontinued after December 31, 2007. We're not sure yet. Why risk it? Join now.